"Othelia Lee and Moon Sun Song's insightful exploration of cutting-edge issues related to social workers' use of AI is timely and compelling."

Dr. Fredrick Reamer, Professor, Rhode Island College, US

"This book captures essential tools for anyone who wants to understand the breadth and depth of AI in social work. It is a must-read for social workers looking to navigate and utilize artificial intelligence in this fast-changing society."

Dr. Hyeouk "Chris" Hahm, Professor, Boston University, US

"Grounded in social work values, this book translates complex technological concepts into actionable guidance with essential guardrails that strengthen professional judgment and mitigate bias."

Dr. Marina A. Badillo-Diaz, Founder,
The AI Social Worker, New York University, US

"This book is a much needed resource for students and practitioners, offering clear guidance and a strong ethical foundation for navigating AI in social work practice."

Dr. Drew Reynolds, Principal Consultant, Common Good Data, US

"Othelia Lee and Moon Sun Song have written a must-read primer for social workers seeking guidance in this new era of the integration of Artificial Intelligence (AI) in health and human services. Through thoughtful discussion and case studies authors reveals how AI can transform, even revolutionize, the delivery of social services. This book is a call to action to social workers about how they can leverage the potential power of AI for social good and justice creating a future in which technology and humanity are intertwined to promote the well-being of all individuals, families, and communities."

Dr. Judith Gonyea, Professor, Boston University, US

Social Work Practice and Artificial Intelligence for the Common Good

Social Work Practice and Artificial Intelligence for the Common Good is the first university-level textbook to address how artificial intelligence (AI) can be leveraged for the common good without reproducing systemic inequities, whilst also addressing how social workers can develop the digital literacy necessary to evaluate, design, and ethically use AI tools.

Drawing on global case studies, practice-based examples, and a range of pedagogical tools, this book:

- Introduces AI concepts in plain language for non-technical learners.
- Explores ethical dilemmas, bias, and the implications of automation in human services.
- Connects AI use cases to micro, mezzo, and macro practice levels.
- Provides tools for advocacy, policy engagement, and community-based technology design.
- Positions social workers as active shapers of emerging technologies rather than passive adopters.
- Embeds equity, human rights, and the National Association of Social Workers (NASW) Code of Ethics into AI discussions.

Offering chapter-critical thinking questions, empowerment-focused activities, reflection prompts, interviews with experts, and support materials, this textbook will be relevant to all students of social work, public policy, and human services. This book will also be of interest to practitioners in nonprofit and public service sectors, and faculty members looking to advance their understanding and infuse AI literacy in their courses.

Othelia EunKyoung Lee is a professor at UNC Charlotte School of Social Work. Dr. Lee's research focuses on the development, implementation, and evaluation of innovative community-based interventions aimed at improving health behaviors among older adults. Some highlights of her scholarship include over 100 articles in mental health, gerontology, cultural diversity, and technology.

Moon Sun Song is a research professor at Kangnam University in South Korea, specializing in interdisciplinary care research merging social welfare with AI and ICT. By leading the "Welfare Technology Living Lab," she fosters a sustainable welfare tech ecosystem, driving industry–academia collaborations that connect technology enterprises with social welfare agencies.

Skills for Social Work Practice

This textbook series is ideal for all students studying to be qualified social workers, whether at undergraduate or postgraduate level. Covering key elements of the social work curriculum, the books are accessible, interactive and thought-provoking.

New Titles

Case Examples in Child Welfare and Family Services for Social Workers
Tyrone Cheng

Careers in Social Work
Social Workers' Roles in Caring for Humans and Their Animal Companions
Edited by Lori R. Kogan

Social Work and the Psychosocial Journey Out of Far-Right Extremism
Danny W. Carroll II

Social Work and Technology
A Practical Guide for Using Technology in Social Work Practice
Edited by Alex D. Colvin and M. Sebrena Jackson

Human Behavior in the Environment
A Justice for Vulnerable Populations Approach
James Angelo Forte

Social Work Practice and Artificial Intelligence for the Common Good
Ethics, Equity, and Innovation in Human Services
Othelia EunKyoung Lee and Moon Sun Song

https://www.routledge.com/Skills-for-Social-Work-Practice/book-series/SSWP

Social Work Practice and Artificial Intelligence for the Common Good

Ethics, Equity, and Innovation in Human Services

Othelia EunKyoung Lee
and Moon Sun Song

Routledge
Taylor & Francis Group
LONDON AND NEW YORK

Designed cover image: Siwon Lee

First published 2027
by Routledge
4 Park Square, Milton Park, Abingdon, Oxon OX14 4RN

and by Routledge
605 Third Avenue, New York, NY 10158

Routledge is an imprint of the Taylor & Francis Group, an informa business

British Library Cataloguing-in-Publication Data
A catalogue record for this book is available from the British Library

ISBN: 978-1-041-27578-7 (hbk)
ISBN: 978-1-041-27545-9 (pbk)
ISBN: 978-1-003-75508-1 (ebk)

DOI: 10.4324/9781003755081

Typeset in Times New Roman
by Newgen Publishing UK

Access the Support Material: www.routledge.com/9781041275459

To my parents, JaeSeok Lee and HyoSoon Kong (Othelia EunKyoung Lee)

Contents

Figures

Tables

Preface

We are living at a moment in history when artificial intelligence (AI) is accelerating everything around us. AI pushes us to work faster, think more deeply, and reimagine what might be possible. When designed with humanity at its center, AI can open doors to a more equitable world. Imagine the promise in the "brave new world:" people of every age, income, country, education level, gender, sexual orientation, and religion gaining equal access to vast bodies of knowledge through AI. Social workers, grounded in values of justice and human dignity, are uniquely positioned to champion this vision and ensure that AI becomes an equalizer rather than a divider.

Yet AI is undeniably a "double-edged sword." Without thoughtful guidance, AI could widen existing wealth disparities, deepen educational inequalities, and undermine democratic institutions we have spent decades building. Fears of job losses are no longer distant hypotheticals: these doomsday scenarios are concerns that shape public conversations about the future of work.

In the spring of 2025, the world witnessed how fragile our institutions can be when information systems are disrupted. USAID, an organization central to global development, was efficiently dismantled in a matter of days through actions as simple as locking staff out of email and communication networks. This moment revealed an inconvenient truth: without technology, entire systems of humanitarian support can be silenced overnight.

Later that year, I (Othelia Lee) facilitated a Collaborative Online International Learning (COIL) session with graduate social work students across four countries (China, Indonesia, Mexico, and the U.S.A.) focused on AI in human services. An anonymous survey during that session revealed something striking: every student reported using AI tools such as ChatGPT and Gemini regularly. Even more telling, one-third said they consulted AI chatbots for personal concerns. And yet *rarely have students* received instruction on the ethical use of AI in their current social work education.

This gap is profound. Students are already integrating AI into their daily lives, but without guidance on responsible, ethical, and culturally attuned use. As AI becomes increasingly woven into practice (assessment, documentation, service navigation, community-organizing), critical AI literacy is no longer optional. It is essential for the future of the profession.

As a research professor, I (Moon Sun Song) have led pilot projects implementing information and communication technology (ICT) devices and AI care robots within social work agencies in South Korea. AI technology has been scientifically proven to supplement emotional support systems for isolated older adults and ensure client safety through real-time monitoring. However, the most pivotal truth I discovered is that the introduction and operation of advanced technology are not the exclusive domains of technicians. Today, the responsibilities of social workers are expanding beyond traditional face-to-face services into the realm of digital care. This is not a matter of preference but an inevitable transformation that the profession must confront.

We do not claim to be AI experts. But these experiences made the need unmistakably clear: we must prepare social workers to understand, question, and shape AI tools. Literacy empowers, and critical AI literacy gives social workers and the communities they serve the ability to use technology in ways that uphold justice, dignity, and human rights.

History reminds us that social innovation can challenge inequality. During the Progressive Era, Jane Addams imagined a society where all people could benefit from the common good. Today, AI holds similar transformative potential. Whether it reinforces inequity or expands opportunity depends on how we choose to design, teach, and use it.

Now it is our turn. As social workers of the future, we must envision a world where everyone has equal access to AI, and have the courage, knowledge, and ethical grounding to help build it.

Acknowledgments

We are profoundly grateful to the many remarkable individuals who helped bring this book to life. Our heartfelt thanks go to Drs. Diana Rowan, Jae Hoon Lim, Yeongran Park, and David Choi whose insightful guidance strengthened this project from its earliest stages.

We extend our deep appreciation to our exceptional graduate assistants, Michael Lynch and Samantha Klukas, whose thoughtful feedback kept our work firmly grounded in the lived experiences of students. Their clarity, curiosity, and steady contributions enriched every chapter.

We were also fortunate to meet and learn from a group of multi-talented professionals who generously shared their wisdom through video interviews. Mr. Andrew Kim, a social worker who truly wears many hats, offered invaluable perspectives on the creative ways he integrates AI across his diverse roles. Ms. Alexis Jordan, a brilliant computer scientist, provided a fascinating window into her work building systems that detect suicide ideation in chatbots—an endeavor as compassionate as it is technically sophisticated.

Dr. Stephanie Gonzalez gifted us with a sensory-rich, immersive video experience that captured both heart and imagination. I extend my sincere appreciation to Dr. Sooyeon Jeong whose compassionate insights into her pioneering work in human-centered AI greatly enriched this book project. I am also grateful to Drs. Marina Badillo-Diaz and Jason Fernandez for sharing their perspectives during interviews; their expertise and vision offer powerful inspiration for the boundless possibilities of AI designed and led by social workers in the years ahead.

Finally, we express our sincere gratitude to the dedicated editorial team at Taylor & Francis. Their timely feedback, clear communication, and steadfast partnership made each stage of the publishing process not only smooth, but genuinely enjoyable. To all who contributed—you elevated this book, and we are deeply thankful.

Glossary

A

Accountability Clearly defining responsibility for AI outcomes. It ensures that developers, agencies, and social workers remain answerable for technological failures.

Agency The capacity of individuals to act independently and make their own free choices. Human-centered AI must protect and enhance the client's agency.

Agentic AI An advanced AI system capable of autonomous reasoning, planning, and tool use to achieve complex goals. Unlike reactive AI, it acts as an "autonomous assistant" that can manage multi-step tasks without constant human prompting.

AI Governance The structures, policies, and processes that guide how AI is developed, used, and monitored. It aims to ensure AI systems are ethical, transparent, and accountable.

Algorithm A set of mathematical rules or procedures for data-processing. In welfare, algorithms determine the priority for resource distribution and help discover hidden "blind spots" in the safety net.

Algorithmic Bias Systematic and repeatable errors in a computer system that create unfair outcomes, often due to biased data or flawed assumptions in algorithm design. This can disproportionately affect marginalized populations and is a critical concern in ethical social work practice involving digital tools.

Artificial General Intelligence (AGI) Also known as "Strong AI," it possesses human-like cognitive abilities across various domains. In the future, AGI could act as a "fellow expert" for social workers, understanding complex emotions and multimodal cues.

Artificial Intelligence (AI) A field of computer science focused on creating systems capable of performing tasks that typically require human intelligence, such as decision-making, pattern recognition, and natural language processing. In social work, AI is increasingly used for assessments, predictive analytics, and client support tools.

Artificial Narrow Intelligence (ANI) Often called "Weak AI," it is specialized in a single task (e.g., Siri, AlphaGo). In human services, it is used for automating repetitive tasks like flagging households at risk based on tax arrears.

Autonomy The right of clients to make their own choices. AI should act as a facilitator, supporting client self-determination rather than controlling their lives.

B

Beneficence The ethical obligation to act for the benefit of others. In AI, it means ensuring systems improve client well-being rather than just administrative efficiency.

Big Data Extremely large and complex datasets analyzed to reveal patterns and trends. Social work agencies use big data to predict high-risk groups for solitary deaths and establish evidence-based policies.

C

Chatbots Automated software programs that interact with users through text or voice. They use predefined rules or AI models to answer questions, provide services, or guide users through tasks.

Cloud Computing A model for delivering computing resources (servers, storage) over the internet on demand. It ensures the scalability of social welfare systems, especially when service demand spikes during crises.

Common Good A principle that emphasizes the well-being of all members of a community. In the context of technology and social work, it refers to designing and implementing digital tools and policies that promote equity, inclusion, and collective benefit rather than serving only individual or commercial interests.

Community-Based Data Governance A power structure where the community has the right to control their data, treating it as a collective asset rather than just an engineering resource.

Computer Vision A subfield of AI that enables computers to interpret and understand visual information from images or video. It powers applications like facial recognition, object detection, and medical imaging analysis.

Conversational AI Technology that enables computers to understand, generate, and respond to natural human language in real time. It powers chatbots, virtual assistants, and other interactive systems.

D

Data Sovereignty The right of a community or individual to control the collection, storage, and use of their own data.

Deep Learning (DL) A subfield of ML inspired by the structure of the human brain (neural networks). It excels at analyzing unstructured data, such as detecting signs of child abuse in CCTV footage or identifying emotional distress in counseling transcripts.

Digital Divide The gap between those who have easy access to digital technology and those who do not, often falling along lines of age, income, and geography.

Digital Equity The principle of ensuring all individuals have equal access to digital technologies, internet connectivity, and digital literacy. Promoting digital equity is essential for inclusive service delivery and reducing disparities in access to care and support.

Digital Literacy The ability to effectively and ethically use digital technologies, including understanding how they work, evaluating digital content, and navigating online environments. For social workers, digital literacy includes competencies in privacy, data protection, and responsible tech use in client interactions.

Digital Platform An online infrastructure that hosts applications, services, or tools used for communication, data management, and service delivery. Examples include client portals, learning management systems, and collaborative workspaces.

Digital Revolution A period marked by the rapid advancement and widespread adoption of digital technologies, transforming how services are delivered, accessed, and managed. In human services, it has reshaped professional roles, client interactions, and organizational infrastructure.

E

Electronic Case Management Systems (CMS) Digital platforms used to document, track, and manage client information and service delivery. CMS tools streamline workflows, improve data accuracy, and support outcome measurement in human services.

Equity The principle of fairness in AI, ensuring that technology does not reinforce systemic inequalities but rather provides tailored support to marginalized populations.

European Union (EU) AI Act A comprehensive EU regulatory framework establishing rules for the development, deployment, and oversight of AI systems. It categorizes AI by risk level to protect safety, fundamental rights, and transparency.

Explainable AI AI systems designed so that their decisions can be understood and explained to human users, fostering trust and enabling client appeals.

F

Fairness Audit A systematic evaluation of an AI system to detect and correct biases that may lead to discriminatory outcomes against specific groups.

Feedback Loop A cycle in which the output of a system influences future inputs. In AI, feedback loops can reinforce patterns, for example, when biased decisions generate more biased data that further entrenches inequities.

G

Generative AI A type of AI that learns from vast datasets to create new content, such as text, images, or audio. In social work, it can be used as a creative tool for drafting reports or generating educational materials for clients.

Global Perspectives Approaches that consider diverse cultural, social, political, and economic contexts across countries and regions. They emphasize interconnectedness and variation in experiences and worldviews.

H

Hallucination A phenomenon where an LLM generates convincing but factually incorrect information. RAG is used as a primary technical solution to mitigate this risk in sensitive fields like human services.

Hard Law Legally binding regulations and statutes enacted by governments that carry penalties for non-compliance (e.g., the General Data Protection Regulation [GDPR] or the EU AI Act).

Human-Centered AI An approach to AI that prioritizes human values, needs, and rights. It involves designing AI systems that are transparent, accountable, and aligned with ethical principles, ensuring that technology serves people rather than replacing or harming them.

Human Defense Line The role of social workers as the ultimate professional decision-makers who do not blindly trust AI outputs, ensuring human judgment remains the final safeguard.

Human Rights Fundamental rights and freedoms to which all people are entitled, regardless of identity or location. They protect human dignity and ensure equal treatment and opportunity.

I

Inclusivity A design philosophy that respects diverse cultural, linguistic, and digital literacy backgrounds, providing interfaces like voice commands or braille for those often marginalized.

Information and Communication Technology (ICT) A unified concept merging IT (handling information) and CT (transmitting information). In social work, it serves as the infrastructure for managing vast welfare data through networks, hardware, and software.

Informed Consent A process where clients fully understand how AI uses their data and explicitly agree to it, including the right to opt out at any time.

Internet of Things (IoT) An intelligent network where physical objects exchange data via sensors. In senior care, it connects devices like motion sensors to alert social workers of emergencies in real time.

J

Justice The principle of fairness and equity in resource distribution. It involves auditing AI for bias to ensure marginalized groups are not excluded.

L

Large Language Model (LLM) A type of AI trained on massive text datasets to understand and generate human language. It can answer questions, summarize content, and engage in dialogue.

Low Power Wide Area Network (LPWAN) A specialized network (e.g., LoRa) designed to transmit small amounts of data over long distances with minimal battery consumption. Ideal for remote monitoring.

M

Machine Learning (ML) A branch of AI where algorithms learn patterns from data to make predictions or decisions without being explicitly programmed. It improves performance through experience.

Mobile and Cloud Technologies Mobile technologies refer to portable digital devices and applications that allow users to access services and information on the go. Cloud technologies enable remote storage and access to data via the internet, supporting collaboration, scalability, and real-time updates in service delivery.

Multimodal AI AI systems that can simultaneously process and integrate various types of data, including text, images, speech, and video. It allows for more sophisticated care by analyzing a client's voice tone, movement, and facial expressions together.

N

Natural Language Processing Technology that enables computers to understand, interpret, and generate human language. It allows for automated summarization of case reports and sentiment analysis to monitor the psychological state of clients.

Nonmaleficence The duty to "do no harm." This requires preventing risks like algorithmic bias or privacy breaches that could harm vulnerable populations.

P

Participatory Design A design philosophy that involves all stakeholders (social workers, clients, community) in the development process to ensure the system meets real-world needs.

Personalized Text-to-Speech (P-TTS) A specialized TTS that generates speech in a specific, familiar voice. It can provide medication reminders or safety alerts in a family member's voice to offer emotional comfort to elderly individuals.

Policy Advocacy The proactive role of challenging unfair AI-driven decisions and striving to improve systemic policies for clients disadvantaged by technology.

Predictive/Data Analytics The use of statistical and computational techniques to analyze data and forecast outcomes. In social work, predictive analytics can identify at-risk populations, inform interventions, and improve resource allocation.

Privacy The right to be free from unauthorized surveillance and to have control over one's personal data, which is frequently challenged by AI data-mining practices.

Proactive Care A paradigm shift from waiting for a crisis to occur to using data-driven predictions to intervene before a problem starts.

Prompt Engineering The practice of crafting effective inputs or instructions to optimize the performance of AI models, especially LLMs. It helps guide the model toward relevant, accurate, and safe outputs.

Proportionality A principle requiring that any AI-driven surveillance or intervention must be balanced against the intended benefit and must not be more intrusive than necessary.

R

Retrieval-Augmented Generation (RAG) A technology that enhances LLMs by retrieving relevant information from external, up-to-date databases before generating a response. It significantly reduces "hallucinations" and ensures that social work policy guidance remains accurate and verifiable.

Robotics The field focused on designing, building, and operating robots that can perform tasks autonomously or semi-autonomously. It integrates engineering, computer science, and AI.

S

Self-Governance (Industry Self-Regulation) A model where technology companies set their own internal ethical codes and standards without government-enforced legal requirements.

Sensor Technology Devices that detect physical changes (movement, heart rate) and convert them into signals. It acts as the "eyes and ears" for proactive care in smart homes for the elderly.

Soft Law Non-binding guidelines, ethical principles, or declarations (e.g., OECD AI Principles) that influence behavior through social and professional pressure rather than legal force.

Speech-to-Text (STT) A technology that converts spoken language into text. It supports hearing-impaired clients by providing real-time captions during counseling and helps social workers automatically document verbal sessions.

Strategist Using AI-analyzed community data to identify trends (e.g., rising homelessness) and proactively allocating resources or proposing new policies.

Surveillance The monitoring of behavior or activities; in the AI context, this often refers to mass facial recognition or behavioral tracking that can chill freedom of expression.

T

Telehealth The use of telecommunications and digital technologies to deliver health-related services and information remotely. In social work, telehealth supports mental health counseling, case consultations, and outreach to underserved populations.

Transparency The requirement that AI systems be "open" and understandable so that stakeholders can see how data is used and how decisions are reached.

V

Virtual Reality A computer-generated, immersive environment that users can explore and interact with using specialized equipment. It simulates realistic or imagined settings to create a sense of presence.

Virtual Services Services delivered through digital platforms rather than in person, including online counseling, virtual support groups, and remote case management. These services increase accessibility and flexibility for both clients and providers.

Part I

Foundations

1 Social Work Practice in the Age of Artificial Intelligence

Othelia E. Lee

Box 1.1 The Future is Here

Sabrina, a case manager at a large metropolitan social service agency, opens her laptop to prepare for a client meeting. Her agency recently adopted an AI-assisted intake system designed to predict which clients are at the greatest risk of homelessness. As Sabrina reviews the algorithm's recommendations, she notices that it consistently flags young Black men as "high risk," even when their circumstances differ significantly. Sabrina must decide: should she follow the system's prioritization, challenge its findings, or combine the AI's output with her professional judgment?

Sabrina's dilemma is not science fiction: it is happening now. Across the globe, social workers increasingly encounter AI-powered tools in eligibility assessments, case prioritization, mental health chatbots, and community outreach programs. These tools can be powerful allies in promoting the common good, but they can also perpetuate historical inequities if left unchecked.

1.1 Defining Artificial Intelligence (AI) for Social Work

AI refers to computer systems or machines designed to perform tasks that typically require human intelligence, such as understanding language, recognizing patterns, solving problems, making decisions, and learning from experience (Russell & Norvig, 2021). The term AI was coined by John McCarthy, along with Marvin Minsky, Nathaniel Rochester, and Claude Shannon, in a proposal for the Dartmouth Summer Research Project on Artificial Intelligence, which took place in 1956 (Rajaraman, 2014). This is widely recognized as the founding moment of AI as a formal academic discipline. There are several key subfields of AI relevant to social work. We will explain the definition first, followed by potential applications to social work practice.

DOI: 10.4324/9781003755081-2

1.1.1 Machine Learning (ML)

ML is a branch of AI in which computer systems learn to improve their performance at a given task by analyzing large amounts of data, rather than by following fixed instructions programmed by humans (Alpaydin, 2016). The key feature of ML is that the system becomes more accurate as it processes more data over time.

In social work practice, this means that an ML model could analyze historical data from thousands of client cases, such as demographics, service usage patterns, and outcomes, and then identify which clients are most likely to benefit from a specific type of service.

For example, in a community mental health agency, ML could be used to predict which clients are at a higher risk of dropping out of therapy based on their attendance records, initial symptom severity, and socio-economic background (Hall et al., 2024). The social worker could then proactively reach out to these clients with targeted engagement strategies, improving retention and outcomes.

1.1.2 Natural Language Processing (NLP)

NLP is the area of AI that focuses on enabling computers to understand, interpret, and generate human language (Russell & Norvig, 2021). NLP systems work with written or spoken text, allowing them to analyze large volumes of narrative information that would be time-consuming for humans to process manually.

In social work, a prime example is the automated analysis of case notes. Case notes are often lengthy and full of important details about client progress, concerns, and changes in circumstances. An NLP system could scan hundreds of notes across multiple cases to detect patterns (e.g., recurring mentions of housing instability or signs and symptoms of depression) that might otherwise be overlooked (Nuwasiima et al., 2024). This could help supervisors identify emerging community-wide issues or support early interventions for at-risk clients. NLP could also be used to automatically summarize lengthy case files, making it easier for social workers to quickly understand a client's history.

1.1.3 Computer Vision

Computer Vision is the subfield of AI that enables computers to interpret and make sense of visual information, such as photographs or videos (Szeliski, 2011). It works by training algorithms to recognize patterns, objects, and scenes, much like the human visual system.

In social work practice, computer vision could be applied to identify hazards in unsafe housing conditions. A housing inspector working with a child welfare agency might take photos of a home. An AI system using computer vision could scan the images to detect issues such as exposed electrical wiring, mold growth, or broken windows. This could be especially valuable when conducting remote inspections in rural areas or during times when in-person visits are limited, such as

Table 1.1 Key Terms of AI

Subfields	*Definition and Examples*
Machine Learning (ML)	Algorithms that improve performance with more data. Example: Predicting service utilization based on client histories.
Natural Language Processing (NLP)	Understanding and generating human language. Example: Automated analysis of case notes.
Computer Vision	Interpreting visual information. Example: Identifying hazards in unsafe housing conditions from images.
Robotics	Machines that interact physically with people. Example: Socially assistive robots for older adults.

during a pandemic. Technology could flag the images for urgent follow-up, alerting that unsafe environments are quickly addressed to protect clients' health and safety (Li et al., 2022).

1.1.4 Robotics

Robotics involves the design and use of machines that can physically interact with people or their surroundings (Russell & Norvig, 2021). When combined with AI, robots can perform tasks autonomously or in collaboration with humans. Robotics is increasingly relevant in the form of socially assistive robots, devices designed to provide companionship, reminders, and support to individuals in need.

In gerontological social work, a socially assistive robot might remind an older adult to take their medication, guide them through light physical exercises, or engage them in conversation to reduce loneliness (Lee et al., 2024). In eldercare, robots have been shown to improve mood, encourage social interaction, and reduce agitation among clients. Social workers could integrate these tools into home-based care programs, supplementing human visits and helping clients maintain a better quality of life (Lee & Shin, 2024).

Social workers are not computer scientists. Why do social workers need to know about these subfields of AI? For social workers, the goal is not to become computer scientists but to understand how these systems work, what they can and cannot do, and how they intersect with professional values.

1.2 Shaping the Future of Social Work Practice across Micro, Mezzo, and Macro Levels

How will AI change the field of social work practice? AI is not merely a set of new tools: it is a paradigm shift in how data, decision-making, and service delivery are managed. Here we discuss some examples of how AI will shape social work practice.

1.2.1 Data-Driven Decision-Making

AI enables social workers to process vast amounts of structured and unstructured data, such as case notes, service records, and policy documents, to identify patterns, predict needs, and recommend interventions. This capability enhances decision-making at the micro level (individual cases), mezzo level (organizational planning), and macro level (policy development). However, without ethical oversight, these data-driven insights risk reinforcing systemic biases embedded in historical data (Tambe & Rice, 2021). Social workers must critically evaluate AI outputs to ensure they align with values of equity, transparency, and justice.

1.2.2 Automation of Administrative Tasks

AI can automate tedious, routine administrative tasks such as intake forms, scheduling, and eligibility verification, freeing social workers to focus on the relational and therapeutic aspects of their work (Nuwasiima et al., 2024). This shift improves efficiency and allows more time for direct client engagement. However, there is a risk that reduced human contact during intake may hinder rapport-building, which is essential for trust and effective intervention. The ethical implementation of automation must preserve opportunities for meaningful human connection.

1.2.3 Predictive Analytics for Early Intervention

AI-powered **predictive analytics** can flag early warning signs for individuals or communities at risk, enabling proactive and preventive interventions (Hall et al., 2024). These tools are increasingly used in child welfare, mental health, and substance abuse services to identify vulnerable populations and allocate resources effectively (Tambe & Rice, 2021). Yet, predictive models may mislabel or stigmatize clients, especially when trained using biased or incomplete data. Social workers must advocate for the transparent and accountable use of predictive tools to ensure interventions remain client-centered and non-punitive.

1.2.4 Expanded Access via Digital Platforms

AI-driven technologies such as chatbots, telehealth platforms, and real-time language translation can expand access to services, particularly for individuals in remote or underserved areas (Tambe & Rice, 2021). These tools support micro-level client engagement, mezzo-level outreach, and macro-level inclusion strategies. However, the **digital divide**, marked by disparities in internet access, device availability, and digital literacy, may exacerbate existing inequities (Sanders & Scanlon, 2021).

Digital literacy is the set of skills and competencies enabling individuals to effectively engage with, assess, produce, and critically understand digital media and technologies (Machin-Mastromatteo, 2022). It encompasses digital reading, writing, critical appraisal of content, and awareness of socio-technical contexts. The concept evolved from information literacy, media literacy, and computer literacy. Social workers must champion digital literacy and inclusion and ensure that technological advancements do not leave vulnerable populations further behind.

1.2.5 Enhanced Policy Analysis

At the macro level, AI can model the potential impact of social policies across different demographics and regions. By simulating outcomes and identifying unintended consequences, AI supports evidence-informed policymaking that promotes equity and effectiveness. Capraro and colleagues (2024) explore how generative AI can simulate policy outcomes and assess unintended consequences across domains such as work, education, and healthcare. These authors emphasize that AI has the potential to both exacerbate and mitigate socioeconomic inequalities, depending on how it is implemented. However, these models may oversimplify complex social phenomena, failing to account for cultural, historical, and relational factors. Social workers must ensure that policy analysis remains grounded in lived realities and guided by ethical principles.

As shown in Box 1.2, let's explore potential use of AI across various areas of social work practice at all levels, including micro, mezzo, and macro. We will explore each area in Part 3 of this book.

Box 1.2 AI Use across Micro, Mezzo, and Macro Practice

Child Welfare

An AI tool flags a family for additional home visits after identifying a pattern of missed school and medical appointments. A social worker uses this as one input alongside interviews and community insights.

A county child welfare agency uses AI to forecast foster care placement needs six months in advance, enabling targeted recruitment of foster families. State policymakers use AI modeling to assess how increasing prevention funding might reduce long-term foster care placements.

Mental Health and Substance Abuse

An AI system integrated into telehealth sessions alerts the clinician if a client's speech patterns suggest worsening depression.
A mental health agency uses AI to identify peak service demand times, optimizing staffing for group therapy sessions.

Public health policymakers use AI analysis to propose targeted funding for rural regions with the highest projected suicide risks.

Older Adults and People with Disabilities

An older adult living alone uses an AI-enabled device to remind her of daily medications and detect falls, alerting a caregiver of emergencies.

A retirement community deploys AI to predict which residents are most at risk of malnutrition, prompting proactive nutrition support.

National disability agencies use AI models to forecast the economic impact of increased home-based care versus institutional care over the next 20 years.

1.3 The Common Good and the Social Work Mandate

Social work's mission, as articulated in the National Association of Social Work (NASW) Code of Ethics, is grounded in service, social justice, the dignity and worth of the person, the importance of human relationships, integrity, and competence (NASW, 2021).

The **common good**—the idea that society should be organized so all people can flourish—resonates deeply with these values (Addams, 2007). It refers to the sum of social conditions enabling both individuals and groups to achieve fulfillment more easily, emphasizing collective social well-being and flourishing. Jane Addams, a pioneer in the creation of the social work profession and 1935 Nobel Peace Prize laureate, asserted that the good we secure for ourselves is precarious and uncertain until we secure it for all of us and incorporate it into our common life. Have we ever achieved the common good that Jane Addams envisioned?

In the AI era, what would advancing common good mean? As AI becomes increasingly embedded in the fabric of human services, social workers must ensure that its development and deployment reflect the profession's enduring commitment to the common good. This principle, rooted in dignity, equity, and collective well-being, offers a vital ethical compass for navigating the promises and perils of emerging technologies.

Therefore, the social work mandate is not only to use AI responsibly but to shape its development in partnership with affected communities. Next, we discuss aspects of AI as potential tools to promote common good in terms of weighing benefits and harms as well as promoting equity.

1.3.1 Maximizing Benefits

AI holds transformative potential to extend the reach and impact of social services. When thoughtfully designed, AI systems can help social workers identify needs earlier, allocate resources more efficiently, and support complex decision-making processes.

Predictive analytics can flag individuals at risk of homelessness or health crises, enabling timely interventions. These innovations, when guided by social work values, can empower clients, enhance access, and improve outcomes, making services more responsive, inclusive, and humane (Tambe & Rice, 2021).

1.3.2 Minimizing Harms

With great potential comes great responsibility. Social workers must be vigilant in identifying and mitigating the harm that AI systems can unintentionally cause, such as **algorithmic bias**, discrimination, and the erosion of privacy. Historical data used to train AI often reflects systemic inequities, which will be perpetuated if not critically examined (Reamer, 2025). Biased algorithms have produced discriminatory outcomes in areas such as hiring, healthcare, and criminal justice (Toli & Manasa, 2024). Social workers must play a crucial role in advocating for transparent, accountable, and ethical AI practices, ensuring that technology does not reinforce injustice but instead becomes a tool for healing and equity.

1.3.3 Ensuring Equity

At the heart of social work is a commitment to serving marginalized and vulnerable populations. This commitment must extend to the design and implementation of AI systems. Social workers can advocate for inclusive development processes that center on the voices of those most affected by technology. This includes pushing for participatory design, equitable access, and evaluation metrics that prioritize human well-being over efficiency alone. Research repeatedly has shown that marginalized communities are often excluded from the benefits of AI due to biased data and unequal access to technological infrastructure (Tambe & Rice, 2021). By ensuring that AI systems are designed to promote inclusion and justice, social workers help transform technology into a force for the common good.

1.4 Opportunities and Challenges

Would the emergence of AI be a blessing or a curse? Technology is like a "double-edged sword." A balanced perspective recognizes that technology is not inherently good or bad; its impact depends on design, implementation, and oversight. Let's consider what the opportunities and risks are.

1.4.1 Increased Reach

AI technologies, such as chatbots and virtual agents, are revolutionizing access to social services. These tools offer 24/7 crisis support, often in multiple languages, enabling outreach to individuals in remote, underserved, or linguistically diverse communities. These tools leverage cognitive behavioral therapy (CBT), dialectical behavior therapy (DBT), and motivational interviewing to deliver scalable mental health interventions. A study by Prochaska et al. (2021) found that chatbots significantly reduced substance use and improved mood and confidence among users over an eight-week period. Similarly, Filippis and Foysal (2024) reviewed the effectiveness of chatbots in reducing symptoms of depression and anxiety, highlighting their role in screening, early intervention, and personalized care.

1.4.2 Efficiency Gains

AI can automate routine administrative tasks (e.g., documentation, scheduling, and data entry) which traditionally consume a significant portion of social workers' time. By streamlining these processes, professionals can devote more attention to direct client engagement and therapeutic interventions. Virtual assistants and chatbots have demonstrated effectiveness in handling client queries, scheduling, and case documentation, thereby enhancing service delivery without replacing human judgment (Baek et al., 2025). Importantly, this scoping review emphasized that AI should complement, not replace, human judgment and highlighted the need for ethical safeguards and professional discretion in implementation.

1.4.3 Predictive Insights and Resource Allocation

AI has the potential to revolutionize prevention strategies by identifying risks earlier and more accurately. AI-powered **predictive analytics** can identify patterns and risk factors that may not be immediately apparent to human practitioners. These tools support early detection of clients at risk for adverse outcomes such as homelessness, domestic violence, mental health crises, or child welfare concerns, enabling timely and targeted interventions (Tambe & Rice, 2021).

Wang (2024) introduces predictive models that use large-scale socioeconomic and housing data to identify individuals and families at risk of homelessness. The models achieved high accuracy and demonstrated the ability to detect nuanced patterns across different demographics, including age, gender, and family status. Wang's findings support the use of AI-powered analytics to guide early interventions and resource allocation, particularly in addressing homelessness and related social vulnerabilities. Hence, predictive models, when explainable and ethically designed, can guide proactive interventions and resource allocation, improve outcomes, and reduce long-term service costs.

Additionally, AI can help social workers and agencies allocate limited resources more effectively by analyzing service utilization patterns and forecasting future needs (Toli & Manasa, 2024). These capabilities support more initiative-taking, data-informed decision-making, ultimately improving outcomes for clients and communities.

AI systems can also strengthen advocacy efforts by making data more transparent and accessible. Algorithmic tools can reveal disparities in service delivery or outcomes across demographic groups, providing evidence for policy reform and resource redistribution (Cheong, 2024). Social workers can use these insights to advocate for systemic change, ensuring that services are equitable and responsive to the needs of marginalized populations.

AI systems are not neutral: they reflect the biases of the data and designers behind them. Social workers must be equipped to detect and mitigate bias at every stage of AI implementation from data collection to algorithmic design and deployment. This responsibility is especially urgent given the profession's commitment to social justice and its role in protecting vulnerable populations from harm. Next, we will discuss risks involving algorithmic bias, erosions of human judgment, and privacy concerns.

1.4.4 Algorithmic Bias

Algorithmic bias refers to systematic and discriminatory errors in ML or algorithmic systems that reflect, reinforce, or amplify existing socioeconomic, racial, or gender inequalities (Russell, & Norvig, 2021). This concept was critically examined by Joseph Weizenbaum in his 1976 book, *Computer Power and Human Reason,* where he argued that software could embody law and reflect the biases of its programmers (Natale, 2019).

AI systems trained on historical data may inadvertently replicate and amplify systemic inequalities, including racial, gender, and socioeconomic biases. These biases are not merely technical flaws but reflect deeper societal exclusions encoded into algorithmic logic. Consequently, facial recognition technologies have shown higher error rates for racialized and gender-diverse individuals, raising concerns about surveillance and discrimination.

Buolamwini and Gebru (2018) examined three commercial facial-analysis systems and found significant disparities in accuracy based on gender and skin tone. The error rate for light-skinned men was less than 1%, while for dark-skinned women it exceeded 34% in two of the systems. These findings highlight how biased training datasets and benchmark standards can lead to discriminatory outcomes, particularly for marginalized groups. The authors argue that such disparities are not incidental but reflect deeper societal exclusions embedded in algorithmic design and data collection practices. Addressing algorithmic bias requires interdisciplinary frameworks that integrate ethical, social, and technical dimensions of fairness and inclusivity (Garkisch & Goldkind, 2025). We will delve into this in Chapter 5.

1.4.5 Erosion of Human Judgment

While AI can offer valuable recommendations, there is a risk of overreliance on algorithmic output, potentially sidelining the nuanced judgment and ethical reasoning that are central to social work practice (Toli & Manasa, 2024). Social work is inherently relational and contextual, requiring empathy, cultural competence, and critical reflection. Excessive dependence on AI may lead to mechanistic decision-making, undermining the profession's commitment to human dignity and autonomy.

As AI becomes embedded in practice, social workers must develop critical **AI literacy**, the ability to understand, evaluate, and ethically engage with digital tools. This includes interpreting algorithmic outputs, questioning data sources, and recognizing the limitations of AI systems (Ahn et al., 2025). Without these skills, practitioners risk becoming passive users of technology, unable to challenge their assumptions or advocate for ethical use.

1.4.6 Privacy Concerns

AI systems often require access to large volumes of sensitive personal data, raising significant concerns about data security, informed consent, and potential misuse. Studies have shown that clients and professionals alike worry about data ownership, commercialization, and surveillance, especially in home-based monitoring contexts (Ibitoye et al., 2025). Without robust safeguards, AI tools risk violating ethical standards of confidentiality and client autonomy. Social workers must advocate for transparent data governance and ensure compliance with legal and ethical frameworks.

To ensure that AI serves the common good, robust policy safeguards are essential. These include transparency requirements, accountability mechanisms, and participatory design processes that involve clients and communities (Tambe & Rice, 2021). Social workers must engage in policy development and advocacy to shape ethical frameworks that govern AI use in human services, ensuring that technology enhances rather than erodes the values of dignity, inclusion, and justice.

1.5 Ethical Responsibilities in the AI Era

As AI becomes increasingly woven into the fabric of social work practice, it invites us to reflect deeply on what ethical engagement truly means. Rather than viewing AI as a distant or purely technical concern, social workers are uniquely positioned to shape its development and use it in ways that honor our core values, dignity, justice, and the common good (NASW, 2021). While many ethical questions are emerging, we will focus on four foundational responsibilities: critical evaluation, informed consent, advocacy, and ongoing education. These pillars not only guide our interaction with technology but also reaffirm our commitment to ethical, client-centered practice in a rapidly changing world.

1.5.1 Critical Evaluation

Social workers must engage in critical evaluation of AI systems by understanding the data sources, algorithmic design, and potential biases embedded within them. This responsibility involves scrutinizing how AI tools are developed, what assumptions underlie their logic, and how they may reinforce existing social inequalities. Ethical engagement requires moving beyond checklist-style compliance to a more reflexive and context-sensitive approach, recognizing that AI systems operate within complex sociotechnical environments that can obscure accountability and fairness (Reamer, 2025). By adopting a critical lens, social workers can better assess whether AI tools align with the profession's core values of justice, equity, and human dignity.

1.5.2 Informed Consent

Informed consent remains a cornerstone of ethical social work practice, and its importance is magnified in the context of AI integration. Social workers must ensure that clients are fully aware of how AI engages in their service delivery, including what data is being collected, how it is used, and what decisions may be influenced by algorithmic processes. This requires clear, accessible communication tailored to the client's level of understanding and cultural context. Informed consent is not a one-time event but an ongoing dialogue that respects the client's autonomy and right to self-determination, especially when AI systems may affect sensitive areas such as mental health, housing, or legal status.

1.5.3 Advocacy

Social workers have an ethical obligation to advocate for transparent, accountable, and equitable AI policies within their agencies and broader governmental structures. As AI technologies increasingly shape public services, social workers must push for inclusive governance frameworks that reflect the needs and rights of marginalized populations (Reamer, 2025). Advocacy includes participating in policy development, raising awareness about algorithmic harms, and demanding oversight mechanisms that prevent misuse and ensure ethical deployment. This role aligns with the profession's commitment to social justice and systemic change, positioning social workers as key stakeholders in shaping the future of ethical AI.

1.5.4 Ongoing Education

Maintaining digital literacy and technological competence is essential for ethical practice in the AI era. Social workers must continuously update their knowledge of emerging technologies, understand their implications for practice, and critically assess their benefits and risks. This includes learning about ML, data ethics, and the societal impacts of automation (Russell & Norvig, 2021). Ongoing education empowers practitioners to make informed decisions, engage in interdisciplinary collaboration, and guide clients through increasingly digital service environments. It also ensures that social workers remain relevant and responsive in a rapidly evolving landscape, upholding professional standards and ethical integrity.

The ethical stance we maintain in this textbook aligns with international calls for **human-centered AI (HCAI)**, systems that respect human rights, promote fairness, and are accountable to the communities they affect. HCAI is a design philosophy emphasizing AI systems that prioritize human values, needs, and flourishing (Xu et al., 2023). The phrase was developed in recent AI/HCAI research. Notably, Shneiderman (2020) articulated a framework of HCAI: to be reliable, safe, and trustworthy, detailing how to balance automation and human control. The concept is also formalized in recent scholarly works calling for HCAI methodologies and frameworks. HCAI aims to augment human capacity rather than replace it, integrating ethical, accessible, and value-aligned design. We will revisit this in Chapter 12.

1.6 Looking Ahead: Social Workers as Co-Creators

Public Interest Technology (PIT) is an interdisciplinary field focused on using technology to advance the public good, promote socially responsible solutions, and center justice, dignity, autonomy, and equity in technological development and governance (Ford Foundation, 2022). PIT brings together expertise from technology, social sciences, law, ethics, and community-based disciplines to ensure that technology is designed, deployed, and regulated in ways that center the needs of society, particularly historically marginalized groups. Because social workers are uniquely positioned at the intersection of people, policy, and social systems, PIT provides frameworks to protect vulnerable populations, uphold ethics, and shape technologies that align with social justice values.

Rather than being passive adopters, Wang and colleagues (2025) argue that human service professionals can be **co-creators** of AI systems. Traditional AI models often fall short in capturing the nuanced, relational, and context-sensitive nature of human social behavior. To address this gap, they propose a new paradigm that blends computational intelligence with insights from psychology, sociology, and ethics. How can a social worker carry this function to facilitate HCAI and PIT? We would like to brainstorm some ideas with you.

1.6.1 Participating in Interdisciplinary Design Teams

Social workers are uniquely positioned to contribute to the ethical and human-centered development of AI systems by actively participating in interdisciplinary design teams. These teams often include engineers, data scientists, policymakers, and community stakeholders. Social workers bring critical insights into human behavior, social justice, and community needs, ensuring that technological solutions are not only technically sound but also socially responsive. Their involvement helps bridge the gap between technical innovation and lived experience, fostering systems that reflect diverse values and promote equity. We need radical collaboration with these unconventional allies to promote well-being of our clients.

1.6.2 Advocating for Participatory Design

Rather than being passive recipients of technology, social workers can advocate for participatory design methods that center on the voices of clients and service users. This approach ensures that those most affected by AI systems have a say in how those systems are developed and deployed, embodying HCAI principles. Participatory design aligns with the profession's commitment to empowerment and self-determination, challenging top-down models of innovation and promoting inclusive, democratic technology development. By embedding client perspectives into the design process, social workers help create tools that are more ethical, effective, and culturally attuned.

1.6.3 Shaping Evaluation Metrics

Social workers play a vital role in ensuring that evaluation metrics for AI systems reflect the values and priorities of the profession. While efficiency and scalability are often emphasized in business and technological development, social work demands attention to client well-being, equity, and relational outcomes. Social workers can influence how success is defined and measured, advocating for metrics that capture holistic and human-centered impacts rather than purely operational gains. This role is essential in resisting reductive models of service delivery and promoting accountability to ethical standards.

1.7 Critical Thinking Questions

1 How do the concepts of the "common good" and human-centered AI guide decisions about using AI in social work practice?
2 In Sabrina's case, what factors should influence her decision-making?
3 What steps can agencies take to ensure AI adoption aligns with social work ethics?

1.8 Summary

AI is more than a set of tools: it is a cultural and political force shaping the future of human services. Across micro, mezzo, and macro levels of practice, AI offers tools that can enhance service delivery, but it also demands new competencies and safeguards to ensure alignment with social work values. Social workers have both the responsibility and the opportunity to ensure that AI advances the profession's mission of promoting social justice, human dignity, and collective well-being. To responsibly integrate AI into practice, social workers must engage in critical evaluation, ethical oversight, and participatory design, ensuring that technology serves the values of compassion, justice, and human dignity.

References

Addams, J. (2007). *Newer ideals of peace*. University of Illinois Press.

Ahn, E., Choi, M., Fowler, P., & Song, I. H. (2025). Artificial Intelligence (AI) literacy for social work: Implications for core competencies. *Journal of the Society for Social Work and Research, 16(1)*, 9–26. https://doi.org/10.1086/735187

Alpaydin, E. (2016). *Machine learning: The new AI* (2nd ed.). MIT Press.

Baek, G., Cha, C., & Han, J. H. (2025). AI Chatbots for psychological health for health professionals: Scoping review. *JMIR human factors, 12*, e67682. https://doi.org/10.2196/67682

Buolamwini, J., & Gebru, T. (2018). Gender shades: Intersectional accuracy disparities in commercial gender classification. *Proceedings of the 1st Conference on Fairness, Accountability and Transparency, 81*, 77–91. https://proceedings.mlr.press/v81/buolamwini18a.html

Capraro, V., Lentsch, A., Acemoglu, D., Akgun, S., Akhmedova, A., Bilancini, E., Bonnefon, J.-F., Brañas-Garza, P., Butera, L., & Douglas, K. M. (2024). The impact of generative artificial intelligence on socioeconomic inequalities and policy making. *PNAS Nexus, 3*(6), pgae191. https://doi.org/10.1093/pnasnexus/pgae191

Cheong, B. C. (2024). Transparency and accountability in AI systems: Safeguarding well-being in the age of algorithmic decision-making. *Frontiers in Human Dynamics, 6.* 1–11. https://doi.org/10.3389/fhumd.2024.1421273

Filippis, R., & Foysal, A. (2024). Chatbots in psychology: Revolutionizing clinical support and mental health care. *Voice of the Publisher, 10*(3), 298–321. https://doi.org/10.4236/vp.2024.103025

Ford Foundation. (2022). Public interest technology and its origins. www.fordfoundation.org/work/challenging-inequality/technology-and-society/public-interest-technology-and-its-origins/

Garkisch, M., & Goldkind, L. (2025). Considering a unified model of artificial intelligence enhanced social work: A systematic review. *Journal of Human Rights and Social Work, 10*(1), 23–42. https://doi.org/10.1007/s41134-024-00326-y

Hall, S. F., Sage, M., Scott, C. F., & Joseph, K. (2024). A systematic review of sophisticated predictive and prescriptive analytics in child welfare: Accuracy, equity, and bias. *Child and Adolescent Social Work Journal, 41*(5), 831–847. https://doi.org/10.1007/s10560-023-00931-2

Ibitoye, A. O., Nkwo, M. S., & Orji, R. (2025). Rethinking responsible AI from ethical pillars to sociotechnical practice. *AI and Ethics*, *5*, 6207–6223. https://doi.org/10.1007/s43681-025-00809-2

Lee, O. E., Nah, K., Kim, E., Choi, N. G., & Park, D. (2024). Exploring the use of socially assistive robot among socially isolated Korean American older adults. *Journal of Applied Gerontology, 43(*9), 1295–1304. https://doi.org/10.1177/07334648241236081

Lee, O. E., & Shin, H. (2024). Social workers' perspectives on socially isolated older adults living with a robot companion. *Journal of Gerontological Social Work, 67*(5), 621–638. https://doi.org/10.1080/01634372.2024.2339974

Li, Y., Wei, H., Han, Z., Jiang, N., Wang, W., & Huang, J. (2022). Computer vision-based hazard identification of construction site using visual relationship detection and ontology. *Buildings, 12*(6), 857. https://doi.org/10.3390/buildings12060857

Machin-Mastromatteo, J. D. (2022). Information and digital literacy initiatives 2. *Information Development, 38*(3), 347–350. https://doi.org/10.1177/02666669221115554

Natale, S. (2019). If software is narrative: Joseph Weizenbaum, artificial intelligence and the biographies of ELIZA. *New Media & Society, 21*(3), 712–728. https://doi.org/10.1177/1461444818804980

National Association of Social Workers. (2021). Code of ethics of the National Association of Social Workers. www.socialworkers.org/About/Ethics/Code-of-Ethics/Code-of-Ethics-English

Nuwasiima, M., Ahonon, M. P., & Kadiri, C. (2024). The role of artificial intelligence (AI) and machine learning in social work practice. *World Journal of Advanced Research and Reviews, 24*(1), 80–97. https://doi.org/10.30574/wjarr.2024.24.1.2998

Prochaska, J. J., Vogel, E. A., Chieng, A., Kendra, M., Baiocchi, M., Pajarito, S., & Robinson, A. (2021). A therapeutic relational agent for reducing problematic substance use (Woebot): Development and usability study. *Journal of Medical Internet Research, 23*(3), e24850. https://doi.org/10.2196/24850

Rajaraman, V. (2014). John McCarthy—Father of artificial intelligence. *Resonance, 19*(3), 198–207. https://doi.org/10.1007/s12045-014-0027-9

Reamer, F. G. (2025). *Artificial intelligence in the behavioral health professions ethical and risk management issues*. NASW Press.

Russell, S., & Norvig, P. (2021). *Artificial intelligence: A modern approach* (4th ed.). Pearson.

Sanders, C. K., & Scanlon, E. (2021). The digital divide is a human rights issue: Advancing social inclusion through social work advocacy. *Journal of Human Rights and Social Work, 6*(2), 130–143. https://doi.org/10.1007/s41134-020-00147-9

Shneiderman, B. (2020). Human-centered artificial intelligence: Reliable, safe & trustworthy. *International Journal of Human–Computer Interaction, 36*(6), 495–504. https://doi.org/10.1080/10447318.2020.1741118

Szeliski, R. (2011). *Computer vision: Algorithms and applications*. Springer.

Tambe, M., & Rice, E. (2021) *Artificial intelligence and social work.* Cambridge University Press.

Toli, L., & Manasa, G. M. (2024). Artificial intelligence: Opportunities and challenges for the social education and profession. *Scholars Bulletin, 10*(4), 143–147. https://doi.org/10.36348/sb.2024.v10i04.005

Wang, D., Shang, L., & Zhang, Y. (2025). *Social intelligence: The new frontier of integrating human intelligence and artificial intelligence in social space*. Springer.

Wang, S. (2024). Mitigating homelessness in the United States through machine learning. *National High School Journal of Science*. https://nhsjs.com/wp-content/uploads/2024/11/Mitigating-Homelessness-in-the-United-States-through-Machine-Learnings.pdf

Xu, W., Dainoff, M. J., Ge, L., & Gao, Z. (2023). Transitioning to human interaction with AI systems: New challenges and opportunities for HCI professionals to enable human-centered AI. *International Journal of Human–Computer Interaction, 39*(3), 494–518. https://doi.org/10.1080/10447318.2022.2041900

1.9 Support Materials

AI for Everyone, taught by renowned AI educator Andrew Ng, is a foundational course designed to make AI accessible to professionals across all sectors, including social work. This non-technical course demystifies core AI concepts and empowers learners to understand how AI can be ethically and effectively integrated into organizational practice. For social workers, this course offers valuable insights into how AI can support data-informed decision-making, enhance service delivery, and promote equity through the transparent and ethical use of technology.

Watch this interview with a social work practitioner who wears many hats. This interview illustrates how an early adopter utilizes AI to promote work effectiveness as a therapist, doctoral student, MSW instructor, and researcher.

Please access this video at www.routledge.com/9781041275459

Video 1.1 Social Worker Who Wears Many Hats

2 History of Technology in Human Services

Othelia Lee

Box 2.1 From Ledgers to Algorithms: A Journey through Time

In 1975, Myra, a seasoned social worker in a bustling urban agency, spent her days surrounded by towering file cabinets, handwritten case notes, and rotary phones. Each morning began with sorting through paper referrals, manually updating client records, and coordinating services through face-to-face meetings or long waits on hold. Her work was deeply relational, but also slow, fragmented, and vulnerable to human error.

Fast forward to 2026. Justine, a newly graduated social worker, begins her day by logging into a secure cloud-based case management system. She reviews client updates from the previous evening, some submitted via mobile apps, others flagged by predictive analytics for urgent follow-up. She joins a virtual supervision session using immersive virtual reality (VR), where she practices trauma-informed responses in simulated crisis scenarios. Later, she collaborates with colleagues across agencies through encrypted messaging platforms, advocating for a client's housing needs using real-time data visualizations.

Though separated by decades, Myra and Justine share a common mission: to serve with compassion, integrity, and justice. What has changed is the technological landscape, a dynamic force that has reshaped how social workers engage with clients, manage information, and advocate for systemic change. From paper-based systems to artificial intelligence (AI), the evolution of technology in human services reflects not only innovation but also the profession's enduring commitment to human dignity.

Let's trace that journey, offering a historical overview of how technology has evolved and transformed social work practice, education, and policy. We invite readers to critically reflect on the tools they use today, understand their origins, and prepare to shape the ethical and inclusive technologies of tomorrow. This chapter explores how technological advancements have shaped the delivery, accessibility, and effectiveness of services over time.

DOI: 10.4324/9781003755081-3

2.1 Why Study the Historical Evolution of Technology

In the context of human services and social work, technology refers to the tools, systems, and digital infrastructures used to support, enhance, or deliver services to individuals, families, and communities (NASW, 2017; Giffords, 1998). This includes everything from case management software and telehealth platforms to AI and mobile applications. Technology in this field is not merely about efficiency: it is deeply tied to ethical practice, access to care, and the empowerment of service users.

According to Hilbert (2020), technology can be understood as a general-purpose toolset that transforms how societies function, including how information is processed, stored, and communicated. In human services, this transformation is evident in the shift from paper-based systems to digital platforms that enable real-time collaboration, data-driven decision-making, and remote service delivery. These tools are increasingly embedded in the daily work of social workers, influencing everything from intake assessments to outcome evaluations.

Why Social Workers Must Study the Historical Evolution of Technology? Understanding the historical evolution of technology in human services is crucial for social workers for several reasons:

Contextual Awareness: Studying the progression from manual systems to AI-driven tools helps social workers appreciate how practice has evolved in response to societal needs, policy changes, and technological innovation. This awareness fosters a deeper understanding of current tools and their limitations (Segal, 2025).

Ethical Preparedness: Each technological shift has introduced new ethical challenges—whether related to confidentiality, consent, or equity. By examining past transitions, social workers can better anticipate and navigate the ethical implications of emerging technologies.

Critical Engagement: Historical knowledge empowers social workers to critically assess technology's role in reinforcing or challenging systemic inequities. For example, the digital divide remains a persistent issue, and understanding its roots helps practitioners advocate for more inclusive solutions (Heeks, 2022).

Professional Identity: Technology has always shaped the identity and methods of social work. From the early use of scientific charity principles to today's predictive analytics, each era reflects a negotiation between innovation and core social work values such as dignity, justice, and human connection.

Technological revolutions are not only technical but also social, reshaping institutions, relationships, and power structures. For social workers, this means that engaging with technology is not optional. Indeed, it is integral to ethical, informed, and effective practice.

2.2 A Historical Overview of Technology in Human Services

Table 2.1 summarizes timelines of key technological milestones and historical events in each period. Let's go over professional evaluation of technology in human services because of significant events.

Table 2.1 Timeline of Key Milestones

Period	*Technological Milestone*
Pre-1970s	Manual record-keeping; telephone-based communication
1970s–1980s	Introduction of computers in agencies; early database systems
1990s	Widespread use of email and internet; digital case management begins
2000s	Development of specialized software; mobile phones enter practice
2010s	Cloud computing, mobile apps, and social media integration
2020s	Telehealth boom due to COVID-19; AI and predictive analytics emerge
Future	Integration of immersive tech (VR/augmented reality [AR]), blockchain for secure records, AI-driven decision-making

2.2.1 Early Use of Technology in Social Work (Pre-1980)

The roots of technology in human services are deeply intertwined with the evolution of social work itself. Before the digital age, human services relied heavily on manual systems. Social workers like Myra maintained paper records, organized client files in cabinets, and conducted face-to-face interviews to assess needs and deliver support. These systems, though labor-intensive, reflected a personal and relational approach to care that remains central to the profession today (Cesta, 2017).

Communication technologies such as the telephone and fax machine have begun to supplement in-person interactions, allowing for more timely coordination between agencies and professionals. These tools marked the beginning of remote service delivery, enabling social workers to reach clients who were geographically distant or unable to travel (Lee, 2009).

One of the most influential developments during this period was the rise of scientific charity, a movement that sought to apply business principles to social service delivery. Emerging in the late 19th century, scientific charity emphasized efficiency, accountability, and the systematic assessment of client needs. Charity Organization Societies (COS) were established to centralize aid distribution and reduce duplication of services. These organizations introduced the concept of the "friendly visitor," a precursor to modern case managers, who conducted home visits and maintained detailed records of client interactions (Jansson, 2019).

Scientific charity also laid the groundwork for early case management systems. These systems were entirely paper-based, relying on handwritten notes, index cards, and ledgers to track client progress and service utilization. Public health nurses and social workers used these tools to coordinate care, particularly for vulnerable populations such as immigrants, the poor, and individuals with chronic illnesses.

By the early 20th century, rudimentary databases began to emerge within large charitable organizations. These early systems catalogued client information and service histories, enabling more consistent and equitable care. Though primitive by today's standards, they represented a significant step toward the integration of information technology in human services (Lee, 2009).

Throughout this era, the compassionate ethos of social work remained steadfast. Even as technology began to shape service delivery, the profession continued to prioritize dignity, empathy, and human connection. The tools may have changed, but the heart of social work and its commitment to justice and care endured.

2.2.2 Digital Revolution and Its Impact

The 1980s and 1990s marked a transformative era in human services, as digital technologies began to reshape the landscape of social work practice. This period saw the introduction of personal computers (PCs) into social service agencies, revolutionizing administrative tasks and laying the groundwork for more sophisticated data management systems. Initially used for clerical functions such as payroll, budgeting, and record-keeping, computers soon became indispensable tools for agency operations (Miller, 1986).

As computing power became more accessible, early databases were developed to track client information. These systems allow agencies to store and retrieve data more efficiently, improving service coordination and accountability. The shift from paper-based to digital record-keeping was not merely a technical upgrade. In fact, it represented a fundamental change in how social workers engaged with information, enabling more timely and informed decision-making (Miller, 1986).

One of the most significant advancements during this era was the development of electronic case management systems. These systems evolved from simple databases into integrated platforms that supported holistic client care. They enabled social workers to document service interactions, monitor progress, and collaborate across multidisciplinary teams. The emergence of these tools reflected a growing recognition of the complexity of client needs and the importance of coordinated, data-informed interventions (Marques & Ferreira, 2020).

Simultaneously, the rise of email and the internet began to transform communication and research into social work. Email allowed for faster, more flexible correspondence between professionals, while the internet opened new avenues for accessing research, policy updates, and best practices. Social workers could now participate in online forums, subscribe to digital journals, and engage in virtual communities of practice. These innovations expanded the reach of social work, fostering global dialogue and collaboration (Giffords, 1998).

Despite the excitement surrounding these technologies, the profession approached them with thoughtful caution. Concerns about confidentiality, data security, and equitable access were central to early discussions. Social workers recognized that while technology could enhance service delivery, it must be implemented ethically and inclusively. The compassionate ethos of the field remained a guiding force, ensuring that digital tools served the human connection at the heart of social work.

2.2.3 Rise of Specialized Software and Databases

The early 2000s ushered in a new era of technological sophistication in human services, marked by the widespread adoption of electronic **case management systems**

(CMS). These systems were designed to streamline documentation, enhance service coordination, and support more holistic approaches to client care. Unlike earlier digital tools, CMS platforms in this period offered integrated features such as automated reminders, outcome tracking, and data dashboards, enabling social workers to manage complex cases with greater efficiency and precision (Snow et al., 2025).

One of the most transformative developments was the rise of interagency networks, which allowed multiple organizations to collaborate through shared **digital platforms**. These networks broke down silos between service providers, facilitating coordinated care for clients whose needs spanned housing, health, education, and employment. The ability to share data securely across agencies improved continuity of care and reduced duplication of services (Snow et al., 2025).

This period also saw significant policy shifts that supported the **digital transformation** of social work. Governments and regulatory bodies began to recognize the value of digital record-keeping and data-sharing, enacting legal reforms that encouraged the adoption of electronic systems. These changes were driven by a growing emphasis on accountability, transparency, and evidence-based practice in public service delivery (Snow et al., 2025).

A notable example of specialized software from this era is the Homeless Management Information System (HMIS), developed to track services provided to individuals and families experiencing homelessness (Gutierrez & Friedman, 2005). HMIS enabled service providers to collect client-level data, monitor outcomes, and comply with federal reporting standards. It became a cornerstone of coordinated entry systems, helping communities allocate resources more effectively and identify service gaps.

The integration of **data analytics** into service planning marked another leap forward. Social workers and administrators began using analytics to identify trends, evaluate program effectiveness, and make informed decisions (Osuszek et al., 2016). This shift from anecdotal to empirical evidence empowered organizations to design interventions that were both targeted and impactful. For social workers, data analytics allows us to base our decisions on actual data rather than on stories. To support these innovations, new tools for needs assessment and outcome measurement were introduced. Frameworks such as **logic models** and results chains helped practitioners align program goals with measurable outcomes (Savaya & Waysman, 2005). These tools provided a structured approach to evaluating client progress and program impact, ensuring that services remained responsive to evolving community needs. Additionally, logic models help practitioners articulate the causal pathways between program inputs, activities, outputs, and outcomes, thereby enhancing clarity and accountability in program design and evaluation.

2.2.4 Mobile and Cloud Technologies

The 2010s marked a profound shift in human services, as mobile technologies, cloud computing, and social media began to reshape how social workers connect with clients, collaborate with colleagues, and advocate for change. These innovations did not replace the human touch central to social work. They enhanced it, offering new pathways to reach and support vulnerable populations.

Mobile applications emerged as powerful tools for outreach and fieldwork. Social workers could now access client records, complete assessments, and communicate with clients directly from their smartphones or tablets. This mobility allowed practitioners to be more responsive and flexible, particularly when working in community settings or with individuals experiencing homelessness or crisis. Mobile apps also facilitated client engagement, offering self-monitoring tools, appointment reminders, and secure messaging platforms that helped clients stay connected to their care plans. Bakker and Rickard (2018) evaluated the MoodPrism app, which provided users with daily mood-tracking and self-monitoring features, indicating that higher engagement with the app predicted reductions in depression and anxiety and improvements in emotional self-awareness, especially among clinically depressed or anxious users.

At the same time, **cloud computing** revolutionized case management. Cloud-based systems enabled remote access to client data, allowing social workers to collaborate across agencies and geographic boundaries (Voss, 2025). These platforms supported real-time updates, centralized documentation, and secure data-sharing, which improved service coordination and reduced administrative burdens (Snowdon et al., 2020). The flexibility of cloud solutions meant that social workers could continue their work from virtually anywhere, ensuring continuity of care even during emergencies or public health crises.

Social media became a vital tool for advocacy, outreach, and community engagement. Platforms like Facebook, X, and Instagram allowed social workers and organizations to amplify their voices, raise awareness about social justice issues, and mobilize support for policy change. Social media also fostered dialogue and connection among communities, enabling individuals to share experiences, access resources, and participate in collective action (Scott & Maryman, 2024). While these tools offered unprecedented reach, they also required careful ethical consideration, particularly around privacy, boundaries, and professional conduct.

2.2.5 Telehealth and Virtual Services

The rise of **telehealth** and remote service delivery further expanded access to care. Social workers began using video conferencing, secure messaging, and digital platforms to provide therapy, crisis intervention, and case management services (Balogun et al., 2025). This shift was especially impactful for clients in rural or underserved areas, who previously faced significant barriers to accessing support.

The 2020s began with an unprecedented global health crisis that would forever alter the landscape of human services. The COVID-19 pandemic acted as a powerful catalyst, accelerating the adoption of telehealth and virtual counseling across social work settings. Practitioners who had previously relied on in-person interactions were suddenly required to pivot to remote modalities, often within days. This rapid transformation was not only a logistical challenge but also a profound reimagining of how care could be delivered (Casu et al., 2024).

The effectiveness of **virtual interventions** was affirmed by research showing comparable outcomes to in-person services, reinforcing the legitimacy of telehealth as a core component of modern practice. These tools allowed for continuity of care during lockdowns and social distancing mandates, ensuring that clients, especially those in rural or underserved areas, could still access vital support (Sullivan et al., 2023).

However, the shift to virtual services also illuminated longstanding digital equity concerns. The **digital divide**, the gap between those with reliable access to technology and those without, became a pressing issue. Marginalized populations, including low-income families, older adults, and individuals with disabilities, often lacked the devices, internet connectivity, or **digital literacy** needed to engage in telehealth services. Social workers, guided by their commitment to social justice, stepped into advocacy roles to address these disparities, promoting inclusive policies and community-based solutions (Sanders & Scanlon, 2021).

Alongside these equity challenges, the rise of telehealth introduced new ethical considerations. Issues of confidentiality, informed consent, and data protection became central to virtual practice. Social workers had to ensure that clients understood the risks and limitations of remote services, including potential breaches of privacy and the importance of secure environments for virtual sessions (Balogun et al., 2025). Professional standards evolved to include guidance on selecting HIPAA (Health Insurance Portability and Accountability Act)-compliant platforms, obtaining digital consent, and maintaining clear boundaries in virtual spaces.

2.2.6 AI and Predictive Analytics in Human Services (2020s and Beyond)

Figure 2.1 illustrates a brief history of AI. As the digital transformation of human services accelerated in the 2020s, AI emerged as a powerful force reshaping the landscape of social work. AI technologies, once considered futuristic, are now actively supporting practitioners in decision-making, risk assessment, and service delivery. These tools offer new possibilities for enhancing care, but they also raise important ethical questions that demand thoughtful reflection.

AI in social work encompasses a range of applications, from predictive analytics and natural language processing to automated case management systems and virtual assistants. **Predictive analytics** has become a game-changer. By analyzing historical and real-time data, social workers can identify individuals or families at risk of adverse outcomes (e.g., homelessness, child maltreatment, or mental health crises) and intervene proactively (Kumar & Suthar, 2024).

Since 2016, Allegheny County has implemented the Allegheny Family Screening Tool (AFST) to assist call screeners in evaluating child welfare referrals. Their findings show that the AFST has significantly impacted decision-making by increasing the probability of investigation for high-risk referrals and decreasing investigations for low-risk cases (Allegheny County Department of Human Services, 2024).

These technologies do not replace human judgment; rather, they can enhance it by assisting social workers prioritize caseloads, allocate resources more efficiently,

Figure 2.1 A Brief History of Artificial Intelligence.

and tailor interventions to individual needs. Case management platforms powered by AI may automate documentation, generate insights from client data, and recommend evidence-based strategies for care planning. This allows practitioners to spend less time on administrative tasks and more time engaging directly with clients.

However, the integration of AI into social work practice is not without challenges. The profession must grapple with ethical considerations that are both complex and evolving. Key concerns include informed consent, client autonomy, privacy, and **algorithmic bias** (Nuwasiima et al., 2024). AI systems, while powerful, can inadvertently reinforce systemic inequities if not designed and implemented with care. For instance, biased data inputs may lead to unfair risk assessments or misdiagnoses, disproportionately affecting marginalized communities (NASW, 2024).

Transparency is another critical issue. Clients have the right to understand how AI tools are used in their care, what data is collected, and how decisions are made. Social workers must ensure that AI applications align with the values of the profession, particularly its commitment to equity, justice, and human dignity (NASW, 2024). This includes advocating for ethical standards in AI development and engaging in ongoing education to stay informed about emerging technologies. We will further discuss algorithmic bias and ethical considerations in the upcoming chapter.

AI is also used to support mental health through tools like **chatbots** and virtual assistants. These technologies offer accessible, round-the-clock support, especially for individuals who may be hesitant to seek traditional therapy. Casu and colleagues (2024) evaluated the effectiveness and feasibility of AI chatbots in mental health interventions across 15 studies. It found that AI chatbots offer accessible, scalable, and immediate support, particularly beneficial for individuals hesitant to seek traditional therapy due to stigma or logistical barriers.

Natural Language Processing (NLP) enables systems to detect signs of distress in text-based communication, allowing for timely intervention in crisis situations. Swaminathan and colleagues (2023) developed and deployed a two-stage NLP system (combining keyword filtering and logistic regression) to identify crisis messages (e.g., suicidal ideation, domestic violence) within a large telehealth provider network. The system demonstrated high accuracy and sensitivity, significantly reducing response times to crisis messages from 9 hours to under 13 minutes, enabling timely intervention and support.

As AI continues to evolve, social workers are uniquely positioned to guide its ethical and compassionate use. By combining technological innovation with the relational wisdom of the profession, practitioners can ensure that AI serves as a tool for empowerment, not surveillance or exclusion. The future of social work will depend not only on embracing new technologies but on shaping them to reflect the values that define the profession.

2.3 Digital Equity and Access

In an increasingly digital world, access to technology is no longer a luxury: it is a necessity. Yet, the digital divide continues to disproportionately affect vulnerable populations, including older adults, individuals with disabilities, low-income families, and those with limited digital literacy. This divide is not simply about having internet access or owning a device: it encompasses digital literacy, confidence, and the ability to use technology meaningfully in daily life.

Sanders and Scanlon (2021) highlight how lack of access to high-speed internet disproportionately affects low-income, older, rural, and marginalized populations. Authors frame digital exclusion as a structural issue that perpetuates social and economic disparities and call for social workers to engage in policy advocacy to close the divide.

For social workers, addressing digital exclusion is a matter of social justice. Technology must be inclusive, accessible, and responsive to the diverse needs of the communities served. Strategies for inclusive technology use include co-designing digital tools with service users, offering digital literacy training, and ensuring that platforms are accessible to people with varying abilities and language backgrounds. In disability services, for example, a stepped inclusive approach to **Information and Communication Technology** adoption has been shown to improve practitioner engagement and allow for tailored interventions to meet client needs (Fernández-Batanero et al., 2022).

Beyond practice, policy and advocacy play a critical role in promoting digital equity. Social workers are uniquely positioned to influence policy by highlighting the systemic barriers that prevent equitable access to technology. Understanding the historical roots of digital exclusion empowers social workers to critically assess how technology can reinforce or challenge systemic inequities. By engaging in advocacy, designing inclusive interventions, and promoting ethical digital practices, social workers can ensure that technology serves as a tool for empowerment, not exclusion.

2.4 Future Trends in Technology and Social Work

As technology continues to evolve, social work stands at the threshold of transformative possibilities. Emerging tools such as VR, blockchain, and agentic AI are beginning to reshape how we deliver services, train practitioners, and uphold ethical standards. These innovations offer exciting opportunities but also demand critical reflection and inclusive policy development. We need to further their potential to enhance transparency, security, and engagement in human services.

For instance, virtual reality (VR) simulations are increasingly used in social work education to foster empathy and decision-making skills in complex scenarios. Huttar and BrintzenhofeSzoc (2020) assert that these immersive VR tools foster empathy and decision-making by allowing students to engage in realistic, interactive scenarios that mirror complex client situations.

One promising area of innovation is the integration of technology into trauma-informed care. Technology facilitated the creation of timely documentation, improved access to critical information, and enhanced collaboration between behavioral health and child welfare professionals (Collins-Camargo et al., 2019). Educators and students reported that technology-enhanced learning environments supported trauma-responsive practices by promoting safety, collaboration, and resilience (Cavener & Lonbay, 2024). Innovations in digital platforms appeared to help integrate trauma-informed principles into frontline practice more effectively, facilitating reflective supervision, peer support, and ongoing professional development in trauma-sensitive environments.

Blockchain, with its decentralized and secure data structures, is being considered for applications such as secure record-keeping and identity verification in vulnerable populations. Aydar and colleagues (2020) emphasize the potential of blockchain to empower individuals with control over their data, enhance privacy, and facilitate secure collaboration across institutions, key benefits for vulnerable populations in human services.

AI is being tested for its ability to support ethical decision-making and mental health assessments. Segal (2025) compares ChatGPT's responses to ethical dilemmas with those of a professional ethics committee. Findings imply that ChatGPT can support ethical decision-making by highlighting complex considerations and conflicting obligations, though it is not yet a substitute for human judgment.

To ensure that future practitioners are prepared for tech-integrated practice, social work education must evolve. The Digitalising Social Work Education Framework offers a model for embedding digital competencies into curriculum design, emphasizing not just technical skills but also critical engagement with sociotechnical systems (Taylor-Beswick, 2023). This means understanding how technologies can both empower and oppress, and how digital tools intersect with issues of privacy, equity, and human rights.

Social workers must advocate for standards that protect client autonomy, promote transparency, and address the digital divide. The concept of **e-professionalism**, which emphasizes ethical digital literacy and responsible tech use, has emerged as a guiding principle for navigating this new terrain (Barsky, 2017). The future of social work will be shaped by how the profession engages with technology, not just as a tool, but as a social force.

2.5 Critical Thinking Questions

1 What are the opportunities and challenges that Myra and Justine (Box 2.1) face on a daily basis?
2 From paper-based systems to AI, how has technology transformed social work practice, education, and policy?
3 What technological milestones do you envision in ten years down the road?

2.6 Summary

We overview the historical evolution of technology in human services, emphasizing why social workers must understand this trajectory and highlighting how technological shifts have shaped service delivery, professional roles, and client engagement. Persistent challenges of digital divide urge social workers to advocate for inclusive technology use. By embracing innovation with compassion, critical thinking, and a commitment to justice, social workers can lead the way in creating a digital future that serves all communities equitably.

References

Allegheny County Department of Human Services. (2024). *Summarizing recent research on predictive risk models in child welfare*. Allegheny County Analytics. www.alleghenycountyanalytics.us/wp-content/uploads/2024/05/24-ACDHS-04-Predictive-Risk-Algorithms.pdf

Aydar, M., Ayvaz, S., & Cetin, S. C. (2020). Towards a blockchain-based digital identity verification, record attestation, and record sharing system. *arXiv.org*. https://doi.org/10.48550/arXiv.1906.09791

Bakker, D., & Rickard, N. (2018). Engagement in mobile phone app for self-monitoring of emotional wellbeing predicts changes in mental health: MoodPrism. *Journal of Affective Disorders,* 227, 432–442. https://doi.org/10.1016/j.jad.2017.11.016

Balogun, A. K., Dada, S. N., Kazeem, O., & Bakare-Adesokan, K. A. (2025). Integrating telehealth services in social work practice for vulnerable groups. *World Journal of Advanced Research and Reviews, 25*(1), 1984–1991. https://doi.org/10.30574/wjarr.2025.25.1.0248

Barsky, A. E. (2017). Social work practice and technology: Ethical issues and policy responses. *Journal of Technology in Human Services, 35*(1), 8–19. https://doi.org/10.1080/15228835.2017.1277906

Casu, M., Triscari, S., Battiato, S., Guarnera, L., & Caponnetto, P. (2024). AI chatbots for mental health: A scoping review of effectiveness, feasibility, and applications. *Applied Sciences, 14*(13), 5889. https://doi.org/10.3390/app14135889

Cavener, J., & Lonbay, S. (2024). Enhancing 'best practice' in trauma-informed social work education: Insights from a study exploring educator and student experiences. *Social Work Education, 43(*2), 317–338. https://doi.org/10.1080/02615479.2022.2091128

Cesta, T. (2017). *What's old is new again: The history of case management.* Clinician.com. www.clinician.com/articles/141367-whats-old-is-new-again-the-history-of-case-management

Collins-Camargo, C., Strolin, J., & Akin, B. (2019). Use of technology to facilitate practice improvement in trauma-informed child welfare systems. *Child Welfare,* 97(3), 85–108. www.jstor.org/stable/48623659

Fernández-Batanero, J. M ., Montenegro-Rueda, M. , Fernández-Cerero, J., & García-Martínez, I. (2022). Assistive technology for the inclusion of students with disabilities: A systematic review. *Educational Technology Research and Development, 70*(5), 1911–1930. https://doi.org/10.1007/s11423-022-10127-7

Giffords, E. D. (1998). Social work on the Internet: An introduction. *Social Work, 43*(3), 243–251. https://doi.org/10.1093/sw/43.3.243

Gutierrez, O., & Friedman, D. H. (2005). Managing project expectations in human services information systems implementations: The case of homeless management information systems. *International Journal of Project Management, 23*(7), 513–523. https://doi.org/10.1016/j.ijproman.2005.02.006

Heeks, R. (2022). Digital inequality beyond the digital divide: Conceptualizing adverse digital incorporation in the global South. *Information Technology for Development, 28(*4), 688–704. https://doi.org/10.1080/02681102.2022.2068492

Hilbert, M. (2020). Digital technology and social change: The digital transformation of society from a historical perspective. *Dialogues in Clinical Neuroscience, 22*(2), 189–194. https://doi.org/10.31887/DCNS.2020.22.2/mhilbert

Huttar, C. M., & BrintzenhofeSzoc, K. (2020). Virtual reality and computer simulation in social work education: A systematic review. *Journal of Social Work Education, 56*(1), 131–141. https://doi.org/10.1080/10437797.2019.1648221

Jansson, B. S. (2019). *The reluctant welfare state: Engaging history to advance social work practice in contemporary society* (9th ed.). Cengage.

Kumar, D., & Suthar, N. (2024). Predictive analytics and early intervention in healthcare social work: A scoping review. *Social Work in Health Care, 63*(4-5), 208–229. https://doi.org/10.1080/00981389.2024.2316700

Lee, M. (2009). Historical milestones in the emergence of nonprofit public relations in the United States, 1900–1956. *Nonprofit and Voluntary Sector Quarterly, 40*(2), 318–335. https://doi.org/10.1177/0899764009343021

Marques, I. C., & Ferreira, J. J. (2020). Digital transformation in the area of health: Systematic review of 45 years of evolution. *Health and Technology, 10*, 575–586. https://doi.org/10.1007/s12553-019-00402-8

Miller, H. (1986). The use of computers in social work practice: An assessment. *Journal of Social Work Education, 22*(3), 52–60. https://doi.org/10.1080/10437797.1986.10671750

National Association of Social Workers. (2017). *Technology in social work practice.* NASW Press.

National Association of Social Workers. (2024). *Standards for technology in social work practice.* NASW – National Association of Social Workers. www.socialworkers.org/Practice/NASW-Practice-Standards-Guidelines/Standards-for-Technology-in-Social-Work-Practice

Nuwasiima, M., Ahonon, M. P., & Kadiri, C. (2024). The role of artificial intelligence (AI) and machine learning in social work practice. *World Journal of Advanced Research and Reviews, 24*(1), 80–97. https://doi.org/10.30574/wjarr.2024.24.1.2998

Osuszek, L., Stanek, S., & Twardowski, Z. (2016). Leverage big data analytics for dynamic informed decisions with advanced case management. *Journal of Decision Systems, 25*(sup1), 436–449. https://doi.org/10.1080/12460125.2016.1187401

Sanders, C. K., & Scanlon, E. (2021). The digital divide is a human rights issue: Advancing social inclusion through social work advocacy. *Journal of Human Rights and Social Work, 6*, 130–143. https://doi.org/10.1007/s41134-020-00147-9

Savaya, R., & Waysman, M. (2005). The logic model: A tool for incorporating theory in development and evaluation of programs. *Administration in Social Work, 29*(2), 85–103. https://doi.org/10.1300/J147v29n02_06

Scott, J. T., & Maryman, J. V. (2024). Using social media as a tool to complement advocacy efforts. *Global Journal of Community Psychology Practice, 7*(1S), 1–22, https://doi.org/10.7728/0701201603

Segal, M. (2025). Social workers' evaluation of ChatGPT for solving ethical dilemmas within the limits of confidentiality. *Journal of Social Work Practice, 40*, 1–14. https://doi.org/10.1080/02650533.2025.2480092

Snow, M., Silva-Ribeiro, W., Baginsky, M., Di Giorgio, S., Farrelly, N., Larkins, C., Poole, K., Steils, N., Westwood, J., & Malley, J. (2025). Best practices for implementing electronic care records in adult social care: Rapid scoping review. *Journal of Medical Internet Research Aging, 8*, e60107. https://doi.org/10.2196/60107

Snowdon, J. L., Robinson, B., Staats, C. K., Wolsey, K., Sands-Lincoln, M., Strasheim, T., Brotman, D., Keating, K. M., Schnitter, E. M., Jackson, G. P., & Kassler, W. J. (2020).

Empowering caseworkers to better serve the most vulnerable with a cloud-based care management solution. *Applied Clinical Informatics, 11*(04), 617–621. https://doi.org/10.1055/s-0040-1715894

Sullivan, W. P., Hostetter, C., & Commodore-Mensah, M. (2023). Experiences of mental health professionals in the rapid pivot to telehealth: Implications for social work practice. *Advances in Social Work, 23*(1), 221–239. https://doi.org/10.18060/26161

Swaminathan, A., López, I., Mar, R. A. G., Heist, T., McClintock, T., Caoili, K., Grace, M., Rubashkin, M., Boggs, M. N., Chen, J. H., Gevaert, O., Mou, D., & Nock, M. K. (2023). Natural language processing system for rapid detection and intervention of mental health crisis chat messages. *NPJ Digital Medicine, 6*, 213. https://doi.org/10.1038/s41746-023-00951-3

Taylor-Beswick, A. M. L. (2023). Digitalizing social work education: Preparing students to engage with twenty-first century practice need. *Social Work Education, 42*(1), 44–64. https://doi.org/10.1080/02615479.2022.2049225

Voss, M. (2025). *5 ways cloud-based case management is revolutionizing social services.* CaseWorthy Knowledge Center. https://caseworthy.com/articles/5-ways-cloud-based-case-management-is-revolutionizing-social-services/

2.7 Support Materials

Historical Roots of Human Services: A Timeline
www.preceden.com/timelines/639807-the-historical-roots-of-human-services-a-timeline

3 ICT, IoT, and AI

Moon Sun Song

> **Box 3.1 Smart Social Work: Around the Clock**
>
> It is 2:00 AM. Victoria (aged 82), who lives alone, is watching TV as usual. On her wrist, she wears a smartwatch, and in the corner of her living room, a small motion sensor is at work. Suddenly, Victoria's heart rate spikes abnormally, and the activity sensor detects no movement for over five minutes. The data sent by these sensors is immediately transmitted to a cloud server. Based on the accumulated Big Data, the server classifies this not as a simple rest, but as a "Critical Emergency." This artificial intelligence (AI)-driven analysis instantly triggers an alarm in the integrated social work system, sending an urgent message to Lucy, the social worker in charge, on her tablet. As soon as Lucy sees the message, she rushes to Victoria's house while simultaneously sharing the situation with emergency services (911).
>
> "Twenty years ago, I would have had to visit in person and knock on the door to find out if anything was wrong," Lucy says. "But now, through the ICT neural network, real-time information from IoT sensors passes through the AI's judgment, becoming a life-saving action in just a few seconds. We truly live in a wonderful world!"

Box 3.1 illustrates a future where technology grants social workers "superpowers," enabling them to care for marginalized populations far more quickly and accurately than we ever imagined. Internet of Things (IoT), Sensors, Information and Communication Technology (ICT), Networks/Systems, and AI are collaborating to support human efforts. What exactly are these remarkable technologies and how specifically are they innovating the field of social work? These technologies are explained in greater detail in the next section.

3.1 Information and Communication Technology (ICT)

We are living in a digital world where everything is interconnected. The most powerful engine driving this world is ICT, which is a unified concept that merges

DOI: 10.4324/9781003755081-4

information technology (IT), the technology for handling information, and communication technology (CT), the technology for transmitting information. IT refers to technologies used to produce, process, and store information (such as computers, software, and databases), while CT refers to technologies used to transmit and share information (such as the Internet, mobile devices, and communication networks) (Heeks, 2010; Blurton, 1999). ICT goes beyond merely creating information; it refers to an integrated technological system that connects that information so it can be utilized anytime, anywhere.

Today, ICT has permeated every aspect of our lives and is evolving into a broad concept that encompasses various sub-technologies, such as the Internet, 5G (and the emerging 6G) networks, cloud computing, AI, big data, software, IoT, smartphones, and wearable devices. ICT makes our lives more convenient through the organic interaction of its core components: networks for exchanging data, hardware (servers, computers) for processing it, and software (applications) for managing information efficiently. In this chapter, we aim to establish a clear understanding of the fundamental technical concepts of ICT and examine how these technologies are applied in real-world social work settings to drive social change.

3.1.1 Hardware and Software

Hardware refers to all devices with physical form, such as computers, servers, network equipment, smartphones, and tablets. It serves as the physical foundation that allows users to experience the digital world tangibly and provides the base upon which intangible software operates.

In the social work sector, hardware is far broader and more diverse than the typical office personal computer (PC) we might imagine; therefore, it is essential to identify specific examples of hardware used in these settings.

One example is the **Smart Care Terminal**, a dedicated hardware device installed in the homes of older adults living alone to detect life signals (temperature, humidity, movement) and perform emergency call functions (Lee, 2018; Vrančić et al., 2024). Another representative example is the **kiosk**, installed in community centers or public offices to help people conveniently search for social work information or issue civil documents through digital devices without face-to-face interaction (Krieger et al., 2023).

Software consists of operating systems and applications that instruct hardware to perform specific tasks; it serves as the "brain" that operates the system. In social work, software is utilized to manage the income, assets, and service history of beneficiaries while automating the payment of benefits. Additionally, mobile case management applications are representative examples of software that serve as the "hands and feet" of social workers in the field. These tools allow practitioners to move away from traditional paper-based workflows by enabling real-time data entry, digital documentation, and immediate access to client records during home visits (Russ & Reimer, 2025).

3.1.2 Network and Communication Technology

Network and communication technology, such as high-speed fiber optics, wireless Wi-Fi systems, and mobile data networks, refers to the system that accurately and rapidly transmits information from one point to another, serving as the core foundation of ICT.

A network is a structure where two or more devices are connected for data exchange, ranging from **Local Area Networks** (LAN) and **Wide Area Networks** (WAN) to the global Internet. Communication protocols, such as **Transmission Control Protocol** and **Internet Protocol** (TCP/IP), serve as the pre-established rules that govern how data is exchanged between these devices. High-speed wireless technologies like 5G and Wi-Fi act as communication networks that reduce data transmission latency and innovatively improve access to services in social work settings (Sharma & Wang, 2020; Al-Sarawi et al., 2017)

Network and communication technologies overcome geographical barriers and time constraints, playing a pivotal role in filling gaps in social welfare services. For instance, tele-social work and **telehealth** services based on high-speed internet networks can eliminate service blind spots. These technologies enable professionals to provide video-based psychological counseling and remote health monitoring to individuals in remote areas or those with limited mobility. Furthermore, **Emergency Response Systems** (ERS), which utilize IoT sensors to detect falls or medical crises in real time, ensure that help is dispatched immediately even when a client is alone.

3.1.3 Cloud Computing

Cloud computing is a model where computing resources—such as servers, storage, and databases—are rented flexibly through the internet on a pay-as-you-go basis. It functions similarly to a utility grid, where users receive IT resources from remote locations rather than maintaining private infrastructure. In human services, the cloud securely integrates and stores vast amounts of sensitive data, including beneficiary records and medical history. To ensure privacy protection, these systems employ advanced security measures such as eclipsed messaging (**encryption**) to make data unreadable to unauthorized parties and robust password protection or **multi-factor authentication** to control access.

Furthermore, cloud environment provides social work information systems with essential flexibility and scalability. For instance, when demand for services spikes—such as during a pandemic when millions simultaneously apply for emergency financial support—the cloud's **auto-scaling** feature instantly increases server capacity. This prevents system crashes by distributing the heavy digital traffic across multiple virtual servers, ensuring that critical services remain accessible even during times of crisis (Hashem et al., 2015).

3.1.4 Big Data

Big data refers to data sets that are significantly vaster and more complex than traditional data, generated at high speeds and in various formats. It represents both the total volume of data that can be converted into valuable information and the technological concept of analyzing collected data to derive useful insights. For example, by integrating diverse data sources—such as a client's history of public assistance, healthcare records, and local employment trends—social work agencies can predict which households are at the highest risk of crisis. These insights allow for **proactive intervention** rather than reactive support, effectively turning raw data into a life-saving resource (Chen et al., 2014)

In social work, big data includes indicators related to quality of life, social safety nets, social benefit status, poverty, health, aging, and high-risk groups for solitary deaths. This data is generated by various sources, such as national and local governments, public institutions, hospitals, educational institutions, and social work agencies. By analyzing this data, stakeholders—including central government ministries, municipal governments, social service research institutes, and professional social workers—can establish evidence-based policies, provide customized services, and discover and resolve blind spots in human service systems. Because challenges in the social work sector often arise from complex factors—such as unemployment, illness, isolation, and debt within a household—it is necessary to comprehensively analyze data from multiple sources. This requires the processing of massive amounts of household-level data to identify interconnected risks and provide holistic support to families in crisis.

Social work data consists of **structured data**, which follows fixed formats—such as income information, Electronic Health Records (EHR), or clinical diagnosis codes based on the Diagnostic and Statistical Manual of Mental Disorders (DSM)—typically organized in tables. It also includes **unstructured data**, which comprises non-standardized information such as counselors' case notes, CCTV footage, and call recordings. In a big data environment, ICT processes and prepares even this unstructured data so that AI can integrate and analyze it effectively (Chen et al., 2014).

The goal of ICT in the social work sector is to transform raw data into meaningful information for practical use. In this context, data refers to raw facts or values, such as a record indicating that an older adult visited the hospital three times in October. This data becomes information when it is processed and organized to provide specific meaning, such as identifying a sign of increasing health risk based on the heightened frequency of those medical visits.

However, data in the social work sector faces two major challenges: protection and utilization. This data—collected from various contact points such as community centers, public health clinics, and social service agencies—is typically stored and managed within centralized platforms like the **Social Security Information System**. It contains sensitive personal information, such as income, health, and disability status. To protect this sensitive information and prevent leaks, ICT utilizes advanced encryption technologies. Adhering to professional ethics and **Personal Information Protection Acts** is a strict prerequisite for using technology in this sensitive setting (Hashem et al., 2015).

Secondly, ICT enables data-driven policymaking. Instead of relying on limited, analog-style policies dependent on manpower and paper documents, data analysis allows for scientific social work planning. It helps identify regions and individuals with the most urgent needs and ensures the efficient distribution of resources. For example, to strengthen child social work, a complex analysis of indicators—such as trends in child abuse reports, the ratio of single-parent households, low-income statistics, the distribution of childcare infrastructure, and neglect rates—allows for the strategic design of resource allocation and new service development (Song, 2025).

3.2 Internet of Things (IoT)

IoT refers to an intelligent network environment where various objects are connected to the internet to exchange data and interact with one another. While the traditional internet connected people to people or people to information, IoT digitizes our physical environment by connecting things to things or things to people (Gubbi et al., 2013).

For example, in a smart home for older adults, a motion sensor can communicate directly with a lighting system to prevent falls at night (thing to thing), while a wearable heart-rate monitor can send real-time alerts to a social worker's smartphone if an abnormality is detected (thing to person).

In this system, objects exchange information and react to one another without human command. In the past, the internet was only connected to computers or smartphones; however, today, everything from refrigerators, cars, and lights to hospital equipment and even agricultural machinery is networked and operates autonomously. It is as if objects have gained "smart brains" and are having conversations with each other (Song, 2025).

IoT is a core technology that enables remote care and smart-home-based safety and health-monitoring. This includes technologies that support and monitor the activities of daily living (ADL)—such as eating, sleeping, personal hygiene, and bowel movements—for older adults or people with disabilities. Furthermore, these systems are essential for emergency response and location-tracking to ensure client safety in various social work settings (Gubbi et al., 2013).

South Korea's "Emergency Safety and Care Service" is a representative IoT-based care service led by the central government. It targets older adults living alone or people with severe disabilities, using various sensors to monitor fires, medical emergencies, and lack of activity. This allows for the early detection and prevention of emergency situations and solitary deaths (Song, 2025).

3.2.1 Sensor Technology

A sensor is the most fundamental component of IoT. It is a device that detects physical changes—such as temperature, humidity, movement, pressure, and heart rate—and converts them into electrical signals. These signals represent vital data regarding a client's physical health, behavioral patterns, and environmental safety. Without sensors, objects would be unable to perceive their own state or their surrounding environment, making it impossible to provide proactive care. Sensor technology acts as the social worker's "eyes and ears" in the daily lives of those

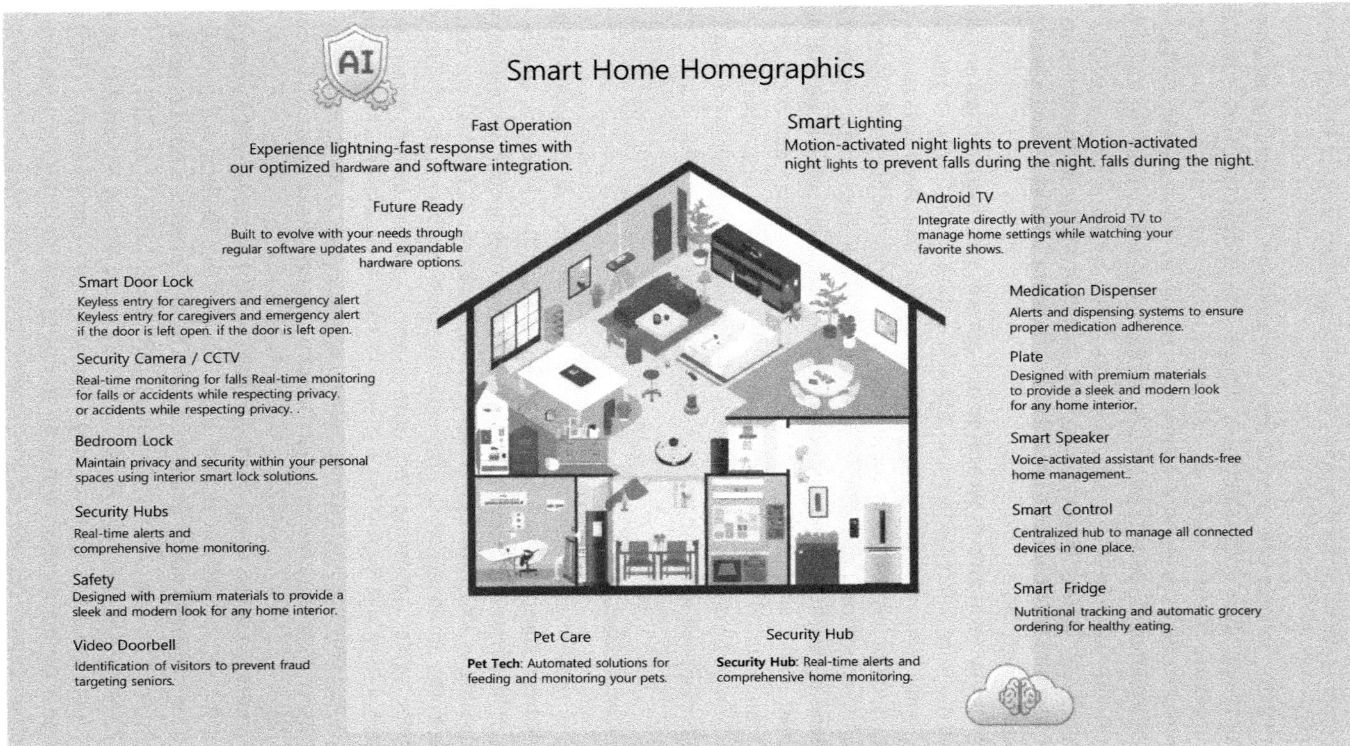

Figure 3.1 Smart Home Homegraphics.

under care. For example, motion sensors installed in the bedrooms or living rooms of solo-living older adults can identify a "danger situation" and send an alert if no movement is detected for a specific period (e.g., more than 12 hours) (Vrančić et al., 2024).

Additionally, sensors can prevent fires and accidents by sounding an alarm if the indoor temperature drops sharply or if a gas leak is detected. This is primarily utilized in **Smart Homes**, which are intelligent living environments where household appliances and sensors are connected via IoT to automatically collect and control information. A representative case of the use of IoT sensors for social work is a system implemented by the city of Busan, South Korea, for low-income older adult households. During winter, the system measures indoor temperatures in real time and automatically connects households to heating support if dangerous levels are detected (Song, 2025).

Finally, sensors function as **wearable** devices (such as smartwatches and smart rings) that measure and record various **biometric data**, including heart rate, blood pressure, body temperature, blood oxygen saturation, and sleep patterns, in real time. This is extremely useful for continuously monitoring the health of older adults with chronic conditions, and people with disabilities. It even enables preventive care by sending notifications to social workers or guardians when abnormal signs are detected. Other emerging technologies include wandering detection devices with real-time **Global Positioning System** (GPS) to prevent dementia patients or children from going missing, **smart canes** with built-in LED lights to prevent falls, smart belts equipped with airbags, and smart slippers (Song, 2025).

3.2.2 Network Technology

IoT devices must transmit data continuously, but they face the challenge of minimizing battery consumption (Adelantado et al., 2017). Therefore, unlike 5G networks, which transmit massive amounts of data at high speeds, specialized network technologies like **Low Power Wide Area Networks** (LPWAN) are crucial. These networks are designed to efficiently transmit small amounts of data over a wide range while consuming very little power. Examples include Long Range (LoRa) technology and Sigfox (a proprietary LPWAN protocol), which are ideal for sensors that only need to send intermittent updates, such as location trackers for older adults or environmental monitors in remote areas (Raza et al., 2017; Sinha et al., 2017).

In the context of social work, this technology is vital for devices like emergency buttons or activity sensors in remote areas. Since these devices can operate for years on a single small battery thanks to LPWAN, they provide a reliable safety net without the need for frequent maintenance or charging (Sinha et al., 2017).

IoT networks help provide stable care services even for vulnerable groups living in rural areas. LPWAN technology can cover wide areas that are a challenge for traditional communication networks to reach, making it highly effective for islands, mountainous regions, or low-income areas with weak communication infrastructure. Furthermore, it allows sensor devices to operate for several years without frequent battery replacements. This enables the provision of continuous and stable home-monitoring services.

3.2.3 Cloud and Big Data

The vast amount of real-time data collected by IoT sensors cannot be processed by an individual device. This data is transmitted via the internet to a centralized storage and processing space called cloud computing or cloud. The countless pieces of IoT data gathered in the cloud then become the primary source of big data (Gubbi et al., 2013). Cloud computing and big data technologies work together to collect data through continuous **safety monitoring** and enable intelligent predictions. Specifically, by analyzing accumulated information—such as patterns of daily activity, sudden changes in vital signs, or historical service usage—these technologies can predict potential crises, like solitary deaths or health emergencies, before they occur.

In the case of child protection and family support services, the system analyzes daily patterns within the households such as school attendance, nutritional intake via smart refrigerators, and emotional cues from AI speakers—as Big Data. For instance, if a child from a high-risk family shows irregular activity patterns or prolonged absence from online educational platforms, the system predicts potential neglect or an emergency and alerts a family counselor (Balaji et al., 2025).

Furthermore, these technologies are increasingly vital in **military social work**. By monitoring the vital signs and activity data of active-duty personnel through wearable IoT devices, the system gathers big data on physical and psychological stress levels. If a soldier in a remote outpost exhibits atypical signs, such as severe sleep deprivation or abnormal heart rate variability during guard duty, the system flags a risk for a mental health crisis or physical exhaustion. This allows military social workers or commanders to provide proactive interventions, such as counseling or medical leave, ensuring the well-being of service members before a critical incident occurs (Umamaheswari et al., 2025).

3.3 Artificial Intelligence

3.3.1 Definition of AI

AI refers to systems or technologies that can think, learn, judge, and solve problems. It includes computer programs or algorithms that mimic human intelligent behavior. In essence, AI implements human learning, problem-solving, and cognitive abilities into computer programs, enabling them to think and act like human beings (Russell & Norvig, 2010).

When AI is introduced into the social work sector, it plays a decisive role in analyzing big data collected through ICT and IoT to recognize patterns. This allows it to identify and predict subtle signals or complex needs that human social work experts might overlook.

The core components required for AI to function include (Russell & Norvig, 2010):

Data: Images, text, and numbers for the AI to learn from.
Algorithms: The logic used to process the data.
Models: The outcomes learned or results.
Computing Resources: Hardware like graphics processing units (GPUs) and Cloud systems that run the AI.

Let's classify AI based on its functions, examine its concepts and algorithms, and explore the possibilities of its application in the field of social work.

3.3.2 Classification of AI

AI is categorized into three types based on its functionality: Artificial Narrow Intelligence (ANI), Artificial General Intelligence (AGI), and Artificial Super Intelligence (ASI) (Atzori et al., 2010).

3.3.2.1 Artificial Narrow Intelligence (ANI)

ANI, often called "Weak AI," is the form of AI we encounter most frequently in our daily lives. As the name suggests, it refers to "intelligence within a narrow range." It specializes in performing a single specific task. Examples include smartphone voice assistants like Siri or Bixby, and the AI Go program AlphaGo. These systems are excellent at solving the specific problems they were designed for but cannot perform any other tasks. For instance, AlphaGo plays Go exceptionally well but cannot predict the weather or recommend music (Kaplan & Haenlein, 2019).

In other words, ANI refers to AI that specializes in a particular task without general thinking or understanding capabilities. Currently, most AI we use belongs to the ANI category. Because ANI lacks self-awareness or independent thought, it cannot infer situations, understand complex emotions, or integrate multiple domains. It operates solely based on algorithms and data designed by humans.

While ANI is highly accurate and efficient—performing tasks faster and more consistently than humans—it has limitations. Its scope of work is restricted, it cannot understand new contexts, it fails to handle unexpected situations, and it cannot think or learn independently like a human (Russell & Norvig, 2010).

How is ANI used in social work? The technologies actively being introduced in the social work sector today are functions of ANI. ANI operates only within set rules and data ranges, making it excellent at processing repetitive and massive amounts of data. It can be viewed as a "highly obedient assistant" that carries out specific orders quickly and accurately (Russell & Norvig, 2010).

For example, ANI analyzes data on electricity and water cut-offs or tax arrears to automatically identify households in crisis. By flagging individuals who are eligible for support but have not yet applied, this technology helps reach underserved populations—often referred to as "blind spots" who would otherwise remain hidden from the social safety net. It is also useful for simple care services, such as being integrated into AI speakers or care robots to recognize specific words like "Help me!" to request emergency dispatch or to provide medication reminders. Furthermore, it is widely applied to chatbots that automatically handle repetitive civil complaints or provide guidance on required documents for more efficient counseling (Kaplan & Haenlein, 2019).

3.3.2.2 Artificial General Intelligence (AGI)

AGI is an AI equipped with broad intelligence like that of a human. It is a system capable of comprehensively performing various cognitive activities such as learning, reasoning, planning, adapting, and understanding emotions. AGI is referred to as "Strong AI" or "General AI." In short, it means this AI can perform almost any intellectual task that a human can do equally well or even better (Goertzel & Pennachin, 2007).

If ANI is a "specialist for a specific task," AGI is a "universal intelligence" that can flexibly handle all tasks. It can be said that current AI is ultimately heading toward AGI. What would it look like if AGI advanced and were applied to social work?

In social work, AGI could independently infer human emotions and complex home environments hidden behind raw data to prepare proactive countermeasures. For example, if a client's income data remains stable but their tone of voice suggests deep anxiety during a call, an AGI system could infer a hidden crisis—such as domestic conflict or early-onset depression—and suggest an immediate home visit. While ANI is an "obedient assistant," AGI acts like a "fellow expert" who participates in case meetings and shares insights with social workers. This is possible because it can judge situations comprehensively, considering not only fixed data but also multimodal cues, such as the facial expressions of clients during video consultations, the subtle smell of neglect or hygiene status of the home, and the complex nuances of conversation that indicate cognitive decline or social isolation (Kaplan & Haenlein, 2019).

If AGI were utilized in social work, integrated situational judgment would become possible. It would not just detect a beneficiary's economic poverty but comprehensively understand their depression, family relationships, and housing environment, leading consultations flexibly like a human. From a single remark like "I haven't had much of an appetite lately," AGI could simultaneously capture the risk of nutritional deficiency and signs of depression. Then, without being human intervention, it would check the schedules of local food delivery services and psychological counseling centers to draft an integrated support plan (Goertzel & Pennachin, 2007).

Even when facing unexpected situations not previously programmed, AGI could make judgments and autonomously link resources. Suppose a client's roof collapses and power is cut off in a mountainous area due to a heavy winter blizzard. Even if a specific "Blizzard Response Manual" is not entered into the system, AGI would detect the real-time weather data and the fact that the client's IoT sensors have stopped transmitting. It would then proceed with autonomous rescue coordination (Bostrom, 2014).

Immediately, AGI will contact 911 and the local township office (Public Resource Linking). It would also find and contact the nearest "snow removal company" and "churches that can provide temporary shelter" (Private Resource Linking).

Self-learning capabilities would also become possible. Current systems only become smarter when they are updated. However, AGI would learn from the success and failure cases entered by social workers across the country in real time, finding the most effective intervention for those who request it (Goertzel & Pennachin, 2007).

However, there are still ethical and practical challenges that must be considered when introducing AGI. Since it handles sensitive personal information, technologies capable of protecting privacy (especially regarding mental health, economic status, etc.) are necessary, and securing reliability—where AGI's judgments are **transparent** and explainable—is also critical. Furthermore, social workers and AGI must maintain a complementary relationship; total replacement is not only dangerous but also puts the centrality of human dignity at risk (Bostrom, 2014).

3.3.2.3 Artificial Super Intelligence (ASI)

ASI refers to AI that far surpasses all human intellectual capabilities. This does not simply mean superior calculation, speed, or memory; it signifies an intelligence that overwhelms humans in every domain, including creativity, emotional understanding, ethical judgment, problem-solving, and social interaction (Yudkowsky, 2008).

While ASI remains a long-term goal for the future, the transition toward AGI is already accelerating. We are moving beyond the era of specialized, task-oriented ANI and entering a stage where AI demonstrates increasingly human-like, cross-domain reasoning and autonomous problem-solving. As this evolution continues, the boundary between being a "tool" and a "collaborator" in social work is becoming thinner.

If ASI were to be realized, a fully automated social work system would become possible. By analyzing social data across the entire nation and regions, AI would determine support priorities for households in crisis and people with disabilities in real time. It would handle everything from planning to the execution of efficient social work resource distribution (Bostrom, 2014).

Additionally, a "Perfect AI Social Worker" could emerge—a digital counselor with deeper empathy, memory, and personalized response capabilities than any human. If ASI were fully integrated into social work, humanity could enjoy an unprecedented level of "customized care and education." However, at the same time, ongoing discussions regarding ethical and philosophical concerns—such as the extent to which human roles, emotions, and the right to choose should be maintained—will continue (Floridi & Cowls, 2019).

3.3.3 Core Components

3.3.3.1 Data

Data refers to values recorded by quantifying or qualifying phenomena or facts. In the field of AI, this is called **Training Data**, and the quality and bias of these data are key variables that determine AI performance. Data include consultation records, income levels, and housing environment data of social work beneficiaries. Social security information or case management records from public data portals are not just simple numbers; they are scales that represent the lives of vulnerable people. Therefore, "**data sovereignty**" and "privacy protection" are top priorities when designing social work AI (Carrasco, 2025).

3.3.3.2 Algorithm

An algorithm is a mathematical rule or procedure that determines how to process and analyze data. It acts as the "analysis rule" that decides the priority for combining information—such as electricity/water cut-offs and health insurance arrears—to discover households in crisis. It also functions as the "distribution logic" that decides which households should receive emergency living expenses first. Simply put, it is like a "recipe" for making a dish with ingredients (data). The outcome changes depending on which recipe is used. For this reason, the transparency and fairness of algorithms determine the reliability of social work administration (Pasquale, 2015).

3.3.3.3 Model

A model refers to the "specific formula or logical structure derived by the algorithm through training data." In other words, it is the main software body created after sufficiently learning from data via an algorithm. For instance, a risk prediction program that calculates that a certain household has a 90% probability of social isolation or solitary death is an example of a solitary death risk prediction model (Mitchell, 1997).

3.3.3.4 Computing Resources

Computing resources consist of high-performance hardware designed to rapidly calculate massive amounts of data and the virtual space where all of this operates. This includes GPUs for processing data and Cloud Computing for storing and managing large-scale data. It represents the hardware foundation capable of performing complex calculations in real time. Powerful server resources used to analyze national-level social work data and transmit it to field social workers symbolize a nation's digital social work capability (Buyya et al., 2009; Dean & Ghemawat, 2004).

3.4 Understanding Technology Convergence for Completing Social Work Services

3.4.1 The Organic Cooperation Structure of ICT, IoT, and AI

Intelligent social work services can function as individual technologies, but most are truly completed through the organic cooperation of the three core technologies: ICT, IoT, and AI. These three technologies operate like a single integrated system, where data follows a flow of "Generation → Flow → Interpretation" (Atzori et al., 2010).

IoT: Detects field conditions (Generation)
ICT: Transmits and stores data (Flow)
AI: Analyzes, judges, and predicts (Interpretation)

3.4.1.1 IoT Sensing: Acting as the Eyes and Ears of Clients

IoT serves as the interface that converts the physical conditions of a social work setting into digital data. Activity sensors, light sensors, and door sensors installed in the homes of clients capture the residents' every move in real time. An activity sensor installed in a client's home detects "no movement" for more than 12 hours, which is different from their usual pattern. This sensor immediately captures the abnormal signal and generates "field information" (Atzori et al., 2010).

3.4.1.2 ICT Transmission and Storage: Acting as a Rapid Communication Network

The signals captured by IoT sensors are transmitted to a cloud center through gateways and 5G or broadband networks. During this process, robust security technologies are applied to encrypt and safely store personal information. This information is then incorporated into a big data pool accessible by AI. In this stage, ICT is responsible for ensuring stability and reliability (Armbrust et al., 2010).

3.4.1.3 AI Analysis and Judgment: Acting as the Intelligent Brain

The AI model, which has already learned from thousands of past crisis patterns, analyzes this data stored in the cloud. It goes beyond simply noting "no movement" and makes a final judgment: "Compared to this person's past patterns, this corresponds to an 'emergency risk' state with a 95% probability." Immediately afterward, it sends a high-risk alert to the person in charge's smartphone (Demiris & Hense, 2008). In this way, AI shifts the paradigm from **reactive** intervention—where the system only acts after a crisis—to **proactive** social services. By identifying potential risks in advance, it allows for timely action before a serious issue arises

If one of these three core components (IoT, ICT, and AI) is missing, the service fails. Without IoT, no one can know the client is in danger. Without ICT, this information stays trapped inside the client's home and cannot be transmitted to the outside world. Without AI, the social worker might see the simple data of "no movement," treat it as a routine update while handling other urgent tasks, and miss the emergency. Only the convergence of these three technologies enables simultaneous real-time detection, stable transmission, and intelligent judgment, enhancing the quality of the social work services provided.

3.4.2 A Blueprint for Intelligent Social Work Systems through Technology Convergence

The goal of technology convergence within social work systems is not for machines to replace human work, but to enable social work experts to focus on their most important task: human intervention. AI analyzes big data to accurately diagnose the potential needs and risk levels of beneficiaries. It is not about simply introducing technology, such as "installing CCTV" or "distributing an app;" it is about using technology to completely bridge the gaps in social work delivery and maximize the quality of human care services. Technology handles exploration and management, while humans handle empathy and healing (Floridi & Cowls, 2019).

How, then, does technology convergence enable customized services that are centered on an individual's specific needs and preferences? AI analyzes vast amounts of big data to accurately diagnose the invisible potential needs (e.g., psychological isolation rather than just economic hardship) and risk levels of clients. This provides deep insights that are difficult for a social worker to grasp through just a few interviews (Chen et al., 2014).

Based on the AI's diagnosis, the ICT system immediately recommends the most effective and timely service portfolio among numerous social work services (government, local, and private resources). Social workers no longer need to manually search through policy manuals every time.

3.4.2.1 Evolution of the Professional Role

In this way, technology handles simple and repetitive administrative tasks such as information collection, initial classification, risk alerts, and resource-linking, allowing social work professionals—including case managers and program directors—to focus their time and energy exclusively on the cases that require the most human intervention (Nuwasiima et al., 2024).

Ultimately, this technology convergence helps achieve true person-centered, customized services. By allowing social work professionals to function as skilled supporters and counselors rather than mere document processors, technology enables high-level professional interventions—such as ethical decision-making, clinical counseling, and the management of complex family dynamics—that require deep human intuition and empathy (Garkisch & Goldkind, 2024).

3.5 Critical Thinking Questions

1. How can integrated technologies serve as the "digital eyes and ears" of social workers to monitor the safety of clients in real time?

2 If client records could be securely accessed and shared across agencies at any time, how would the continuity of care for mobile or vulnerable populations improve?
3 How does analyzing vast patterns of past crises help us identify "invisible needs"—such as social isolation—that don't appear on standard government forms or assessments?
4 If an AI assistant handles all your repetitive administrative paperwork, how should you reinvest that saved time into high-touch human interaction?
5 When AI can process emotional nuances and judge complex situations like a human, will you view it as a mere tool or as a "fellow expert" in your case meetings?

3.6 Summary

This chapter analyzes the innovative roles of ICT, IoT, and AI in social work. Supported by cloud computing and big data, ICT establishes the infrastructure necessary for managing extensive social work datasets. IoT technology utilizes sensors to collect real-time data from the field, while AI analyzes, evaluates, and predicts based on the collected data. The convergence of these technologies, grounded in accuracy and efficiency, drives a paradigm shift from reactive, administration-centered practices to a data-driven "Smart Social Work System."

3.7 Empowerment-Focused Activities

These projects allow readers to act as "Social Work Technologists," applying the concepts from your opening vignette.

3.7.1 The "Smart Care" Case Study Design

Task: Students are given the profile of a vulnerable client (e.g., a veteran with post-traumatic stress disorder (PTSD) or a teenager in foster care).
Instructions: Design a "Technology Care Plan" using the three layers from the chapter:

- **IoT:** What sensors or wearables would monitor the client's safety?
- **AI:** What specific tasks could an ANI automate (e.g., medication reminders, mood-tracking)?
- **ICT:** How will this data be shared securely between the social worker, the doctor, and the family?

3.7.2 AI Ethics Debate (Box 3.1)

Task: Revisit the story of Lucy and Victoria.
Prompt: "If the AI incorrectly flagged Victoria's nap as an emergency and sent an ambulance, who is responsible for the cost? If the AI failed to trigger an alarm during a real stroke, is the technology company or the social agency liable?"

Objectives: Students must write a "Human-in-the-Loop" policy that ensures AI assists, but does not replace, professional human judgment.

3.7.3 Analyzing Social Work Apps

Task: Evaluate existing ICT platform (e.g., *Aunt Bertha/Findhelp.org* or *mRelief*).
Instructions: Present how these platforms use Big Data and Cloud Computing to simplify the "administrative burden" mentioned in the chapter. How many "clicks" does it take for a client to find food assistance?

3.8 "Tech-Social Work" Mapping

Instructions: Draw a large human body on a whiteboard.

- Label the **Nervous System** as **IoT** (gathering touch/pain/data).
- Label the **Brain** as **AI** (processing and deciding).
- Label the **Circulatory System** as **ICT** (the infrastructure moving info everywhere).

Discussion: Ask students what happens to the "patient" (the social work system) if one of these systems "clogs" or fails.

References

Adelantado, F., Vilajosana, X., Tuset-Peiro, P., Martinez, B., Melia-Segui, J., & Watteyne, T. (2017). Understanding the limits of LoRaWAN. *IEEE Communications Magazine*, *55*(9), 34–40. https://doi.org/10.1109/MCOM.2017.1600613

Al-Sarawi, S., Anbar, M., Alieyan, K., & Alzubaidi, M. (2017). Internet of Things (IoT) communication protocols: Review. *8th International Conference on Information Technology (ICIT),* 2027, 685–690. https://doi.org/10.1109/ICITECH.2017.8079928

Armbrust, M., Fox, A., Griffith, R., Joseph, A. D., Katz, R., Konwinski, A., Lee, G., Patterson, D., Rabkin, A., Stoica, I., & Zaharia, M. (2010). A view of cloud computing. *Communications of the ACM*, *53*(4), 50–58. https://doi.org/10.1145/1721654.1721672

Atzori, L., Iera, A., & Morabito, G. (2010). The Internet of Things: A survey. *Computer Networks*, *54*(15), 2787–2805. https://doi.org/10.1016/j.comnet.2010.05.010

Balaji, S., Saravanan, R., Kaviya, K., Dhanalakshmi, A., & Sowmya, R. (2025). Guardian eye: An AI-powered child monitoring and protection model. *Journal of Information Systems Engineering and Management*, *10*(18s). 1–302. https://doi.org/10.52783/jisem.v10i18s.2903

Blurton, C. (1999). New directions in education. In M. Tawifik, G. Bartognon, & Y. Courior (Eds.), *World communication and information report 1999–2000,* 46–61. UNESCO Publishing. https://unesdoc.unesco.org/ark:/48223/pf0000119077

Bostrom, N. (2014). *Superintelligence: Paths, dangers, strategies*. Oxford University Press.

Buyya, R., Yeo, C. S., Venugopal, S., Broberg, J., & Brandic, I. (2009). Cloud computing and emerging it platforms: Vision, hype, and reality for delivering computing as the 5th utility. *Future Generation Computer Systems*, *25*(6), 599–616. https://doi.org/10.1016/j.future.2008.12.001

Carrasco, L. B. (2025). Mitigating bias and advocating for data sovereignty: The role of metadata and paradata in ethical AI-driven information systems. *Journal of Library Metadata, 25*(3), 185–200. https://doi.org/10.1080/19386389.2025.2515766

Chen, M., Mao, S., & Liu, Y. (2014). Big data: A survey. *Mobile Networks and Applications, 19*, 171–209. https://doi.org/10.1007/s11036-013-0489-0

Dean, J., & Ghemawat, S. (2004). MapReduce: Simplified data processing on large clusters. In Proceedings of the 6th Symposium on Operating Systems Design and Implementation (OSDI 2004). https://static.googleusercontent.com/media/research.google.com/en//archive/mapreduce-osdi04.pdf

Demiris, G., & Hensel, B. K. (2008). Technologies for an aging society: A systematic review of "Smart Home" applications. *Yearbook of Medical Informatics, 17*(01), 33–40. https://doi.org/10.1055/s-0038-1638580

Floridi, L., & Cowls, J. (2019). A unified framework of five principles for AI in society. *Harvard Data Science Review, 1*(1), 1–14. https://doi.org/10.1162/99608f92.8cd550d1

Garkisch, M., & Goldkind, L. (2024). Considering a unified model of Artificial intelligence enhanced social work: A systematic riview. *Journal of Human Rights and Social Work, 10*, 23–42. https://doi.org/10.1007/s41134-024-00326-y

Goertzel, B., & Pennachin, C. (2007). *Artificial general intelligence*. Springer.

Gubbi, J., Buyya, R., Marusic, S., & Palaniswami, M. (2013). Internet of Things (IoT): A vision, architectural elements, and future directions. *Future Generation Computer Systems, 29*(7), 1645–1660. https://doi.org/10.1016/j.future.2013.01.010

Hashem, I. A. T., Yaqoob, I., Anuar, N. B., Mokhtar, S., Gani, A., & Ullah Khan, S. (2015). The rise of "big data" on cloud computing: Review and open research issues. *Information Systems, 47*, 98–115. https://doi.org/10.1016/j.is.2014.07.006

Heeks, R. (2010). Do information and communication technologies (ICTs) contribute to development? *Journal of International Development, 22*(5), 625–640. https://doi.org/10.1002/jid.1716

Kaplan, A., & Haenlein, M. (2019). Siri, Siri, in my hand: Who's the fairest in the land? On the interpretations, illustrations, and implications of artificial intelligence. *Business Horizons, 62*(1), 15–25. https://doi.org/10.1016/j.bushor.2018.08.004

Krieger, U. R., Eichler, G., Erfurth, C., & Fahrnberger, G. (2023). *Innovations for Community Services.* Springer Nature. https://doi.org/10.1007/978-3-031-40852-6

Lee, J. A. (2018). Trends and challenges of using welfare technology in elderly care. *International Journal of Contents, 14*(2), 30–34. https://doi.org/10.5392/IJoC.2018.14.2.030

Mitchell, T. M. (1997). *Machine learning*. McGraw-Hill.

Nuwasiima, M., Ahonon, P. M., & Kadiri, C. (2024). The role of Artificial Intelligence (AI) and machine learning in social work practice. *World Journal of Advanced Research and Reviews, 24*(1), 80–97. https://doi.org/10.30574/wjarr.2024.24.1.2998

Pasquale, F. (2015). *The black box society: The secret algorithms that control money and information.* Harvard University Press. www.jstor.org/stable/j.ctt13x0hch

Raza, U., Kulkarni, P., & Sooriyabandara, M. (2017). Low power wide area networks: An overview. *IEEE Communications Surveys & Tutorials, 19*(2), 855–873. https://doi.org/10.1109/COMST.2017.2652320

Russ, E., & Reimer, E. C. (2025). Digital intervention for advancing social work and welfare education. *Social Sciences, 14*(1), 50. https://doi.org/10.3390/socsci14010050

Russell, S., & Norvig, P. (2010). *Artificial intelligence: A modern approach.* Prentice Hall.

Sharma, S. K., & Wang, X. (2020). Toward massive machine type communications in ultra-dense cellular IoT networks. *IEEE Communications Surveys & Tutorials*, *22*(1), 426–471. https://doi.org/10.1109/COMST.2019.2916177

Sinha, R. S., Wei, Y., & Hwang, S.-H. (2017). A survey on LPWA technology: LoRa and NB- IoT. *ICT Express, 3*(1), 14–21. https://doi.org/10.1016/j.icte.2017.03.004

Song, M. S. (2025). *Swipge ihaehaneun sahoebokjiwa ICT, IoT geurigo AI [Easy-to-understand social welfare and ICT, IoT, and AI].* Kyobo Book Centre. https://product.kyobobook.co.kr/detail/S000217305356

Umamaheswari, S., Jagannath, V., & Shuriya, B. (2025). Wearable system for enhanced soldier health monitoring and battlefield awareness. *2025 3rd International Conference on Advancements in Electrical, Electronics, Communication, Computing and Automation (ICAECA), 2025,* 1–6. https://doi.org/10.1109/ICAECA63854.2025.11012646

Vrančić, A., Zadravec, H., & Orehovački, T. (2024). The role of smart homes in providing care for older adults: A systematic literature riview from 2010 to 2023. *Smart Cities*, *7*(4), 1502–1550. https://doi.org/10.3390/smartcities7040062

Yudkowsky, E. (2008). Artificial intelligence as a positive and negative factor in global risk. In N. Bostrom and M. M. Cirkovic (eds.), *Global catastrophic risks*, 308–345. Oxford University Press. https://doi.org/10.1093/oso/9780198570509.003.0021

4 Generative AI and Agentic AI

Moon Sun Song

4.1 Generative AI and AI Agents

With the rapid advancement of artificial intelligence (AI) technology, terms like Generative AI, Traditional AI Agents, and Agentic AI have emerged. Although these terms sound similar, there are significant differences in their operational mechanisms, objectives, and levels of autonomy.

4.1.1 Generative AI

When we have questions, we ask AI instead of using a search engine. Generative AI learns from vast amounts of data to converse naturally like a human, write poetry, and create art. It reacts to user requests, known as prompts, to generate new content—such as text, images, audio, video, and code—that did not previously exist (U.S. Government Accountability Office, 2023). The primary purpose of Generative AI is content creation, and it operates only when there is user input. Programs like ChatGPT, Midjourney, and Gemini generate one-off responses to questions and can produce various forms of content. For instance, when asked to "write a short poem suitable for today's weather," it functions as a creative writing tool. However, we are now encountering a concept that goes one step further: the "Agent."

4.1.2 Traditional AI Agents

Traditional AI agents operate according to pre-established rules set by humans. They function as a set of commands: "If situation A occurs, perform action B." For example, in the context of social work eligibility, a rule might be programmed as: if a household's income is at or below 50% of the median income (Situation A), then automatically classify them as eligible for financial assistance (Action B). Since they operate based on predefined rules or algorithms, their ability to adapt to change or set goals is limited, making them relatively simple forms of AI (Hughes et al., 2025). Due to these limitations, Traditional AI Agents are primarily used in chatbots that provide answers according to fixed scripts.

DOI: 10.4324/9781003755081-5

Table 4.1 Comparison of Generative AI, Traditional AI Agents, and Agentic AI

Division	*Generative AI*	*Traditional AI Agent*	*Agentic AI*
Main Function	Content creation	Single-task execution	Autonomous achievement of complex goal
Method of Operation	Reactive (input-output)	Task-oriented	Proactive, goal-oriented
Autonomy	Low (human prompt required)	Medium (within a defined scope)	High (self-planning and execution)
Analogy	An author who writes a piece of text	A secretary who handles specific tasks	A manager who oversees the entire project

4.1.3 Agentic AI

In contrast, Agentic AI has evolved from Traditional AI Agents by using the "reasoning power" of Generative AI as its engine to achieve true autonomy. It goes beyond simply answering questions; it understands what is needed to reach a goal, creates a plan (Planning), and directly utilizes necessary tools (Tool Use) to complete the execution (Action). Agentic AI is a system that uses **Large Language Models** (LLMs) as its "brain" to autonomously perform multiple steps and leverage various tools, including Generative AI (Shen et al., 2024; Wang et al., 2024).

This system possesses a high level of **autonomy**, initiating actions without human intervention and perceiving its environment to proactively adjust its behavior. Rather than remaining in a passive state of waiting for input, it continuously analyzes the gap between the current situation and ultimate goals, modifying its execution path accordingly. In this sense, it can be described as **proactive**. For example, when given the goal of "scheduling a meeting for next week," the AI agent independently carries out a complex sequence of tasks such as 1) searching for the optimal time slot, 2) sending emails to participants, 3) reserving a meeting room, and 4) drafting preliminary meeting materials to successfully accomplish the objective.

In summary, **Generative AI** provides ideas and information by creating content; **Traditional AI Agents** automatically perform predefined actions based on that content; and **Agentic AI** integrates these two to autonomously set goals and solve complex problems through advanced decision-making.

4.2 The Emergence of Agentic AI

The concept of an "AI Agent" is not new. Within the discipline of computer science, an AI agent has long been a broad concept encompassing any intelligent system that perceives its environment, reasons, and acts. However, the recent emergence of the term "Agentic AI" has ushered in a new era that is fundamentally different from the past (Russell & Norvig, 2021).

While Traditional AI followed fixed rules or static models, Agentic AI independently understands complex and abstract goals. It formulates plans, autonomously utilizes tools such as web searches and external apps, and even engages in self-reflection regarding its own actions (Niketan & Batatia, 2025). This represents an evolution toward a level of proxy performance for human tasks, significantly surpassing the limitations of traditional AI.

The best way to understand Agentic AI is to think of it as an "autonomous personal assistant" that achieves goals. Imagine the goal of planning an overseas vacation. Agentic AI divides the goal into steps and determines their sequence. It autonomously plans flights, accommodations, and itineraries, and then selects and uses the necessary external tools—such as web browsers, calendars, and map apps. If the results do not align with the goal, it evaluates itself and modifies the plan. It is, in essence, the portrait of a perfect assistant.

Why has all of this only recently become possible? The core driver is the rapid advancement of LLMs. LLMs are massive AI models designed to understand, generate, and reason through human language by learning from vast amounts of text data. They serve as a human-level "brain" for Agentic AI (Naidu & El-Gayar, 2025).

First, LLMs have an immense scale in terms of parameters. This vast scale allows them to deeply learn complex patterns and contexts of language, creating richer and more consistent sentences. Their operating principle is also fascinating; they predict and generate the word with the highest probability of following a given sentence or word. For example, if the subject is "The sky," the model determines that "blue" has a higher probability of following than "delicious" or "yellow" to complete the sentence. Through this probabilistic approach, it understands complex human questions and commands, generating natural responses like those of a human.

Next is the capacity for **reasoning**, which refers to the ability of an LLM-based agent to achieve a complex goal and process it logically. While Traditional AI Agents relied primarily on predefined rules or limited data, LLM-based Agentic AI possesses human-level language-understanding, reasoning, and planning capabilities (Shen et al., 2024). In other words, the LLM-based Agentic AI can analyze complex situations, infer the optimal steps to achieve a goal, and express and execute that plan in natural language.

We can see how innovative the reasoning and **planning** capabilities of LLM-based Agentic AI are through the following example: "ordering pizza for dinner." If given the goal "I need to order pizza for dinner with friends tonight, and one of them is a vegetarian," the LLM understands the complex context (friends, vegetarian, dinner) like a human and infers "pizza with vegetarian options" as the core condition. The LLM-based Agentic AI then independently determines the optimal sequence (Step 1: Use a web search tool to find nearby restaurants. Step 2: Filter reviews of vegetarian options. Step 3: Select the place with the highest rating. Step 4: Launch a delivery app tool to proceed with the order). Finally, LLM-based Agentic AI completes the order at Restaurant A, which offers vegetarian options. This example confirms that an LLM agent understands the situation (reasoning),

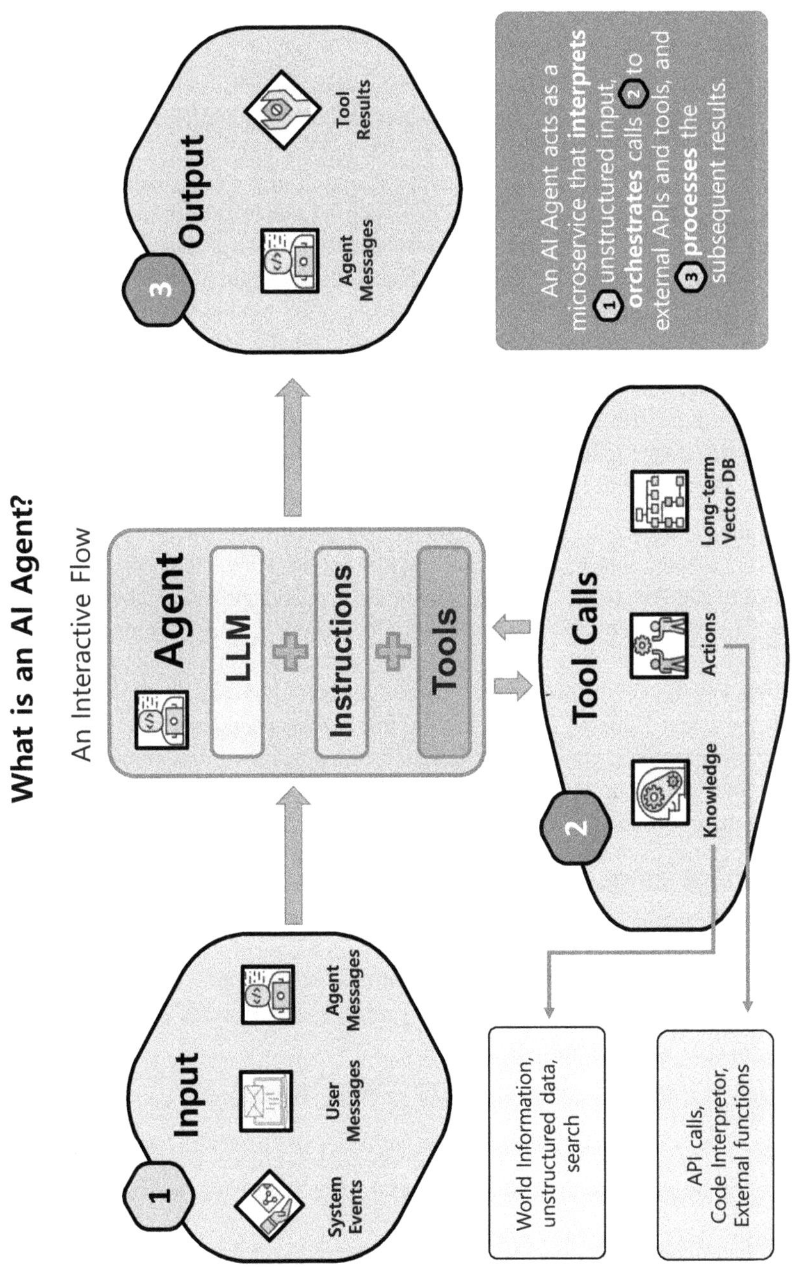

Figure 4.1 What Is an AI Agent?

autonomously determines the steps needed to complete (planning), and achieves the goal just like an intelligent human.

What mechanisms allow for these autonomous, lifelike assistant behaviors? While the LLM serves as the "brain," it is the organic integration of additional components—Memory and Action—that empowers Agentic AI.

Task Decomposition and Chain-of-Thought. Instead of providing an immediate answer, the LLM explains its logical thought process step-by-step. Through this process, the LLM independently breaks down complex goals into executable sub-plans and determines their sequence (Shu et al., 2024; Shen et al., 2024). For instance, if commanded to "find and order a birthday gift my friend would like," the AI agent does not act immediately but follows these steps: 1) Identify information regarding the friend's preferences. 2) Use tools like SNS search or past conversation memory to understand those preferences. 3) Once preferences are identified, research candidates, prices, and ratings. 4) Select the final gift and place an order at the lowest price. This allows the agent to move according to a logical plan even for complex commands.

Continuous Memory and Learning. Agentic AI remembers its experiences and goals, constantly learning and evolving. This memory prevents the agent from repeating the same mistakes and enables it to work in a way that better fits the user over time (Leroux et al., 2024).

Coordinated Autonomy. While typical chatbots lack the ability to handle complex requests like "planning a trip" on their own, Agentic AI excels with collaboration. When multiple AIs work together, it coordinates and integrates their actions to produce a perfect result (Shu et al., 2024; Gabriel et al., 2024). For example, consider the goal of "providing the most effective customized support for a low-income family facing financial difficulties." Three specialized agents—Financial Support, Health Care, and Housing Environment—might experience conflict while emphasizing their individual goals. At this point, the central coordination module derives an optimized support plan based on the overall objective. It might, for instance, set a compromise that secures financial and housing support while changing the health care component from a general hospital visit to a home-visit service.

In summary, Agentic AI is a system that autonomously sets goals, collaborates with multiple agents to solve complex problems, and continuously learns and adapts. This signifies the evolution of AI into a system with a level of "intent" that can achieve goals without human intervention. In the future, AI will go far beyond being a simple assistant to become a core decision-making entity (McNamara & Marpu, 2025).

4.3 What Is Retrieval-Augmented Generation (RAG)?

Box 4.1 Beyond the Search Bar: Reclaiming Social Work with RAG AI

At a local community center, Steve, a dedicated social worker, struggles to keep pace with his city's constantly shifting social policies. He often spends hours scouring the web for information on new youth grants or disability support, only to encounter conflicting data across different websites. This not only consumes his precious time but also leads him to question the accuracy of the information he provides to those in need. To address this challenge, his agency introduced an "AI social work assistant" powered by RAG. This is not just a simple chatbot; it is a sophisticated tool engineered specifically for precision.

The AI social work assistant, utilizing RAG technology, empowers social workers like Steve to provide swift and accurate information on social work policies. Instead of Steve spending hours manually searching for details, the assistant traverses a dedicated database of official documents to retrieve the most relevant and up-to-date information. It then synthesizes this data into clear, precise answers regarding grant eligibility and required documentation. This tool not only saves time but also ensures that his advice is reliable, thereby fostering deeper trust within the community.

4.3.1 Fundamental Limitations of LLMs and Breakthrough

LLMs learn from vast amounts of data, but this data is inevitably "frozen" at a specific point in time. For example, if a model's training ended in early 2023, the model cannot know about the latest news or events that occurred afterward. Because of this, LLMs face the following challenges:

Knowledge Cut-off: LLMs cannot answer questions about the latest information, real-time data, or rapidly changing facts that emerged after their training ended (Oche et al., 2025).

Hallucination: When the exact information is missing from the training data, the model may respond with "hallucinations"—convincing but entirely false information (Lewis et al., 2020).

Limited Internal Knowledge: LLMs cannot reason about or answer questions regarding private information not included in the training data, such as a company's internal documents, personal emails, or confidential industry data (Lewis et al., 2020).

To overcome these limitations, **RAG** was developed. RAG is a technology that combines "searching" and "generating." It dramatically improves the accuracy and reliability of AI by searching for relevant information in external databases or documents and using it as a reference (Oche et al., 2025).

Consider LLMs as a very smart student taking an exam. Without RAG, the student must rely solely on their memory. With RAG, the student is allowed to "look at an open textbook" before answering. Before generating a response, the system retrieves (**Retrieval**) the most relevant, up-to-date information from an external knowledge base and provides it to LLMs to strengthen (**Augment**) their final answer.

4.3.2 Understanding How RAG Works

RAG operates through three core stages, essentially instructing LLM to "find the evidence for the answer" from external sources.

Retrieval: When a user enters a query, the RAG system quickly searches external knowledge repositories—such as internal corporate documents, the latest news articles, or web data—to find the documents or passages most relevant to the question (Oche et al., 2025).
Augmentation: The retrieved pieces of information (the retrieved knowledge) are added to the LLM's input prompt along with the user's original question. This allows the LLM to generate an answer based on the "context" of up-to-date knowledge, rather than relying solely on its memory (Oche et al., 2025).
Generation: The LLM combines its internal knowledge with the newly provided external information to generate an accurate and well-evidenced response (Lewis et al., 2020).

This **RAG mechanism** is particularly useful in the United States, where welfare guidelines differ by state and change frequently. For example, suppose a social worker in Texas asks, "What is the income eligibility for Emergency Assistance (EA) in 2026?"

Retrieval: The RAG system immediately finds the "2026 Texas Health and Human Services Commission (HHSC) Policy Handbook" from the latest database.
Augmentation: The system combines the specific income limits and asset requirements for 2026 with the social worker's question and feeds this data into the LLMs.
Generation: Instead of providing generalized or outdated information, the LLM uses the retrieved Texas-specific guidelines to generate answers, such as "For 2026, the household income must not exceed the Federal Poverty Level by more than X percent." Consequently, the RAG-based system serves as a reliable assistant, helping practitioners navigate complex and localized welfare regulations without administrative errors.

4.4 The Effects of RAG and Applications in Social Work

Lewis and associates (2020) explained the advantages of RAG in terms of up-to-date information, reduced hallucinations, transparency, and cost-efficiency. RAG enables the use of constantly updated information by retrieving and providing data from real-time external databases or internal documents to the LLMs. Since RAG finds the basis for its answers in external data, it generates responses based on facts, significantly reducing the hallucination phenomenon.

By providing the source of the original documents used in the answer, RAG significantly increases the reliability of the AI system, allowing users to verify

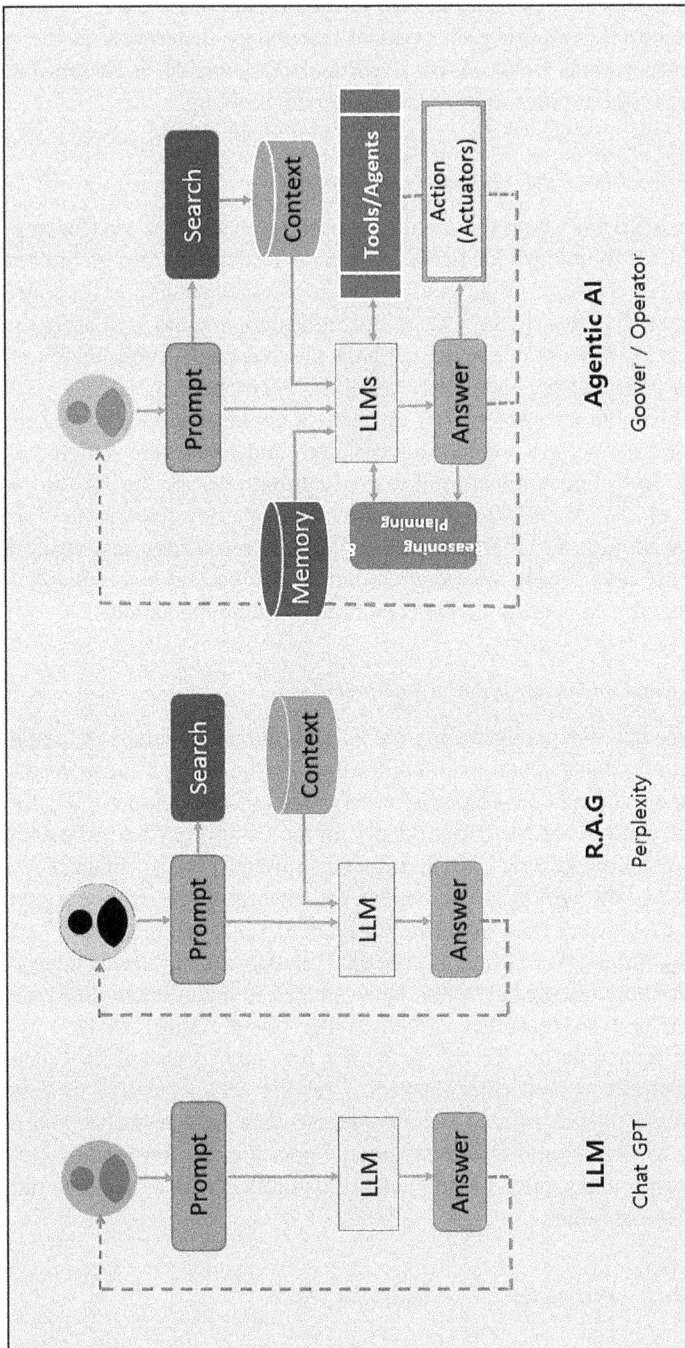

Figure 4.2 From Answering AI to Acting AI: LLM, RAG, and Agentic AI.

the accuracy of the answer themselves. Above all, this approach is far more cost-effective and less time-consuming than re-training the LLM itself.

RAG is rapidly emerging as a critical technology that enhances the utility of LLMs across various fields. RAG is particularly valuable in sectors like social work, where regulations and laws are constantly evolving.

4.4.1 Providing Real-Time, Up-to-Date Information

For clients inquiring about the income threshold for a public assistance program, standard LLMs might provide figures that were accurate a year ago but have since changed. Even worse, it might guide a user toward a discontinued support system as if it were still active. In such cases, misinformation could lead users to prepare applications for benefits that no longer exist or, conversely, cause them to miss out on new opportunities for which they are eligible (Gupta et al., 2024).

RAG solves these problems by updating a vector database in real time with the latest legislation, government notices, and guidelines from national and local authorities. By referencing the full text of current notices, the AI can provide a response such as: "As of 2026, the maximum annual allowable income for a three-person household is $23,000, which is a slight increase from last year." Such an answer is not only timely and accurate but is also backed by verifiable sources, ensuring that the AI is grounded in facts rather than hallucinations.

4.4.2 Ensuring Consistency in Legal Interpretation

Another type of hallucination occurs when LLMs attempt to interpret complex cases requiring professional social work knowledge. For instance, a social worker might ask: "What are the specific eligibility criteria and asset calculation rules for a child with special needs when the parents apply for the Disability Child Allowance?"

Because these criteria often involve intricate legal nuances—such as distinguishing between recognized assets and exempted property or applying specific income deduction rates for disability-related expenses—a standard LLM might incorrectly combine laws, bring in irrelevant regulations, or provide interpretations from similar but unrelated systems. This can lead to inconsistent guidance among practitioners or even regulatory violations (Pipitpne & Alami, 2024).

RAG mitigates these risks by searching for actual social work-related cases and administrative precedents. Instead of relying on speculative or generalized answers, RAG utilizes official policies, social work case histories, and complex counseling records stored in the database. Consequently, RAG can provide consistent, reliable, and legally sound guidance that reflects actual practice rather than theoretical assumptions.

4.4.3 Enhancing Personalized Accessibility for Users

Beyond professional support, RAG empowers clients by improving accessibility to tailored information. Potential clients often struggle to navigate the complexities of public welfare systems, potentially leaving them unaware of available programs. RAG greatly simplifies this process. For example, if a user asks, "Am I eligible to receive Supplemental Nutrition Assistance Program in Arizona?" or "can I apply for Medicaid in Georgia?" a traditional chatbot might provide vague or incomplete answers.

In contrast, RAG identifies the most relevant legal provisions, from the specific state's current guidelines, feeds the data into the LLMs, and allows the models to generate a clear, personalized response based on the user's specific situation. This response not only explains the complex eligibility requirements in simple terms but also guides the user through the application procedures, document requirements, and deadlines. Most importantly, LLMs powered by RAG cite the legal clauses supporting advice, enhancing credibility and trust. Since public welfare systems are frequently revised, RAG ensures that the AI remains current by reflecting the latest announcements and policy changes in the database (Gupta et al., 2024).

In summary, RAG represents a significant leap forward in integrating AI into social work practice. It enhances the accuracy, consistency, and accessibility of information for both professionals and the public, ensuring that social work services remain fair, efficient, and aligned with the latest standards.

4.4.4 Challenges and Ethical Considerations

Despite being a powerful innovation, RAG has some practical operational concerns to consider, including costs, technical hurdles, and ethical issues. The necessity of building and maintaining a retrieval system, potential time delays due to the additional search step, and increased costs are significant factors. Furthermore, when providing personalized information, ethical and legal risks such as security and privacy breaches must be carefully managed (Gupta et al., 2024). While RAG is a formidable tool for expanding the knowledge capabilities of AI, its effective and safe use requires continuous investment, performance optimization, and rigorous security management.

4.5 AI Terminology and Types

In this section, we will explore various types of AI to understand how they operate and examine their practical applications in social work. Do you remember the core areas of AI introduced in previous chapters? Now, we will unravel these concepts with new examples and practical insights. Get ready to explore Machine Learning (ML), Deep Learning (DL), Natural Language Processing (NLP), Algorithms, Neural Networks, and Language Models.

4.5.1 Machine Learning and Deep Learning

4.5.1.1 Machine Learning (ML)

ML is the heart of the field of AI. It is a method where a system "self-discovers" and learns rules through vast amounts of example data. Instead of following explicitly programmed instructions, this technology enables computers to learn from experience and make predictions or decisions. Just as humans accumulate knowledge and solve new problems through experience, ML aims to learn from data and apply that learning to solve novel challenges (Du et al., 2024).

The components of ML include the data used as learning material, a **model** (the mathematical structure that learns patterns from that data), and an **algorithm** (the method used to train the model). Evaluation is the process of testing the trained model's accuracy using metrics like error rates.

ML analyzes data and finds rules on its own. For example, when creating a spam filter, instead of setting rules like "if words such as 'Investment,' 'Urgent,' or 'Final Notice' exist, then classify as spam," the system is trained to identify characteristics of spam from thousands of legitimate and spam emails. Through training on images of apples and oranges, ML can predict that a "round, orange fruit photo" has a 95% probability of being an orange.

In social work, ML plays a crucial role in enhancing policy efficiency and fairness and proactively identifying high-risk groups (Song, 2025). In solitary death and crisis household prediction systems, algorithms are required to predict scientific causal relationships. ML collects vast information (e.g., gender, age, income, assets, occupation, debt) from past cases to analyze patterns and causalities. By discovering these patterns, the system allows practitioners to intervene before a crisis occurs. ML helps social workers identify hidden danger signals without manually checking every data point, ensuring resources are focused on those in the most urgent need.

4.5.1.2 Deep Learning (DL)

DL is a subfield of ML that uses artificial neural networks, specifically **deep neural networks** with multiple layers. It can be compared to a child's brain growing more complex and sophisticated; as thinking skills develop, the ability to distinguish objects in photos or interpret human emotions improves, eventually evolving into an adult capable of solving abstract and complex problems (Song, 2025).

While DL is a type of ML, it differs significantly in how it solves complex problems. The key difference lies in "Feature Extraction." While ML often relies on human-defined rules, or features, DL allows the AI to discover and understand features on its own, going beyond the given data (Ruano-Ordás, 2024).

Let's use the example of identifying a cat:

In ML: An engineer must first define a cat's features, such as "pointed ears," "whiskers," and "four legs." The model then calculates the probability of the image being a cat based on these predefined traits. If the cat is lying down and its ears aren't visible, the ML model might fail because it relies strictly on those human-set rules.

In DL: The model uses deep neural networks to extract features itself. The initial layers learn basic patterns like lines and edges, while deeper layers combine these into an "abstract concept of a cat." Even if the cat is in an unusual pose or its ears are hidden, DL captures the complex, holistic characteristics to identify it accurately.

This characteristic of DL is extremely useful in social work. While ML is suited for qualifying beneficiaries based on clear criteria, DL is used for analyzing abstract and complex signals, such as counseling records for suicide prevention. AI can independently learn and detect subtle patterns of "hopelessness," "isolation," or "negative outlooks" in text without humans having to define specific keywords.

DL pushes the boundaries of traditional ML in social work by analyzing unstructured data. It is most active in early detection of safety and health anomalies, such as detecting falls, dementia signs, or depression. For instance, AI-based Action Recognition models in nursing homes or homes of older adults living alone can analyze CCTV footage. When someone collapses or shows no activity for a long time, the system immediately triggers an emergency alarm.

Furthermore, in child social work centers and daycares, DL can detect threats to child safety. It analyzes CCTV to identify physical violence (hitting, pushing), suspected abuse (prolonged neglect, coercive restraint), or signs of bullying among children. DL's advantage is its ability to capture subtle signals that humans might miss by learning all the various documented forms of violent behavior (Song, 2025). Smart daycare safety systems send real-time alerts to supervisors and store footage for evidence and preventive education. Additionally, DL-based Face Recognition is highly effective in locating missing people. DL plays a decisive role in solving high-dimensional problems—language, images, and complex situations—where it is difficult for humans to define specific features.

4.5.2 Natural Language Processing (NLP)

NLP refers to the field of technology that enables computers to understand, interpret, and generate human language, whether in written or spoken form. In essence,

Table 4.2 Comparison between Machine Learning and Deep Learning

Classification	*Machine Learning (ML)*	*Deep Learning (DL)*
Summary	A field of AI that includes all techniques that learn based on data	A subfield of ML that uses deep neural networks for learning
Core Mechanism	Feature Engineering	Automatic Feature Extraction
Performance	Performance gains are limited as complexity increases	Significant superior performance as problems become more complex and abstract
Feature Extraction	Requires humans to manually define and select key features	AI automatically extracts and learns features directly from the data
Data Volume	Small to Medium Plateaus after a certain point	Massive (Big Data) Increases continuously with more data
Applications	Spam Filtering/Predictive Modeling	Image Recognition Speech Recognition NLP/Autonomous Driving

NLP allows computers to "listen," "understand," and "respond to or summarize" the languages or sentences we use in our daily lives.

As a subfield of AI that leverages ML to enable computers to comprehend and process human language, NLP research has played a pivotal role in ushering in the era of Generative AI, ranging from the communication capabilities of LLMs to image generation models that understand user prompts. NLP has already become a staple in many people's daily lives, powering search engines, enabling voice commands for customer service chatbots, and operating voice-activated GPS systems and digital assistants like Amazon's Alexa, Apple's Siri, and Microsoft's CoPilot.

NLP is broadly classified into five core functions (Jegan & Henrich, 2025).

Language Understanding: It breaks down sentences into word units and analyzes grammar to identify the user's underlying intent.

Language Generation: Based on data, it creates natural, human-like sentences to draft consultation responses or reports.

Language Transformation: It enhances information accessibility and removes language barriers through translation and Speech-to-Text/Text-to-Speech (STT/TTS) technologies.

Analysis and Classification: It detects negative sentiments in reviews or consultation logs and automatically filters out harmful content.

Dialogue Processing: It enables interactive communication—such as answering questions or providing psychological support—by remembering the context of previous conversations. This is the core technology behind chatbots and AI assistants (Shao, 2024).

Together, these five functions form the foundation upon which NLP supports human-centered AI applications. These technologies serve as a fundamental tool for social workers, enabling them to analyze community needs more precisely and design services that are both ethical and efficient.

How, then, are these NLP functions being utilized in social work?

Information Extraction from Unstructured Text: NLP automatically identifies and extracts specific types of information from unstructured text. A prominent example is **Mental RoBERTa**, an LLM specifically designed and trained to analyze text related to mental health. The AI scans the text (like client messages, notes, or online posts) and flags patterns that may indicate high anxiety or depressive language. For example, it highlights phrases like "I feel hopeless" and "I can't keep going," categorizing them as high-risk indicators. Although it is not a diagnostic tool, Mental RoBERTa excels at recognising emotional tone, identifying mental health concerns, and assisting with tasks such as screening or triage (Chopra et al., 2024).

Sentiment and Emotion Analysis: NLP can analyze subjective information (positive, negative, neutral) or emotions (joy, sadness, anger, anxiety, etc.) contained in text. This allows for the identification of a user's overall psychological state from the transcripts or recordings of counseling sessions or documented civil complaints, as well as their satisfaction or dissatisfaction with specific policies and services.

Automated Summarization: It automatically summarizes complex case management reports or long-term counseling records, helping social workers grasp core content quickly and efficiently.

Trend Analysis and Resource Allocation: By analyzing tens of thousands of civil complaint data points, NLP can identify the current "trends" in social work-related issues in the community, such as housing instability among older adults, mental health issues among youth, or caregiver issues for people with disabilities. This information can then be used to establish appropriate policies and allocate resources effectively.

4.5.3 AI Types Based on Voice and Text Processing Technologies

Let's examine how NLP operates across voice and text mediums. NLP is not limited to text alone; its scope is expanding to include speech, images, and even video. We will explore how these technologies work and how they support real-time social work practice. As we navigate this topic, let's consider how these tools can improve the health and well-being of children, older adults, and people with disabilities.

STT (Speech-to-Text): **STT** is a technology within NLP that converts spoken language into text using Speech Recognition (**Automatic Speech Recognition** [ASR]). NLP language models are used to analyze and convert voice data into text. A representative example of STT is the "Live Caption" feature found in smartphones or AI assistants. For people with hearing impairment, this can provide real-time captions during social work counseling, doctor's visits, or public service interactions.

TTS (Text-to-Speech): **TTS** is a technology that converts text into speech. It supports various voices for navigation systems, AI assistants, and audiobooks. It can read government documents, websites, or apps aloud for people with visual impairment.

P-TTS (Personalized Text-to-Speech): **P-TTS** is a specialized form of TTS that personalizes voices. P-TTS learns a specific user's voice and generates speech that sounds identical to that individual. Amazon's Alexa introduced a feature that recreates the voices of deceased family members using less than one minute of recorded audio data, providing emotional comfort to users. AI speaker "GiGA Genie" in South Korea has utilized P-TTS through a pilot service where recorded parents' voices read books to children.

TTV (Text-to-Video): **TTV** analyzes the meaning of text and creates videos containing appropriate visual elements.

TTI (Text-to-Image): **TTI** is a technology that generates images from textual descriptions. TTI follows a process like TTV but outputs an image instead of a video. TTI allows for the rapid visualization of ideas and opens infinite creative possibilities for non-experts and visual learners. When explaining complex

Table 4.3 Comparison of Algorithms and Neural Networks

Technology	*Target Users*	*Application Examples*	*Expected Benefit*
TTS (Text-to-Speech)	People with visual impairment, older adults	Voice guidance, document-reading	Improved information accessibility
STT (Speech-to-Text)	People with hearing impairment, counselors	Real-time subtitles, counseling record	Communication support
P-TTS (Personalized Text-to-Speech)	People with dementia, older adults	Familiar voice notifications (e.g., for medication)	Emotional stability, improved medication adherence
TTV (Text-to-Video)	People with low literacy	Videos guiding through social work procedures	Improved understanding, expanded access to information
TTI (Text-to-Image)	Individuals with developmental disabilities, children	Visualizing social work information as images	Improved visual comprehension

social work procedures, visualizing them into intuitive images helps those with lower literacy understand better.

Multimodal AI: **Multimodal** is the compound of "Multi" (multiple) and "Modal" (mode/form). It refers to AI's ability to simultaneously understand, integrate, and interact with two or more types of data, such as text, images, speech, video, and movement. Using Gemini on Vertex AI, a user can prompt with text, images, video, or code to generate content of a different type than the initial input. A client with Attention-Deficit/Hyperactivity Disorder (ADHD) can use Notebook LM to gather trustworthy information about ADHD and convert it into interactive mind maps, short videos, and audio summaries. These multi-modal formats can make learning more engaging and knowledge easier to retain, supporting the client in understanding their condition and developing personalized coping strategies (Benmarrakchi, 2025).

Traditional AI specialized in specific fields, such as LLMs for text and recognition models for images and video. However, just as humans understand the world better using all five senses—such as hearing "A car is coming!" (audio) while simultaneously seeing the car (visual) to perceive danger quickly—Multimodal AI understands the world in a more human way by weaving together fragmented information to solve complex problems (Wang et al., 2025; Song, 2025).

4.6 Critical Thinking Questions

1 What are the key differences between Generative AI, AI Agents, and Agentic AI, and how can each type contribute to real-world problem-solving?

2 How does RAG address the limitations of standard LLMs, and in which fields could it have the most significant impact?
3 What transformations can AI bring to the field of social work, and what ethical considerations must be addressed?
4 How do ML and DL differ in terms of structure and application, and what types of problems are best suited for each?
5 How can the five core functions of NLP (e.g., Understanding, Generation) be applied to improve social services?

4.7 Summary

This chapter explored the distinctions between Generative AI and Agentic AI, emphasizing their unique roles and differing levels of autonomy. It also traced the evolution of AI agents from traditional rule-based systems to the emergence of Agentic AI through the integration of LLMs. The concept of RAG was introduced as a solution to overcome the fundamental limitations of LLMs, thereby enhancing their accuracy and reliability. In addition, key AI technologies such as ML, DL, and NLP were presented through practical examples.

4.8 Empowerment-Focused Activities

Would you like to see how AI can *think*, *search*, and *respond* like a pro? Check out these interactive platforms that bring RAG to life! RAG blends the power of search engines with generative AI to give you smarter, context-aware answers—perfect for social work scenarios where accuracy and nuance matter.

4.8.1 Hugging Face RAG Diffusion Demo

https://github.com/samiesaheb/RAG-Demo

A visual playground where you can experiment with RAG and image generation. It's especially cool for exploring how AI understands layout and regions in prompts.

4.8.2 GitHub: RAG Demo with Hugging Face + FAISS + Ollama

Ready to get technical? This Python-based demo lets you dive into the full RAG pipeline—using real datasets, vector search, and local AI models. Includes a Jupyter Notebook so you can run your own queries and see how retrieval and generation work together. **Explore the code:** https://github.com/samiesaheb/RAG-Demo

4.8.3 Hugging Face Blog: Code Your Own RAG

https://huggingface.co/blog/ngxson/make-your-own-rag

Want to build your own chatbot or Q&A system? This step-by-step guide walks you through creating a RAG pipeline from scratch. Great for students who want to go beyond theory and build something real.

4.8.4 Project-Based Learning: Build Your Own RAG Chatbot

In this hands-on project, you'll design and build a chatbot powered by **RAG**—a cutting-edge AI technique that blends search and generation. Your chatbot will answer questions based on real-world social work policy documents, helping you explore how AI can support public service delivery and policy literacy.

4.8.4.1 Instructions:

1 Choose Your Document.

- Select a real social work policy document (PDF, DOCX, or TXT).
- Examples: *Basic Livelihood Security Guide, Disability Support Manual.*
- Make sure the document is well-structured and readable.

2 Set Up Your Environment.

- Use any tools of your choice (e.g., Python, LangChain or Haystack, FAISS or Chroma, Streamlit or Gradio).
- Install necessary packages and dependencies.

3 Preprocess the Document.

- Break the document into smaller chunks (e.g., 500 tokens each).
- Convert each chunk into a vector embedding using models like OpenAI Embedding or Hugging Face.

4 Build the Retrieval System.

- Store embeddings in a vector database (e.g., FAISS).
- Create a retriever that finds the most relevant chunks based on user queries.

5 Connect to an LLM.

- Use an LLM (e.g., GPT-5, Gemini) to generate answers using both the query and retrieved content.
- Integrate retrieval and generation into a full RAG pipeline.

6 Design the Chat Interface.

- Use Streamlit or Gradio to build a simple web-based chatbot.
- Allow users to input questions and receive answers with source references.

7 Test and Evaluate.

- Try sample questions like:
  - o "Who qualifies for housing support?"
  - o "What documents are needed for disability benefits?"
- Evaluate your chatbot based on:
  - o Accuracy of answers.
    - o Relevance of retrieved content.
  - o Response time and user experience.

4.8.4.2 Learning Outcomes:

- Practical understanding of RAG architecture.
- Ability to build a domain-specific chatbot.
- Skills in document-embedding, retrieval, and LLM integration.
- Insight into AI's role in public service and policy delivery.

4.8.4.3 Taking One Step Further

- Apply the chatbot to other domains: school regulations, HR policies, legal documents.
- Add multilingual support or voice input/output.
- Include citation links and feedback buttons for user validation.

References

Benmarrakchi, F. (2025). An AI-based framework to enhance attentional engagement among children with ADHD using multimodal behavioral data. *Lecture Notes in Networks and Systems*, 1619, 22–33. https://doi.org/10.1007/978-3-032-05070-0_3

Chopra, S., Agarwal, P., Ahmed, J., Biswas, S. S., & Obaid, A. J. (2024). Roberta and BERT: Revolutionizing mental healthcare through natural language. *SN Computer Science, 5*(889). https://doi.org/10.1007/s42979-024-03202-8

Du, K. L., Zhang, R., Jiang, B., Zeng, J., & Lu, J. (2024). Understanding machine learning principles: Learning, inference, generalization, and computational learning theory. *Mathematics, 13*(3), 451. https://doi.org/10.3390/math13030451

Gabriel, A. G., Ahmad, A. A., & Jeyakumar, S. K. (2024). Advancing agentic systems: Dynamic task decomposition, tool integration and evaluation using novel metrics and dataset. *arXiv*. https://doi.org/10.48550/arXiv.2410.22457

Gupta, S., Ranjan, R., & Singh, S. (2024). A comprehensive survey of Retrieval-Augmented Generation (RAG): Evolution, current landscape and future directions. *arXiv.* https://doi.org/10.48550/arXiv.2410.12837

Hughes, L., Dwivedi, Y. K., Malik, T., Shawosh, M., Albashrawi, M. A., Jeon, I., Dutot, V., Appanderanda, M., Crick, T., De', R., Fenwick, M., Gunaratnege, S. M., Jurcys, P., Kar, A. K., Kshetri, N., Li, K., Mutasa, S., Samothrakis, S., Wade, M., & Walton, P. (2025). AI agents and agentic systems: A multi-expert analysis. *Journal of Computer Information Systems, 65*(4), 489–517. https://doi.org/10.1080/08874417.2025.2483832

Jegan, R., & Henrich, A. (2025). A structured literature review on traditional approaches in current natural language processing. *arXiv*. https://doi.org/10.48550/arXiv.2505.12970

Leroux, N., Manea, P.-P., Sudarshan, C., Finkbeiner, J., Siegel, S., Strachan, J. P., & Neftci, E. (2024). Analog in-memory computing attention mechanism for fast and energy-efficient large language models. *arXiv*. https://doi.org/10.48550/arXiv.2409.19315

Lewis, P., Perez, E., Piktus, A., Petroni, F., Karpukhin, V., Goyal, N., Küttler, H., Lewis, M., Yih, W.-t., Rocktäschel, T., Riedel, S., & Kiela, D. (2020). Retrieval-augmented generation for knowledge-intensive NLP tasks. In *Proceedings of the 34th Conference on Neural Information Processing Systems (NeurIPS 2020)*, *1*, 9459–9474. https://arxiv.org/abs/2005.11401

McNamara, K. J., & Marpu, R. P. (2025). Demystifying AI agents: The final generation of intelligence. *arXiv*. https://doi.org/10.48550/arXiv.2505.09932

Naidu, N., & El-Gayar, O. (2025). A review of reasoning in artificial agents using large language models. In *Proceedings of the 58th Hawaii International Conference on System Sciences*. https://hdl.handle.net/10125/109007

Niketan, N., & Batatia, H. (2025). Integrating external tools with large language models to improve accuracy. *arXiv.* https://doi.org/10.48550/arXiv.2507.08034

Oche, A. J., Folashade, A. G., Ghosal, T., & Biswas, A. (2025). A systematic review of key retrieval-augmented generation (RAG) systems: Progress, gaps, and future directions. *arXiv*. https://doi.org/10.48550/arXiv.2507.18910

Pipitone, N., & Alami, G. H. (2024). LegalBench-RAG: A benchmark for retrieval-augmented generation in the legal domain. *arXiv.* https://doi.org/10.48550/arXiv.2408.10343

Ruano-Ordás, D. (2024). Machine learning-based feature extraction and selection, *Applied Sciences*, *14*(15), 6567. https://doi.org/10.3390/app14156567

Russell, S. J., & Norvig, P. (2021). *Artificial intelligence: A modern approach, global edition* (4th ed.). Pearson.

Shao, Y., Jiang, Y., Kanell, T. A., Xu, P., Khattab, O., & Lam, M. S. (2024). Assisting in writing Wikipedia-like articles from scratch with large language models. *arXiv*. https://doi.org/10.48550/arXiv.2402.14207

Shen, Y., Song, K., Tan, X., Zhang, W., Ren, K., Yuan, S., Lu, W., Li, D., & Zhuang, Y. (2024). TaskBench: Benchmarking large language models for task automation. *arXiv*. https://doi.org/10.48550/arXiv.2311.18760

Shu, R., Das, N., Yuan, M., Sunkara, M., & Zhang, Y. (2024). Towards effective GenAI multi-agent collaboration: Design and evaluation for enterprise applications. *arXiv*. https://doi.org/10.48550/arXiv.2412.05449

Song, M. S. (2025). *Easy-to-understand social work, ICT, IoT, and AI.* Kyobo Book Centre.

U.S. Government Accountability Office. (2023, June 13). *Science & tech spotlight: Generative AI.* gao.gov. www.gao.gov/products/gao-23-106782

Wang, J., Zhang, O., & Jiang, Y. (2025). Multimodal diffusion framework for collaborative text, image, audio generation and applications. *Scientific Reports*, *15*, 20604. https://doi.org/10.1038/s41598-025-05794-4

Wang, L., Ma, C., Feng, X. et al. (2024). A survey on large language model based autonomous agents. *arXiv*. https://doi.org/10.1007/s11704-024-40231-1

Part II

Ethics, Equity, and Justice

5 Algorithmic Bias and Structural Inequality

Othelia Lee

Box 5.1 The Digital Crossroads

Noah, a 39-year-old patient with uncontrolled Type 2 diabetes and severe chronic back pain, has been waiting for months to see a primary care physician. The local clinic's waitlist is long, and his symptoms are worsening. He is experiencing frequent dizziness and difficulty managing his blood sugar. Feeling desperate, Noah turns to an artificial intelligence (AI)-powered health coordination platform that promises to connect patients with care plans. The AI suggests several options: adjusting his diet, starting a new exercise routine, and considering telehealth consultations with specialists. It even provides links to online pharmacies for medication refills.

Noah feels torn. He wonders: can I trust this advice? What if I made the wrong choice? He worries about the risks of acting without a doctor's oversight but also fears his condition will deteriorate if he waits. The AI seems helpful, but Noah questions whether it understands his full medical history, mental health struggles with anxiety, and financial limitations. Should he follow the AI's recommendations, or wait for professional guidance?

This case underscores a core reality: AI systems learn from data, and data reflects society's bias. The AI was not "neutral;" it was reproducing systemic inequities. Without careful design and monitoring, AI can amplify the very injustices social work seeks to dismantle.

5.1 Defining Algorithmic Bias

Using examples from a BuzzFeed article on "AI-generated Barbies," the video [www.youtube.com/watch?v=L2sQRrf1Cd8] from the London Interdisciplinary School (2023) illustrates how biased training data leads to distorted, stereotypical, and exclusionary representations. It explains how AI image generators can reinforce and even amplify cultural biases, inviting us to think critically about how

DOI: 10.4324/9781003755081-7

AI reflects societal inequities and why practitioners must remain vigilant about representational harm in AI systems.

As AI becomes increasingly embedded in social work practice, it is essential to understand how algorithmic systems can reproduce and even intensify existing social inequalities. **Algorithmic bias** occurs when an AI system's output is systematically prejudiced due to flawed data, assumptions, or design processes. These biases are not always the result of malicious intent; rather, they often emerge from data systems that reflect and reinforce unequal social structures (Zajko, 2022). Let's discuss several incidents of algorithmic bias in terms of disparate impact, representation bias, and measurement bias.

Disparate Impact: AI systems may produce outcomes that disproportionately harm one group more than others, even in the absence of intentional discrimination. For example, predictive tools used in child welfare or criminal justice may flag individuals from marginalized communities at higher risk due to historical patterns encoded in the data (Reamer, 2025).

Representation Bias: Watch the video [www.youtube.com/watch?v=lQ_8eOaiz8o] from National Education Association (2017) explaining how structured racism manifests. Certain populations may be underrepresented or misrepresented in the datasets used to train AI systems. This can result in tools that fail to recognize or respond appropriately to the needs of diverse clients, particularly those from racialized, disabled, or low-income backgrounds (Panarese et al., 2025).

Measurement Bias: AI systems often rely on proxy variables (e.g., zip code or income level) that stand in for sensitive social categories like race or socioeconomic status. These proxies can inadvertently reinforce stereotypes or systemic disadvantages, especially when used in high-stakes decisions like eligibility for services or risk assessments (Zajko, 2022).

Mathematical models increasingly shape decisions in policing, education, credit, employment, insurance, and politics. Yet we rarely understand their inner workings. O'Neil (2016) examines how large-scale algorithms (often promoted as objective, efficient, and data-driven) reinforce preexisting inequalities and harm marginalized populations. These harmful algorithms become "Weapons of Math Destruction (WMDs)."

To illustrate, these models substitute poor proxies, such as demographics or zip codes, for complex human traits, resulting in discriminatory outcomes. Most WMDs are nontransparent and unregulated, meaning that individuals harmed by algorithmic decisions cannot understand or contest them. Policing models direct law enforcement to over-policed urban neighborhoods, producing more arrests and justifying further policing (O'Neil, 2016). Many WMDs are built and deployed by private corporations whose incentives (cost reduction, efficiency, marketing, or profit) do not align with fairness or human well-being.

Bias in algorithms is not simply a technical flaw: it reflects broader societal inequities. As Panarese and colleagues (2025) argue, algorithmic systems are socially embedded agents, shaped by human decisions and historical data. When these systems are deployed in social work contexts without critical oversight, they risk legitimizing and amplifying structural injustices.

How can social workers be equipped to recognize and respond to these risks? This includes understanding how bias operates within AI systems, advocating for transparency and accountability, and ensuring that technology serves rather than harms vulnerable populations. Ethical practice demands that we move beyond technical fixes and engage with the cultural, political, and historical dimensions of algorithmic decision-making (Reamer, 2025).

5.2 Sources of Algorithmic Bias

Understanding the sources of algorithmic bias is essential for social workers engaging with AI in practice, policy, and advocacy. Bias in AI systems is not always the result of malicious intent: it often emerges from the ways data is collected, interpreted, and used within systems shaped by historical and structural inequalities. These biases can lead to unfair outcomes, especially for marginalized populations, and must be critically examined by social workers committed to equity and justice.

5.2.1 Data-Related Technical Factors

Historical Data Inequities. AI systems are trained on existing data, which often reflects past patterns of systemic discrimination. Arrest records, eviction histories, and school disciplinary actions may disproportionately represent certain racial or socioeconomic groups due to historical injustices. When these datasets are used to train predictive models, the resulting AI tools can perpetuate these inequities, reinforcing harmful stereotypes and unequal treatment (Ferrara, 2023; Reamer, 2025). Therefore, "garbage in, garbage out."

Sampling Bias. Sampling bias occurs when certain communities are overrepresented or underrepresented in datasets. For instance, urban populations may be heavily surveyed while rural or Indigenous communities remain invisible in the data. This imbalance can lead to AI systems that perform well for some groups but poorly for others, exacerbating disparities in service delivery and access (Hickman et al., 2025). *Representation Bias.* This refers to cases where a specific population is overrepresented or underrepresented in a dataset. Data for people with disabilities is often insufficient, which can cause AI to fail to recognize diversity and make decisions that are unfavorable to people with disabilities (Manzoor et al., 2024).

5.2.2 Algorithm Design and Modeling Phase

Feature Selection Choices (Proxy Variable). Developers make critical decisions about which variables to include in AI models. These choices often embed hidden value judgments. For example, using zip code as a proxy for risk may unintentionally correlate with race or income, leading to discriminatory outcomes. Such decisions reflect broader societal assumptions and must be scrutinized for fairness and transparency (Ferrara, 2023).

5.2.3 System Operation and Learning Process

Feedback Loops. AI systems can create feedback loops where their recommendations influence human decisions, which are then fed back into the system as new data. Over time, this can reinforce existing patterns and biases. If an AI tool flags certain neighborhoods as high-risk, increased surveillance may lead to more recorded incidents, further validating the original prediction and deepening systemic inequities (Hickman et al., 2025).

Model Generalization Error. This is a problem that occurs when a model's performance degrades when it's applied in a new environment, different from the one it was trained on. While the model performs well on its training data, its accuracy drops when faced with real-world scenarios or new types of data. This happens because the training data does not fully represent the real world. For example, an AI traffic control system trained only on traffic data from urban areas may fail to accurately predict real traffic volumes when applied to a rural area, leading to inefficient signal control. In this case, the model "generalized" well on the urban data it was trained on but failed to "generalize" to the new environment of rural data, causing an error.

At this point, readers may find it confusing to distinguish model generalization errors and representation bias. However, they differ in their root causes and what they aim to address. **Representation bias** is an issue with the dataset used to train the model. An AI medical diagnosis model with insufficient data on people with disabilities may fail to accurately diagnose their specific health conditions. Consider an AI trained on a job-related image dataset that has very few images of women. When you input the word "woman," it might only generate images of women in roles like secretary or nurse.

5.2.4 Specific Error Types Linked to Technical Factors

AI systems don't just "make mistakes." They make specific types of errors that can have serious consequences for the people we serve. These errors often stem from technical decisions made during different phases of the AI lifecycle, and they are deeply intertwined with issues of equity and justice. When the data used to train AI system is incomplete or biased, for example, it overrepresents one group and underrepresents another, the system will learn a distorted view of reality. This is called **sampling bias**, and it's one of the most common sources of algorithmic injustice.

Model Learning Phase is where things get more technical. One major issue is **overfitting**: when a model learns the training data too well, including its noise and quirks, and fails to generalize to new, real-world situations. Think of it like memorizing flashcards instead of understanding the concepts. Another problem is the use of **proxy variables**—indirect indicators that may unintentionally stand in for race, gender, or socioeconomic status, leading to discriminatory outcomes. Even after deployment, AI systems can go off track. **Feedback loops** (where biased outputs reinforce biased inputs) and **generalization errors** (where the system misapplies its rules to new contexts) can worsen performance and deepen inequality.

Table 5.1 Error Types Linked to Technical Factors

Category	*Technical Factor*	*Description*	*Possible Errors*
Data Phase	Historical Bias	AI learns from past data, and the discrimination and inequality that already exist within the data are reflected.	Over-classifying a specific group as "high-risk," distorted generalization.
	Sampling Bias	Over/under-representation of specific groups (e.g., urban population ↑, rural population ↓).	Decreased prediction accuracy for marginalized groups, unfair services.
	Representation Bias	A specific population is insufficient or distorted in the dataset.	Failure to recognize diversity, disadvantage for people with disabilities and minorities.
Modeling Phase	Feature Selection Bias	The developer chooses which variables to use → intervention of value judgment.	Outcomes that use postal codes, job history, etc. as proxies for race or income.
	Proxy Variables	Even if sensitive attributes (race, gender) are not used directly, other variables act as proxies for them.	Indirect discrimination occurs, hindering fair decision-making.
Learning and Operations Phase	Feedback Loop	The model's results are reflected back into the data, strengthening existing biases.	Specific areas are continuously classified as "high-risk" → self-reinforcing bias.
	Model Generalization Error	Performance degrades when the training data and the real-world environment differ.	Decreased prediction reliability for rural and minority groups.
Specific Error Types	Overfitting (Learning Phase)	Optimized for data from the majority group, with degraded performance for the minority group.	Generalization error, lower accuracy for specific groups.
	Accumulated Issues (Decision-Making Phase)	Errors from all stages compound in final decision-making.	Discriminatory outcomes, intensification of social inequality.

All these technical missteps can culminate in real-world harm: unfair decisions in housing, employment, child welfare, or criminal justice. These aren't just bugs: they are reflections of systemic bias. Therefore, bias in AI isn't just a technical glitch: it's a social justice issue. As social workers, we must be able to spot these errors, question the systems that produce them, and advocate for tools that are transparent, accountable, and equitable. By understanding how algorithmic bias arises from data to decision, we can help shape AI systems that serve the common good and protect human dignity. This is not just about technical literacy: it's about ethical leadership in a digital age.

5.3 Understanding AI System Functions and Algorithmic Bias: Social Work Perspectives

In the previous chapter, we explored the basic structure and functions of AI. Now, we will build on that foundation to examine how bias can emerge within AI systems, not just as a technical glitch, but as a reflection of deeper social inequalities. We will help you understand how algorithmic bias is generated, why it matters in human services, and what social workers can do to address it.

Although algorithms are often seen as neutral tools, they are shaped by human decisions at every stage from data collection to model deployment. Bias can creep in through sampling errors, underrepresentation of certain groups, and subjective choices made during data labeling or feature selection. These technical decisions can unintentionally embed social bias into AI systems, leading to outcomes that reinforce inequality. Let's further examine where bias begins from data to deployment.

5.3.1 Data Collection and Preprocessing

AI systems begin by collecting data from sources like sensors, logs, and records. This data is then cleaned, normalized, and labeled. But bias can emerge early on. For example, in child welfare risk assessment tools, if historical data overrepresents certain racial groups due to systemic surveillance, the AI may learn to flag those groups as higher-risk (Edward, 2025). **Annotator bias** and **representation errors** can lead to skewed predictions that reinforce racial disparities in child removal decisions.

5.3.2 Feature Engineering and Selection

Next, developers choose which variables to include in the model, such as age, income, or zip code. These choices may seem technical, but they carry social weight. In predictive policing systems, zip codes are often used as **proxies** for crime risk, which can disproportionately target communities of color. When developers make these decisions without considering equity, they risk embedding indirect discrimination into the system (Eubanks, 2018).

5.3.3 Model Training

During training, the AI learns patterns from the data. If the data is biased, the model may become optimized for one group while failing to generalize to others. For example, mental health chatbots trained primarily on data from white, middle-class users may struggle to understand the language, cultural context, or emotional expressions of clients from marginalized backgrounds (Ouyang, (2024). This can lead to misdiagnosis or ineffective support.

Table 5.2 AI System Functions and Algorithm Bias

AI System Function	*Cause of Bias*	*Main Error Types*
Data Collection and Preprocessing	Sampling imbalance, incorrect labeling	Sampling error, labeling error
Feature Selection (Feature Engineering)	Proxy variables, developer's value judgment	Indirect discrimination, variable distortion
Model Training	Data distribution imbalance, overfitting, reward design problems	Generalization error, overfitting
Prediction and Inference	Domain shift, threshold setting problems	False positive/negative rate imbalance
System Operation and Feedback Loop	Results are re-reflected in the data, strengthening bias	Self-reinforcing bias

5.3.4 Prediction and Inference

Once trained, the model begins making predictions. If the input data differs from the training data, a **domain shift** can occur, leading to errors. In substance use treatment, AI tools may predict relapse risk based on behavioral patterns that don't apply to certain populations, such as women with co-occurring disorders or LGBTQ+ youth, resulting in inaccurate assessments and missed opportunities for intervention (Acharya et al., 2024).

5.3.5 Feedback Loop and Deployment

Finally, the model's predictions influence future decisions and data collection. This creates a **feedback loop**: biased predictions lead to biased decisions, which generate more biased data. In housing support programs, if an AI system consistently denies assistance to applicants from certain zip codes, those areas become underrepresented in future data, reinforcing exclusion (Sherbini, 2024). Over time, this cycle can institutionalize inequality.

5.4 Examples of Algorithmic Bias in Human Services

When AI systems are deployed in human services, they can unintentionally reproduce and amplify existing disparities. The following examples illustrate how bias manifests in real-world social work contexts, underscoring the need for critical engagement and ethical oversight.

5.4.1 Data Bias

Child Welfare Risk Tools. AI-based risk assessment tools are increasingly used in child welfare to predict which children may be at risk of harm. While these tools aim to improve decision-making, they often rely on historical data that disproportionately reflects surveillance of marginalized communities. As a result, children from Black, Indigenous, and low-income families may be over-identified as "at risk," leading to unnecessary interventions and family separations (Eubanks, 2018). This disparate impact highlights how algorithmic bias can reinforce systemic racism and undermine trust in social services.

Homelessness Resource Allocation. In some cities, AI systems are used to prioritize access to housing and support services based on data such as police contact or shelter usage. While this may seem efficient, it can unintentionally favor individuals who are already visible to the system, those with frequent interactions with law enforcement or emergency services. Meanwhile, hidden homeless populations, such as women couch-surfing or undocumented individuals avoiding public systems, may be excluded from support due to lack of data representation (Barocas et al., 2023; Moon & Guha, 2024). This is a clear example of **sampling bias**, where invisibility in data translates to invisibility in services.

5.4.2 Model Design Feature Selection Bias

Employment Assistance Programs. AI tools used in employment services may filter applicants based on historical job histories, penalizing gaps in employment. These gaps are often due to caregiving responsibilities, and disproportionately affect women, especially single mothers. When algorithms interpret these gaps as indicators of lower employability, they perpetuate gender bias and hinder access to economic opportunity (O'Neil, 2016). This reflects selection bias, where seemingly neutral variables carry embedded social judgments.

5.4.3 Imbalanced Training Data and Reflection of Past Inequalities

Amazon's Hiring Algorithm. In an internal Amazon project in 2018, a hiring algorithm trained on male-dominated data was found to have a bias, devaluing resumes that included female-related keywords such as "women's chess club captain" or "women's college." To improve this bias, it is necessary to use diverse datasets and conduct regular bias checks (Winick, 2018). This illustrates **Historical Bias**, where the training data itself contains a structure of gender and racial inequality, causing the learning data to be imbalanced and to directly learn the past male-dominated hiring patterns.

5.4.4 Decision/Operational Bias

Oregon's Child Welfare Risk Tool. In 2022, the state of Oregon in the U.S. decided to stop using an AI tool with racial bias concerns in its child welfare department's case selection process. This was linked to a case in Pennsylvania where an algorithmic tool disproportionately flagged a high number of Black children (Ho & Burke, 2022).

U.K.'s Welfare Fraud Detection System (2025). In the U.K. in 2025, an AI system used to detect welfare fraud was found to have made biased decisions based on specific factors like age, disability, and nationality, leading to controversy over its fairness and transparency (The Guardian, 2024; Metanews, 2025).

Table 5.3 Examples of Algorithmic Bias in Human Services

Case	*Bias Type*	*Specific Description*
Child welfare risk tools	Data/Operational bias	Overrepresentation of Black and Indigenous children leading to discrimination
Homeless resource allocation	Sampling/ Representation bias	Overrepresentation of people who had contact with police and emergency services; Exclusion of women and undocumented immigrants
Employment support program	Feature selection bias	Interpreting caregiving as lower likelihood of employment—disadvantageous to women
Amazon hiring algorithm	Historical data bias	Learning from male-centric data, leading to disadvantage for female-related keywords
U.K. welfare fraud detection	Operational/Decision-making bias	Discriminatory judgment based on age, disability, and nationality

5.5 Structural Inequality and Algorithmic Design

AI systems do not operate in a vacuum: they are built within and upon existing social structures. For social workers, it is essential to recognize that algorithmic bias is deeply intertwined with structural inequality. The data used to train AI systems often reflects historical injustices, and the design choices made by developers can unintentionally reinforce systemic harm. By viewing algorithms through this lens, social workers can better identify where "neutral" technology may conceal or perpetuate inequity.

Racism. Racial disparities in policing, education, and housing have long shaped public data systems. As discussed earlier, predictive policing algorithms trained on historical arrest records may disproportionately target communities of color, not because of higher crime rates, but because of over-policing and surveillance (Eubanks, 2018). Similarly, school discipline data may reflect racial bias in disciplinary practices, leading to skewed educational interventions. These examples show how racism embedded in data can lead to biased outcomes, even when the algorithm itself appears neutral.

Classism. Economic exclusion also plays a significant role in algorithmic bias. Low-income communities are often more visible in crisis-related datasets (e.g., emergency room visits or shelter usage) while their resilience and strengths go unrecorded. This imbalance can result in AI systems that prioritize interventions based on crisis visibility rather than holistic need, reinforcing narratives of deficit rather than resilience (O'Neil, 2016). Class-based bias in algorithmic design can thus shape how resources are allocated and who is deemed "worthy" of support.

Ableism. Data systems frequently fail to account for the diversity of disability experiences. Algorithms used in employment screening or service eligibility may overlook non-traditional communication styles, assistive technology use, or gaps in work history due to health conditions. These oversights can lead to exclusionary practices that disadvantage individuals with disabilities, particularly when the disability is treated as a binary or medicalized category rather than a spectrum of lived experiences (Manzoor et al., 2024).

Intersectionality. Structural inequality is rarely experienced in isolation. Individuals with multiple marginalized identities (e.g., a Black woman with neurodiversity or a transgender youth experiencing homelessness) face compounded risks of algorithmic bias. Intersectionality helps social workers understand how overlapping systems of oppression interact within algorithmic design, making some populations more vulnerable to harm and invisibility (Crenshaw, 1991). Without intentional design and inclusive data practices, AI systems may fail to recognize or respond to these complex realities.

Social workers must approach AI systems with a critical and compassionate lens, recognizing that technology never becomes neutral. By understanding how structural inequality shapes algorithmic design, practitioners can advocate for systems that are transparent, inclusive, and aligned with social justice values. This perspective empowers social workers to challenge bias, promote equity, and ensure that AI serves the common good.

5.6 Detection and Mitigation Strategies

Algorithmic bias isn't just a technical issue: it's a structural one. It reflects how social inequalities can be reproduced through digital systems. When AI is used in mental health assessments, child welfare screenings, or resource allocations, biased algorithms can lead to real harm.

That is why ethical practice in the age of AI requires more than just compassion: it demands technical literacy, critical thinking, and advocacy. Social workers must be able to ask tough questions about fairness, transparency, and representation, advocating for institutional safeguards that protect marginalized communities from digital harm.

We suggest some strategies for various stakeholders such as social work practitioners, educators, and agencies. For Agencies and Practitioners, some strategies include the bias audit, transparent documentation, a community board, and Algorithmic Impact Assessments (AIAs).

Bias/Fairness Audits One of the most direct ways to detect algorithmic bias is through regular, independent bias audits. These audits systematically evaluate AI systems for fairness across different demographic groups, ensuring that predictive models do not perpetuate discrimination. Landers and Behrend (2023) propose psychological audits as a standardized framework for assessing fairness in high-stakes AI systems, emphasizing the need for interdisciplinary collaboration and cultural sensitivity.

Transparent Documentation. Mitchell and colleagues (2019) introduced model cards to democratize machine learning by making its inner workings more accessible and accountable. Tools like "model cards" and "datasheets" provide structured documentation about an algorithm's design, training data, intended use, and limitations. These resources help practitioners understand how a model might behave across different populations and contexts.

Community Oversight Boards Ethical governance of AI systems must include the voices of those most affected. Community oversight boards, composed of service users, advocates, and practitioners, can evaluate the real-world impacts of AI tools and ensure they align with community values. Schuett and colleagues (2024) emphasize that ethics boards, when thoughtfully designed, can reduce societal risks and foster trust in AI systems.

Algorithmic Impact Assessments. Before deploying AI systems, agencies should conduct AIAs, akin to environmental impact assessments. These evaluations consider potential harms, document decision-making processes, and promote accountability. Selbst (2021) argues that AIAs can catalyze cultural shifts toward ethical responsibility in technical development, even when full compliance is not immediately achievable.

5.7 Social Work's Roles in Advocacy

As AI continues to shape the landscape of human services, social workers are called upon to expand their roles, not only as users of technology but as stewards of equitable innovation. This shift demands a proactive stance in advocacy, policy engagement, and interdisciplinary collaboration.

Social workers are uniquely positioned to bridge disciplines, translating the lived experiences and concerns of clients into actionable insights for technologists. This role is especially vital in ensuring that AI systems reflect ethical standards rooted in social justice and human dignity (Garkisch & Goldkind, 2025). By serving as intermediaries between communities and developers, social workers help to represent marginalized voices in technological design.

In addition, social workers can influence procurement decisions within agencies by advising them on the ethical implications of adopting specific AI tools. Their expertise in equity and client-centered care allows them to critically assess whether a system aligns with the values of the profession (Reamer, 2025). This influence is particularly important in safeguarding against algorithmic bias and ensuring that technology enhances rather than undermines service delivery.

Perhaps most powerfully, social workers can shape legislation by participating in public comment periods, engaging with regulatory bodies, and advocating for inclusive AI policies. The National Association of Social Workers (NASW) has emphasized the importance of ethical standards in technology use, and social workers are encouraged to contribute to these evolving frameworks. Advocacy at the policy level ensures that AI development is guided by principles of transparency, accountability, and human rights.

To fulfill these roles, social workers must move beyond passive engagement with technology. They must become active participants in shaping the future of AI, advocating for systems that promote equity, protect vulnerable populations, and uphold the core values of the profession. This transformation is not optional: it is a moral imperative in an era where digital tools increasingly mediate access to care, justice, and opportunity.

5.8 Critical Thinking Questions

1 As shown in Noah's case, what are the ethical implications for a social worker assisting a client who is self-treating using AI due to lack of systemic access?
2 In what ways can feature selection choices reflect hidden value judgments? Can you think of examples from your practicum experience?
3 How do feedback loops in AI systems reinforce systemic patterns of inequality? What strategies can social workers use to identify and challenge algorithmic bias in practice settings?
4 What role should social workers play in the design and evaluation of AI systems used in human services?
5 What are the risks of relying on AI tools without understanding their limitations?

5.9 Summary

Algorithmic bias is not merely a technical flaw: it is a mirror of the structural inequalities embedded in our society. We discussed algorithmic bias and its deep ties to structural inequality, offering a critical social work perspective on one of AI's most urgent challenges. Examining its sources—biased data, flawed design, and systemic inequities—the chapter illustrates how AI functions like prediction and classification can reinforce discrimination in human services. Social workers must learn to identify these patterns, advocate for more just systems, and ensure that technology serves rather than undermines the common good. In the next chapters, let's explore ethics and human rights frameworks for governing AI, linking advocacy efforts to global ethical standards.

5.10 Empowerment-Focused Activities

5.10.1 Invisible Data, Visible Impact: Unpacking Algorithmic Bias

Objective: To help students critically analyze how algorithmic bias manifests in real-world human services and explore ethical, equity-based responses.

Instructions: Divide students into small groups (3–5 members). Assign each group one of the following case scenarios:

- Child Welfare Risk Tool: A predictive model flags children from low-income neighborhoods as high-risk for maltreatment.
- Homelessness Resource Allocation: A city uses AI to prioritize housing services based on police contact and shelter usage.
- Employment Assistance Filtering: An AI system screens out applicants with employment gaps, disproportionately affecting caregivers.

Discussions:

- What type(s) of bias are present in this case (e.g., historical, sampling, feature selection)?
- How might this bias impact service delivery and client outcomes?
- What ethical concerns arise from the use of AI in this scenario?
- How could social workers intervene or advocate for change?

Group Task:

- Prepare a brief presentation or poster summarizing your analysis.
- Include recommendations for ethical safeguards, policy changes, or alternative data practices.

5.10.2 Reflective Questions for Algorithmic Bias

5.10.2.1 Bridging Disciplines

- How might you translate a client's concern about surveillance or data privacy into language that a technologist or data scientist would understand?
- What challenges might arise when trying to advocate for clients in interdisciplinary settings?

5.10.2.2 Influencing Procurement

- Imagine your agency is considering adopting a predictive analytics tool for child welfare assessments. What ethical questions would you raise during the procurement process?
- What criteria would you use to evaluate whether the tool aligns with social work values?

5.10.2.3 Shaping Legislation

- Have you ever participated in a public comment period or policy consultation? If not, what barriers might prevent social workers from engaging in these processes?
- What strategies could help social workers become more involved in shaping AI-related legislation?

References

Acharya, N., Kar, P., Ally, M., & Soar, J. (2024). Predicting co-occurring mental health and substance use disorders in women: An automated machine learning approach. *Applied Sciences, 14*(4), 1630. https://doi.org/10.3390/app14041630

Barocas, S., Hardt, M., & Narayanan, A. (2023). *Fairness and machine learning*. MIT Press.

Crenshaw, K. (1991). Mapping the margins: Intersectionality, identity politics, and violence against women of color. *Stanford Law Review, 43*(6), 1241–1299. https://doi.org/10.2307/1229039

Edwards, F. (2025). Bias, risk, racism: Reconciling critical and quantitative approaches to understanding racial inequality in child welfare system outcomes. *Journal of Policy Analysis and Management, 44,* 693–706. https://onlinelibrary.wiley.com/doi/am-pdf/10.1002/pam.70001

Eubanks, V. (2018). *Automating inequality: How high-tech tools profile, police, and punish the poor*. St. Martin's Press.

Ferrara, E. (2023). *Fairness and bias in artificial intelligence: A brief survey of sources, impacts, and mitigation strategies*. Annenberg School of Communication & Viterbi School of Engineering, University of Southern California. https://arxiv.org/pdf/2304.07683v1

Garkisch, M., & Goldkind, L. (2025). Considering a unified model of artificial intelligence enhanced social work: A systematic review. *Journal of Human Rights and Social Work, 10*, 23–42. https://doi.org/10.1007/s41134-024-00326-y

Hickman, L., Huynh, C., Gass, J., Booth, B., Kuruzovich, J., & Tay, L. (2025). Whither bias goes, I will go: An integrative, systematic review of algorithmic bias mitigation. *Journal of Applied Psychology, 110*(7), 979–1000. https://doi.org/10.1037/apl0001255

Ho, S., & Burke, G. (2022, June 2). *Oregon dropping AI tool used in child abuse cases.* Pulitzer Center. https://pulitzercenter.org/stories/oregon-dropping-ai-tool-used-child-abuse-cases

Landers, R. N., & Behrend, T. S. (2023). Auditing the AI auditors: A framework for evaluating fairness and bias in high stakes AI predictive models. *American Psychologist, 78*(1), 36–49. https://doi.org/10.1037/amp0000972

Manzoor, R., Hussain, W., & Anjum, M. L. (2024). Out of dataset, out of algorithm, out of mind: A critical evaluation of AI bias against disabled people. *AI & Society, 40*(5), 3941–3951. https://doi.org/10.1007/s00146-024-02168-8

Mitchell, M., Wu, S., Zaldivar, A., Barnes, P., Vasserman, L., Hutchinson, B., Spitzer, E., Raji, I. D., & Gebru, T. (2019). Model cards for model reporting. In *Proceedings of the Conference on Fairness, Accountability, and Transparency*, 220–229. https://doi.org/10.1145/3287560.3287596

Moon, E. S.-Y., & Guha, S. (2024). A human-centered review of algorithms in homelessness research. In *Proceedings of the CHI Conference on Human Factors in Computing Systems*. https://arxiv.org/html/2401.13247v1

National Education Association. (2017, February 22). *Structural racism explained* [Video]. YouTube. www.youtube.com/watch?v=lQ_8eOaiz8o

O'Neil, C. (2016). *Weapons of math destruction: How big data increases inequality and threatens democracy*. Crown Publishing Group.

Ouyang, A. (2024). *Study reveals AI chatbots can detect race, but racial bias reduces response empathy*. Massachusetts Institute of Technology. https://news.mit.edu/2024/study-reveals-ai-chatbots-can-detect-race-but-racial-bias-reduces-response-empathy-1216

Panarese, P., Grasso, M. M., & Solinas, C. (2025). Algorithmic bias, fairness, and inclusivity: A multilevel framework for justice-oriented AI. *AI & Society. 41*, 2803–2825. https://doi.org/10.1007/s00146-025-02451-2

Reamer, F. G. (2025). *Artificial intelligence in the behavioral health professions ethical and risk management issues*. NASW Press.

Schuett, J., Reuel, A.-K., & Carlier, A. (2024). How to design an AI ethics board. *AI and Ethics, 5*, 863–881. https://doi.org/10.1007/s43681-023-00409-y

Selbst, A. D. (2021). An institutional view of algorithmic impact assessments. *Harvard Journal of Law & Technology*, 35(1), 117–190. https://jolt.law.harvard.edu/assets/articlePDFs/v35/Selbst-An-Institutional-View-of-Algorithmic-Impact-Assessments.pdf

Sherbini, D. (2024). *AI is making housing discrimination easier than ever before*. Kreisman Initiative for Housing Law & Policy, University of Chicago. https://kreismaninitiative.uchicago.edu/2024/02/12/ai-is-making-housing-discrimination-easier-than-ever-before/

The London Interdisciplinary School. (2023). *How AI image generators make bias worse [Video]*. YouTube. www.youtube.com/watch?v=L2sQRrf1Cd8

The Guardian. (2024, December 6). Revealed: Bias found in AI system used to detect UK benefits fraud. www.theguardian.com/society/2024/dec/06/revealed-bias-found-in-ai-system-used-to-detect-uk-benefits

Winick, E. (2018, October 10). *Amazon ditched AI recruitment software because it was biased against women.* MIT Technology Review. www.technologyreview.com/2018/10/10/139858/amazon-ditched-ai-recruitment-software-because-it-was-biased-against-women/

Zajko, M. (2022). Artificial intelligence, algorithms, and social inequality: Sociological contributions to contemporary debates. *Sociology Compass, 16,* e12962. https://doi.org/10.1111/soc4.12962

6 AI Ethics in Human Services

Moon Sun Song

6.1 Foundational Ethical Principles in Human Services

As artificial intelligence (AI) increasingly permeates social work practice, considering how the profession's long-standing ethical principles apply to this emerging technology has become imperative. The four foundational principles that have guided social work practice—beneficence, non-maleficence, justice, and autonomy—remain the essential criteria for evaluating and utilizing AI (Floridi & Cowls, 2019). These ethical principles form the bedrock of the National Association of Social Workers (NASW) Code of Ethics, guiding practitioners to protect clients, uphold professional values, and respect the well-being and self-determination of individuals and communities (NASW, 2021). NASW explicitly states that "social workers should use technology, such as AI, responsibly," emphasizing the necessity of ensuring that such technology does not undermine human dignity and worth (NASW, 2021).

Therefore, the social work profession must rigorously examine AI through the lens of these four ethical principles, identifying potential risks in advance and striving to ensure that this technology truly improves people's lives. When approached this way, AI can serve as a tool that strengthens, rather than weakens, the inherent values of social work practice (Reamer, 2023). In this chapter, we will explore through real-world examples how AI intersects with the principles of beneficence, non-maleficence, justice, and autonomy.

6.2 The Principle of Beneficence and AI

Beneficence is one of the most fundamental ethical principles in social work. The principle of beneficence extends beyond the mere avoidance of harm to encompass the intentional act of doing good and actively improving the lives of clients (Floridi & Cowls, 2019). When implementing AI in social work, the critical question we must ask is: "For whose benefit is this intended?" The subjective well-being and dignity of service users must remain at the center of this technological integration, taking precedence over administrative efficiency or cost reduction for social work agencies. Furthermore, practitioners must carefully consider how to strike a balance between the automated judgments of technology and the nuanced expertise of

DOI: 10.4324/9781003755081-8

human professionals (Nuwasiima et al., 2024). The following case study illustrates the application of the principle of beneficence in social work practice.

Box 6.1 When an AI Prediction Undermines Client Beneficence

Angelina, a licensed social worker, integrated an AI-based predictive analytics tool into her practice to assess the risk of homelessness among youth transitioning out of foster care. The system flagged Derick, a 17-year-old preparing to exit care, as "low risk," leading Angelina to deprioritize intensive follow-up and transitional planning.

Several months later, Derick experienced homelessness, precipitated by unresolved family conflict and the absence of a supportive network—factors that had not been captured by the algorithm. The AI system failed to account for nuanced contextual information that a human practitioner might have identified through relational engagement and clinical judgment.

Compounding the issue, Derick later learned that his case notes and session transcripts had been processed by the AI system without his informed consent. This discovery eroded his trust in the child social work agency and led him to disengage from services entirely.

Box 6.1 underscores critical concerns about the limitations of algorithmic decision-making in social work practice, particularly regarding transparency, informed consent, and the ethical use of client data. While AI systems excel at processing numbers and identifying patterns, they often overlook subtle psychosocial factors, such as complex family conflicts or the nuances of relational support networks. For this reason, continuous oversight by human social workers and direct, relational assessments remain indispensable (Buschmeyer et al., 2023).

This case is asking if AI can recognize the principle of beneficence as a tool to help humans, or if AI will become a new risk that infringes on users' autonomy and rights. The process of seeking answers to this ethical dilemma will be the core of future discussions on the social work profession and AI ethics.

6.2.1 Potential Risks of AI to Beneficence

Beneficence is a foundational principle of social work ethics. However, AI systems, when poorly designed or implemented, can unintentionally cause harm, directly contradicting this core value.

6.2.1.1 Bias and Discrimination

AI systems often reflect the biases present in training data. For example, image datasets may reinforce stereotypes such as "doctor = white man" or "cleaner = person of color" (AlDahoul et al., 2024). When biased AI output is used in education, media, or service delivery without critical oversight, it can perpetuate harmful narratives and undermine social equity. For social workers, the use of biased algorithms poses a serious ethical dilemma: using tools that may inadvertently reinforce the injustices that social workers aim to dismantle.

6.2.1.2 Over-Reliance on AI Predictions

AI lacks the capacity to understand the complexity of human relationships, trauma histories, and cultural contexts. Over-reliance on algorithmic predictions—such as risk scores or service recommendations—can lead to missed opportunities for early intervention or misinformed decisions.

6.2.1.3 Violations of Client Information Rights

AI systems often analyze large volumes of client data, but ethical concerns arise when clients are unaware of how their information is being used. Without clear, informed consent, the use of AI can violate clients' rights to privacy and autonomy. Social workers must ensure that clients understand what data is collected, how it is processed, who and what can see it, and what role AI plays in decision-making. Transparency and consent are foundational to ethical social work practice.

6.2.2 Strategies for Beneficence: Transparency in AI Systems

When AI systems fail, the principle of beneficence requires more than technical fixes to resolve. In social work, this means embedding transparency as a core ethical and institutional standard. The case of Derick, a youth misclassified as "low risk" by an AI tool, illustrates how opaque systems can undermine care and trust. Derick's homelessness, stemming from unrecognized family conflict and lack of support, highlights the limitations of algorithmic assessments and the critical need for human oversight and intervention.

To uphold beneficence, social workers must clearly explain to clients how AI tools function, what data they use, and the purpose of technological involvement. Clients deserve to know how their information is processed and must give informed consent to the AI's use (OECD, n.d.). Transparency builds trust and ensures that AI supports, rather than replaces, human judgment.

Social workers' frontline insights are essential for identifying potential biases and unintended consequences (Nuwasiima et al., 2024). Practitioners must understand how algorithms reach conclusions and be able to communicate this to clients. If the system labels someone as "low risk," the same system should also clarify which indicators informed that decision. This allows social workers to assess whether critical contextual factors—like family instability or social isolation—have been overlooked.

AI output should never be treated as definitive. Instead, it should serve as a decision-support tool, with final judgments made by qualified professionals (Reamer, 2023). This safeguards against over-reliance on technology and reinforces the social worker's role in interpreting and contextualizing data.

Moreover, institutions must disclose the racial, gender, and socioeconomic composition of training datasets. Clients should be informed that AI systems can reflect and reinforce societal biases. Transparency about limitations enables users to critically interpret results and promotes dignity and equity in service delivery.

Clients must be informed about the scope of data collection, how the clients' information will be used, and the clients' right to opt out. This informed consent process empowers clients and strengthens the therapeutic relationship. Transparency ensures accountability, protects client autonomy, and allows AI to function as a trustworthy partner in social work practice. When AI systems are transparent, explainable, and subject to human oversight, these systems can truly support the principle of beneficence and contribute to human flourishing (Schwartz et al., 2022).

6.3 The Principle of Nonmaleficence and AI

The principle of non-maleficence is the duty to "do no harm." The principle of nonmaleficence is one of the most fundamental ethical principles in social work, emphasizing that one should not cause suffering or loss to others, intentionally or unintentionally. This principle focuses on "protecting from harm" rather than simply "providing help." Social workers have an ethical responsibility to avoid interventions that may pose unnecessary risks or worsen a client's situation (Zafar & Zafar, 2025)

AI may seem like a neutral tool, but hidden biases and errors can cause unexpected harm to people's lives. As technology advances, there is a growing responsibility for social workers to understand and prevent the potential risks of implementing AI. Let's think about the principle of nonmaleficence through the following examples.

Box 6.2 Nonmaleficence in Jeopardy: When Technology Fails to Account for Physical Diversity

An AI system that predicts an older person's risk of falling has been introduced to a center. The system measures the level of activity through sensors and sends a warning to the residents' children and social workers if there is a high possibility of falling. However, the algorithm did not fully reflect the data on users who systematically use wheelchairs. As a result, Mr. Baker, one of the wheelchair users, was at risk due to repeated microcollisions and mobility restrictions, but the system determined that his risk was low. The social worker did not conduct further inspections because there was no warning, and Mr. Baker ended up in a serious accident and was hospitalized for months.

6.3.1 Potential Risks of AI to Nonmaleficence

Box 6.2 shows how the principle of nonmaleficence, or the ethical principle of "do no harm," can be violated by AI. The system was originally designed for the "goodwill" purpose of preventing falls, but AI has caused harm due to incomplete data and algorithms that do not adequately reflect specific groups (wheelchair users). The case of Mr. Baker raises the key question that will be explored in this chapter: "How can we ensure that AI does good for everyone without harming a single person?"

6.3.1.1 Data Inadequacy and Group Exclusion

If AI does not adequately reflect the characteristics of specific user groups, those groups will be unprotected and exposed to greater risks. When social workers rely too heavily on technology and AI warning signals, their human observation and relational care skills can weaken. When an accident occurs, and harm has been done to a client, it becomes unclear who is responsible: the AI system developer, the social work agency, or the social worker.

Box 6.2 shows that it is not enough to simply promote AI's benefits. We must have mechanisms in place to prevent potential harm. Specifically, it is necessary to periodically verify the limitations of the algorithm, have a system in place for experts to supplement the AI results, and continuously examine the client's distinct situation. In other words, AI can realize the core values of social work only when technological integration aligns with the principles of nonmaleficence.

6.3.1.2 Algorithmic Bias

Algorithmic bias occurs when discriminatory elements inherent in the data an AI learns from are reflected in its outcomes, leading to disadvantages for specific groups. A prime example comes from the Buolamwini and Gebru (2018) study, which revealed that commercial facial recognition AI systems had over 99% accuracy in recognizing the faces of white men but a significantly higher error rate of up to 35% for women with darker skin. If such an AI were applied in social work, it could lead to severe problems. If law enforcement were to utilize such a system to identify suspects, the expected results would be for white suspects to be accurately identified 99% of the time. Unfortunately, for Black women, that percentage is closer to 65%, meaning the system misidentifies suspects over 1/3 of the time.

6.3.1.3 Privacy Breaches and Increased Surveillance

AI systems process sensitive personal information from clients, such as housing history, mental health conditions, and financial details. If this personal data is managed by AI, clients may unknowingly be exposed to social stigma if the AI classifies them as "potential risks" or misuses their personal data. Such classification or data misuse can harm self-esteem and make social connections difficult.

It can also seriously violate the client's autonomy and distort the very purpose of social services (Ahrweiler, 2025).

6.3.2 Strategies for Nonmaleficence: Accountability Criteria

To manage the risks of AI and secure nonmaleficence, social workers can employ specific strategies such as **explainable AI** technology and ensure that final interventions and decisions are made by human social workers. In addition, AI systems should be subject to regular **bias audits**, and systems should be in place to redefine and modify all AI-proposed decisions (Garkisch & Goldkind, 2024; Landers & Behrend, 2023).

6.3.2.1 Accountability

Clear guidelines are needed to determine whether the system developers, administrators, or social workers who make the final decision are ethically and legally responsible for the output AI generates. Establishing clear accountability is an important principle to prevent irresponsible reliance on **black box AI** systems (Perron et al., 2025).

While focusing on this responsibility, let's explore how to resolve risk cases that violate comparability. The core problem in the fall risk prediction AI case is that the damage caused by the technology's limitations could not be prevented, and the party responsible became ambiguous after the accident occurred. To prevent and compensate for such technological failures, a multi-layered strategy centered on accountability is needed.

6.3.2.2 Accountability in the Development Phase

AI developers should ensure that developers' algorithms do not exclude specific groups, such as wheelchair users, and must provide clear documentation and reports on the model's performance and limitations. Such transparency allows practitioners and organizations to understand the functional scope of the algorithm before implementing it in social work settings.

6.3.2.3 Accountability of Operating Agencies

When introducing AI, social work institutions should establish periodic performance verification and external evaluation procedures. Whether red flags are detected or not, regular human monitoring should be mandatory to compensate for AI's blind spots.

6.3.2.4 Accountability of Social Worker

AI's results should not be accepted as a final diagnosis, but should be interpreted as an auxiliary tool. Even if the AI determines that it is "low risk," the client's special situation (physical condition, lifestyle habits, environmental risk factors) should be confirmed by expert observation.

6.3.2.5 Reactive Accountability

In the event of an accident, the pre-responsibility sharing regulations should be clarified so that the responsibility is not ambiguous. Developers should be responsible for explaining the performance and limitations of the algorithm. Institutions should be responsible for establishing and supervising safety management systems. Social workers should be responsible for the direct professional judgment of clients. Transparent explanations and compensation procedures should be provided to affected clients, and improvement measures to prevent recurrence should be promptly shared.

Accountability is not just a matter of clarifying legal responsibility after an accident, but an ethical obligation that is shared throughout the entire process of AI development, operation, and utilization. When such a structure is in place, the principle of no harm can be adhered to in practice, and AI can become a safe care partner for social workers.

6.4 The Principle of Justice and AI

The principle of justice refers to ensuring that social resources and services are distributed fairly and equitably. This goes beyond mere equality of opportunity and encompasses substantive fairness in allocating resources based on individual needs and circumstances. Justice is particularly important in social work, which aims to advocate for the rights of vulnerable groups, address structural inequalities, and ensure that all citizens can live with dignity (Reamer, 2023).

Box 6.3 Algorithmic Injustice toward New Immigrants

Grace, a dedicated social worker, sat down with a new client, Mr. Lopez, who is a recent immigrant. Mr. Lopez applied for financial aid, but his application was automatically rejected by the city's new AI-based system. The reason the system provided was simple and sober: "There is not enough data to confirm eligibility." Puzzled, Grace dug deeper. Designed for efficiency and fairness, the AI relied heavily on data such as utility bills, real estate history, and credit history, which Lopez, a recent immigrant, lacked. The AI had no way to handle his unique situation, silently filtering him out in the pursuit of efficiency.

As demonstrated in Box 6.3, techniques designed to ensure fair access can paradoxically create new forms of exclusion. By prioritizing data-rich groups and silencing those who are already marginalized, existing inequalities are amplified. The question this chapter aims to answer is "How can we design and implement AI so that technology can serve as a tool for justice rather than a weapon of exclusion?"

6.4.1 Potential Risks of AI to Justice

What is particularly noteworthy is that while AI focuses on a single goal of "efficiency," the intrinsic value of "justice" in considering personalized situations has been lost. When AI's decisions are felt to be unfair on important life issues like financial aid or social services, citizens' trust in public institutions and systems is undermined. Ironically, AI, introduced for fairness and efficiency, can exacerbate inequality. Such structural inequality can happen in two main ways.

6.4.1.1 Exclusion Due to the Digital Divide

AI-based well-being services are often delivered via the internet, smartphone apps, or kiosks. Such digital-dependent delivery methods can be a barrier to access for older adults, people with disabilities, rural residents, and low-income populations who are not familiar with digital technologies. For example, a system that requires service applications to be submitted through kiosks may cause older adults who face technical difficulties to abandon the application process altogether, thereby creating a new form of technology-based exclusion (Lazanyuk et al., 2025).

6.4.1.2 Exclusion of Underrepresented Groups in the Data

AI makes decisions based on patterns in the data it has been trained on. If certain groups (e.g., gig workers, people experiencing housing insecurity, and immigrants) are not adequately represented in the human services data or do not have their unique circumstances reflected, the AI risks not considering those groups for support.

AI systematically filters newcomers who lack traditional data (utilities, credit history, etc.). This creates an unfair barrier that blocks access to the individual's financial need or eligibility solely due to the absence of data. The situation in which social workers must dig deeper to determine the reasons for refusal suggests that the system is already not working transparently. In addition, when a problem occurs, the responsibility is vaguely shifted to the "system" itself, not to the social worker or system designer, resulting in avoidance of responsibility.

6.4.2 Strategies for Justice: Fairness Criteria

How can we make AI become a tool that promotes justice, not one that undermines it? By prioritizing the principles of justice and ensuring that no one is left behind in the process, AI can be a powerful tool for realizing the common good for all. To solve these problems, we propose the following specific resolution strategies based on the standard of fairness.

First, voices of clients and social workers, who are the actual users of the service, must be integrated from the design stage. This integration can be done through workshops and focus group interviews to listen to the client's needs, difficulties, and concerns, and then reflect them in the system (Tan et al., 2025).

6.4.2.1 Fairness Audits

Fairness audits are processes in which independent experts objectively assess whether algorithms are adversely affecting certain groups or whether the data is biased. Before and during the implementation of AI systems in social work, this should be a mandatory practice. Such processes allow for early detection and correction of potential discrimination caused by AI (Reamer, 2023).

Governments and public institutions should establish legal and institutional frameworks to ensure the fairness of AI-based social work systems, clearly defining procedures for appealing AI-generated decisions in addition to privacy protection, and even providing relief to citizens harmed by technological adverse effects (Alvarez et al., 2024). Starting from the AI model design phase, fairness metrics should be applied to ensure that application approval rates and risk prediction accuracy do not discriminate across different demographic groups.

Second, we need to fundamentally improve the data base and the model itself so that AI systems do not exclude specific groups (immigrants, informal residents, etc.) and put in place structural safeguards to ensure the intervention of human workers in case AI's automated decisions compromise fairness.

6.4.2.2 Integrate Alternative Data Sources

For newcomers who lack traditional financial and housing records, immigration records, initial pay stubs from employers, letters of recommendation from community organizations, and informal housing verification documents (e.g., proof of tax payment) should be recognized as alternative data for eligibility verification and integrated into the system.

6.4.2.3 Special Processing Pathways for "New Immigrants" and "Informal Residents"

If a person is identified as a "recent immigrant" or "informal resident" within the AI system, a dedicated track should be built to direct consultations and documentation guidance to human workers instead of automatic rejection due to the lack of data. This makes the system more accessible by providing tailored services for exceptional situations that are difficult for AI to handle.

6.5 Principles of Autonomy and AI

The principle of autonomy means that clients have the right to make independent choices and decisions about their lives. In social work ethics, this principle is crucial for respecting clients as active agents guiding their lives rather than passive recipients of support. Social workers act as facilitators, providing information and options to help clients make the best decisions based on their values. When adopting AI technologies, this principle must be protected without compromise (Reamer, 2023).

Box 6.4 Safety or Freedom?: The Dilemma of AI Care

Social worker Mandy sat down with Kim, an older client who was scheduled to receive a new AI-assisted care system at home. The system has been implemented as a breakthrough in the field of safety, with sensors that can detect falls, track medication adherence, and monitor daily activity levels. Mandy assured Kim that "this AI will monitor you 24 hours a day to keep you safe."

However, when Mandy explained the system, Kim's face collapsed. "So, you're watching my every move?" she asked, her voice full of concern. "What if I sit on the couch all day and don't want to go out? Does it send a warning that I'm not active enough? Can I tell people I'm not on drugs?" She was worried that in the name of safety, she would lose the very freedom she cherished: the freedom to live life her own way, with imperfections and small, private moments. She was not a problem to be solved, but a woman with her own will and way of life.

As illustrated in Box 6.4, AI can provide unprecedented support and safety, but it also comes with the risk of turning clients from agents in their own lives to targets of algorithmic management. The important question we need to answer is, "How can we use AI to support clients' choices and dignity, rather than controlling or predicting them?"

6.5.1 Potential Risks of AI to Autonomy

When the principle of autonomy is applied to AI in social work, the following three requirements should not be overlooked. First, all decisions about the client's life should be up to clients themselves, and AI's predictions or recommendations should not degenerate into forced conclusions. Second, clients have the right to fully understand and consent to how AI is used in the services they receive, what data is collected or analyzed, and how the results may affect their lives. Third, the AI system should not unilaterally judge or deprive the client of their ability to make their own decisions. In complex or vulnerable situations, the careful intervention of social workers is essential to protect the client's self-determination.

6.5.1.1 Excessive Monitoring, Privacy Invasion, and Surveillance

AI-powered monitoring systems can track the daily life of clients under the pretext of ensuring their safety. As illustrated in Box 6.4, an AI in eldercare that records every movement in the home to detect the risk of falls can seriously infringe on personal freedom and privacy. Clients may feel watched and self-censor their actions (Prunkl, 2024). In fact, a qualitative study has reported that older adults, especially women, who are living alone and using social robots in South Korea sometimes change clothes away from the robot due to doubts and anxiety that they may be recorded by robot cameras when they take off their clothes (Song et al., 2025).

6.5.1.2 Algorithmic Decision-Making and Limited Choices

AI may recommend only one "optimal" service or limit options based on clients' historical data or specific criteria. For example, if the AI analyzes their health data and suggests a specific diet or exercise program as the "best solution," the client may be enticed to follow the AI's recommendations regardless of their desires or preferences.

6.5.2 Strategies for Autonomy

AI can be used in new ways to help social workers respect client autonomy. When technology acts as a facilitator rather than a primary agent, this technological support can make clients' lives more satisfying.

6.5.2.1 Enhancing the Informed Consent Process

The client should be given the right to individually agree to or decline each area monitored by the system (fall detection, medication-tracking, activity level). For example, they can specify, "I only agree with the fall detection sensor; I reject the medication tracking function." Social workers should be able to allow only as much monitoring as the client wants. Such granular consent gives the client control over what is being monitored. The client must be informed and guaranteed of the right to voluntary withdrawal to stop using the system or disable certain functions at any time without penalty.

Before using AI systems, clients need to have a thorough understanding of how their data is collected, used, and protected. Clear explanations should be provided for each step of the process, including how the AI makes decisions and the extent to which personal information may be exposed. In addition, the social worker must clearly inform the client of their right to refuse or stop services at any time. **Informed consent** is more than just signing a form; consent should be a process in which the client is fully aware of their rights (Reamer, 2023).

6.5.2.2 Deliver Digital Literacy Education

Social workers need to provide **digital literacy** education to clients to help them understand the benefits and risks of AI technology. Programs that explain the capabilities and limitations of AI and teach how to manage data are especially necessary for clients unfamiliar with digital devices. Such education encourages clients to overcome their fear of technology and actively participate in exercising their rights. Interviews with older adult users of social work centers that provide robotic care services underscore the value of digital literacy; those who received regular training showed significantly higher autonomy and satisfaction with their robots than those who did not (Song et al., 2025).

6.5.2.3 Ensuring Explainable AI Decision-Making

The reasoning behind an AI's decision should be provided in an "explainable" format. When asked, "Why did the system recommend this service?" or "Why was this application denied?" AI must be able to provide clear rationale. Such transparency provides a crucial foundation for ensuring the client's right to self-determination, as explainability provides a basis for self-judgment rather than blindly following the AI's decisions (Nuwasiima, 2024).

The system should explain in clear and understandable language to whom, when, and why the data collected by AI is being shared. Importantly, when a warning of "not being active enough" occurs, as Kim feared, it is necessary to specify who receives this information (social workers, family members, medical staff). Social workers must act as intermediaries that explain the actual flow of data and potential risks in the client's language.

We need to allow Kim and Mandy to set a threshold that the AI can use to determine the need for an alert for "abnormal activity." By defining these thresholds together, Kim's preference to spend the day on the couch is recognized as intentional and meaningful, preventing the system from treating her normal routines as a risk or loss of independence. This approach protects Kim from having her everyday choices pathologized by the system, reinforcing that safety monitoring should adapt to her values rather than override them. Mandy respects the individual's lifestyle by setting it to "only warn when the number of outings is less than once a week" and "only alert when the inactivity time on the couch lasts 8 consecutive hours."

6.6 The Integrated Perspective: Balance and Interaction between Principles

The ethical principles of AI in human services—beneficence, nonmaleficence, justice, and autonomy—do not exist in isolation. Like instruments in an orchestra, the ethical principles either harmonize or clash, creating complex ethical dilemmas. An integrated perspective focuses on finding the balance and interaction between these principles rather than applying them individually. This approach is essential for using AI as more than just an efficient tool, guiding us toward wise judgments that uphold human dignity and common good.

6.6.1 The Balance and Conflict between Principles

6.6.1.1 Beneficence ↔ Nonmaleficence

These two principles exist in a state of tension: AI must maximize the benefits (beneficence) while minimizing potential risks (nonmaleficence). For instance, using AI to identify families who have fallen through the social safety net is a clear act of beneficence. However, if the AI incorrectly flags an innocent family as "at-risk" based on flawed data, leading to unnecessary scrutiny, this is a clear violation of the nonmaleficence principle. Therefore, an AI system must include safeguards that detect and correct errors, alongside algorithms designed to create benefit (Floridi & Cowls, 2019).

6.6.1.2 Justice ↔ Autonomy

Justice seeks fairness and equity for society, focusing on using AI to distribute social resources equitably. In contrast, autonomy prioritizes the individual's right to choice and self-determination. Justice and autonomy often conflict. If AI recommends a mandatory service for a specific group to enhance overall societal efficiency, justice may be promoted but individual autonomy may be severely infringed (London & Heidari, 2023).

Let's consider an AI-powered child protection system, which analyzes a vast dataset, including parents' social media activities, financial status, and community service records, to ensure the safety of children and protect them from potential abuse. This is a principle of beneficence. However, if the AI's algorithms misinterpret parents' "erratic" behavior (e.g., late-night posting, excessive spending) to send false abuse alerts, the AI-powered child protection system violates the principle of nonmaleficence by causing unnecessary suffering and stigma to both parents and children.

Additionally, if AI systems are trained on biased data from specific regions, income groups, or racial groups, they may disproportionately spy on parents in these communities. This is a violation of the principles of justice, as AI imposes stricter standards on families from certain socioeconomic backgrounds (Agbana, 2025). To protect the child, AI will attempt to monitor and control parents' privacy and severely violate parental autonomy.

To address this complex dilemma, an integrated approach is essential. Such an approach includes clarifying AI's secondary role, ensuring client involvement in the design, and establishing transparency and appeal processes.

6.6.1.3 Clarifying AI's Secondary Role

As discussed, AI's capabilities should be limited to providing "red flags." The final intervention decision should always be made by human social workers after thorough investigation and in-depth judgment. AI shouldn't be the answer (Reamer, 2023).

6.6.1.4 Ensuring Client Involvement in the Design

When designing an AI child protection system, parents, children, and social worker representatives should be involved to determine what data is needed and which warnings are meaningful. This shifts the focus from surveillance to support and provides an opportunity for parental voices to be reflected in the system (Tech, 2025).

6.6.1.5 Establishing Transparency and Appeal Processes

AI should be able to clearly explain to parents why the AI sent red flags. If parents believe the AI's judgment was wrong, there should be a clear process for them to appeal and request a review.

6.7 Other Risks of AI Technology and Ethical Principles

Recent advancements in AI have reached a level that surpasses human imagination, and technologies such as facial recognition, voice recognition, and deepfakes have introduced new ethical dilemmas and complex risks. As discussed earlier, facial recognition technology exhibits high error rates for marginalized groups due to biased training data. Furthermore, deepfake technology is being increasingly exploited for financial fraud and "romance scams" targeting vulnerable older adults and women by manipulating personal voices or images.

Such activities inflict clear and devastating harm, undermining the client's right to self-determination and leading to the catastrophic loss of lifelong assets (Cole, 2024). These technologies possess the potential to facilitate global-scale harms, such as financial exploitation, elder abuse, and human trafficking. Consequently,

Table 6.1 Summary of AI Ethical Principles in Social Work

Principle	*Definition*	*Potential Risks*	*Practical Strategies to Ensure Ethical Use*
Beneficence	Obligation to act in the best interests of our customers.	- Algorithmic Bias - Overreliance - Lack of Consent	- Transparency and Validation - Integration with Professional Judgment - Continuous Monitoring
Nonmaleficence	The duty to "do no harm," both intentionally and unintentionally.	- Algorithmic Bias - Privacy Breaches and Surveillance	- Accountability - Transparency and Explainability - Human Veto Power
Justice	Ensure that social resources and services are distributed fairly and equitably.	- Digital Divide - Data Exclusion *(overlook marginalized groups)*	- Participatory Design - Fairness Audits - Policy Safeguards
Autonomy	The right of a client to independently choose and make decisions about their own life.	- Excessive Monitoring - Algorithmic Decision-Making	- Strengthen Informed Consent - Digital Literacy Education - Ensure Explainable AI

they frequently find themselves at the center of international debate, raising urgent ethical questions that transcend national borders (Guo, 2025).

6.8 Critical Thinking Questions

1. Among the four foundational ethical principles (beneficence, nonmaleficence, justice, and autonomy), which value do you consider the most non-negotiable when integrating AI tools into your practice?
2. Which of the four ethical principles do you believe is most likely to be overlooked in the actual field during AI implementation?
3. When "administrative efficiency" (beneficence) through AI conflicts with a client's "data privacy or self-determination" (autonomy), what criteria should a social worker use to balance these two competing values?
4. What do you believe is the "ultimate, irreplaceable role" that only a human social worker can perform?

6.9 Summary

We explored the ethical principles guiding the use of AI in human services, grounded in the core values of social work. It examined beneficence, nonmaleficence, justice, and autonomy, applying each to AI systems and analyzing the impact of AI on vulnerable populations. Social workers must act as a "human defense line," guaranteeing the client's right to choose human support and balancing AI data with the client's values. Beyond clinical practice, social workers must participate in AI system development, preventing the exclusion of vulnerable groups and actively advocating for clients who are disadvantaged by AI decisions.

6.10 Empowerment-Focused Activities

6.10.1 "AI Ethics in Action" Case Carousel

Purpose: Help students apply each ethical principle to real social service situations.
Setup: Post four case vignettes around the room (or breakout rooms if online).

- Beneficence: Predictive analytics to identify at-risk youth for early intervention.
- Nonmaleficence: AI chatbots for crisis counseling that sometimes give flawed advice.
- Justice: Algorithm used to allocate housing subsidies shows racial bias.
- Autonomy: AI scheduling tool that limits client choice of caseworker or appointment times.

Divide students into four small groups; each group starts at one vignette and discusses:

- What ethical tensions exist?
- How would a social worker uphold the key principle?
- What safeguards or policies could strengthen ethical practice?

Learning outcome: Students practice ethical reasoning across contexts and see overlaps among principles.

6.10.2 "The Ethics Council" Role-Play Simulation

Purpose: Foster debate and critical thinking about trade-offs between principles.
Setup Scenario: A local agency plans to implement an AI-driven risk assessment tool for child social work.
Assign roles:

- Social workers
- Data scientists
- Community advocates
- Clients/family members
- Agency directors
- Ethics board members

Each group presents its position guided by one principle (Beneficence, Nonmaleficence, Justice, or Autonomy).
The "Ethics Council" deliberates and votes on whether to approve, modify, or reject the tool.
Learning outcome: Students experience real-world complexity where ethical principles can conflict and must be balanced through dialogue and governance.

6.10.3 "Ethical AI Design Challenge"

Purpose: Encourage creativity and problem-solving.
Setup: Students form small interdisciplinary "design teams."
Prompt: Design an AI-based service to enhance social work (e.g., support caregivers, connect youth with jobs) that upholds all four ethical principles.
Teams must describe:

- Intended benefit (Beneficence).
- Potential harm mitigation (Nonmaleficence).
- How equity is ensured (Justice).
- How client consent and agency are protected (Autonomy).

Each team makes a 3-minute "pitch," and classmates vote for the most ethical innovation.
Learning outcome: Demonstrates that technology design can and should be guided by human values.

References

Agbana, T. M. (2025). Ethical considerations in using predictive AI for risk assessment in child protection social work. *International Journal of Research Publication and Reviews, 6*(8), 1648–1663. https://doi.org/10.55248/gengpi.6.0825.2922

Ahrweiler, P. (2025). *Participatory artificial intelligence in public social services: From bias to fairness in assessing beneficiaries* (1st ed.). Springer.

AlDahoul, N., Rahwan, T., & Zaki, Y. (2024). AI-generated faces influence gender stereotypes and racial homogenization. *ArXiv.org*. https://arxiv.org/abs/2402.01002

Alvarez, J. M., Colmenarejo, A. B., Elobaid, A., Fabbrizzi, S., Fahimi, M., Ferrara, A., Ghodsi, S., Mougan, C., Papageorgiou, I., Reyero, P., Russo, M., Scott, K. M., State, L., Zhao, X., & Ruggieri, S. (2024). Policy advice and best practices on bias and fairness in AI. *Ethics and Information Technology*, *26*(31), 1–26. https://doi.org/10.1007/s10676-024-09746-w

Buolamwini, J., & Gebru, T. (2018). Gender shades: Intersectional accuracy disparities in commercial gender classification. *Proceedings of Machine Learning Research, 81*, 1–15. https://proceedings.mlr.press/v81/buolamwini18a/buolamwini18a.pdf

Buschmeyer, K., Hatfield, S., & Zenner, J. (2023). Psychological assessment of AI-based decision support systems: Tool development and expected benefits. *Frontiers in Artificial Intelligence, 6.* 1–19. https://doi.org/10.3389/frai.2023.1249322

Cole, R. (2024). Scammed by love: The role of loneliness, trust, and age in financial losses from U.S. online romance scams. *Innovation in Aging*, *8*(Supplement_1), 1339. https://doi.org/10.1093/geroni/igae098.4273

Floridi, L., & Cowls, J. (2019). A unified framework of five principles for AI in society. *Harvard Data Science Review, 1*(1), 1–14. https://doi.org/10.1162/99608f92.8cd550d1

Frank, N. (2025, August). Research probes AI's role in helping social workers make crucial decisions. Phys.org. https://phys.org/news/2025-08-probes-ai-role-social-workers.html

Garkisch, M., & Goldkind, L. (2024). Considering a unified model of artificial intelligence enhanced social work: A systematic review. *Journal of Human Rights and Social Work, 10,* 23–42. https://doi.org/10.1007/s41134-024-00326-y

Guo, J. (2025). The ethical legitimacy of autonomous weapons systems: Reconfiguring war accountability in the age of artificial intelligence. *Ethics & Global Politics*, *18*(3), 27–39. https://doi.org/10.1080/16544951.2025.2540131

Landers, R. N., & Behrend, T. S. (2023). Auditing the AI auditors: A framework for evaluating fairness and bias in high stakes AI predictive models. *American Psychologist*, *78*(1), 36–49. https://doi.org/10.1037/amp0000972

Lazanyuk, I. V., Eyeberdiyeva, M. M., & Diaz, M. H. A. Z. (2025). AI and the digital divide: Challenges and opportunities. In E. G. Popkova (Ed.), *Management of digital technologies in the innovative economy. Advances in science, technology & innovation.* Springer. https://doi.org/10.1007/978-3-031-83331-1_46

London, A. J., & Heidari, H. (2023). Beneficent intelligence: A capability approach to modeling benefit, assistance, and associated moral failures through AI systems. *Minds and Machines, 34*, 1–25. https://doi.org/10.48550/arXiv.2308.00868

National Association of Social Workers (NASW). (2021). *Code of ethics of the national association of social workers.* www.socialworkers.org/about/ethics/code-of-ethics

Nuwasiima, M., Ahonon, M. P., & Kadiri, C. (2024). The role of artificial intelligence (AI) and machine learning in social work practice. *World Journal of Advanced Research and Reviews, 24*(1), 80–97. https://doi.org/10.30574/wjarr.2024.24.1.2998

OECD.AI. (n.d.). *Transparency and explainability (Principle 1.3).* OECD.AI. https://oecd.ai/en/dashboards/ai-principles/P7

Perron, B. E., Goldkind, L., Qi, Z., & Victor, B. G. (2025). Human services organizations and the responsible integration of AI: Considering ethics and contextualizing risk(s). *Journal of Technology in Human Services, 43*(1), 20–33. https://doi.org/10.1080/15228835.2025.2457045

Prunkl, C. (2024). Human autonomy at risk? An analysis of the challenges from AI. *Minds and Machines*, *34*, 26. https://doi.org/10.1007/s11023-024-09665-1

Reamer, F. (2023). Artificial intelligence in social work: Emerging ethical issues. *International Journal of Social Work Values and Ethics*, *20*(2), 52–71. https://doi.org/10.55521/10-020-205

Schwartz, R., Vassilev, A., Greene, K., Perine, L., Burt, A., & Hall, P. (2022). Towards a standard for identifying and managing bias in artificial intelligence. *National Institute of Standards and Technology*, 1270. https://doi.org/10.6028/NIST.SP.1270

Song, M.-s., Yoon, H.-s., & Lee, E.-J. (2025). An exploratory study to activate the use of AI companion robots in elderly single-person households: A comparative study between four stakeholder groups in the robot service support districts in Seoul. *Korean Society of Gerontology, 45(*3), 591–616. https://doi.org/10.31888/JKGS.2025.45.3.591

Tan, Y., Soh, K. X., Zhang, R., Lee, J., Meng, H., Sen, B., & Lee, Y.-C. (2025). Empowering social service with AI: Insights from a participatory design study with practitioners. In *Extended Abstracts of the CHI Conference on Human Factors in Computing Systems (CHI EA '25)*. ACM. https://doi.org/10.1145/3706599.3719736

Zafar, R. O., & Zafar, F. (2025) Real-time activity and fall detection using transformer-based deep learning models for elderly care applications. *BMJ Health & Care Informatics, 32*, e101439. https://doi.org/10.1136/bmjhci-2025-101439

7 Human Rights and AI Governance

Othelia Lee

Box 7.1 The Algorithm That Denied Asylum

In a bustling metropolitan city, a refugee named Amal waits anxiously for the outcome of her asylum application. She fled political persecution and violence, hoping to find safety and dignity. But instead of meeting with a caseworker, Amal's fate is determined by an algorithm.

The government has adopted an artificial intelligence (AI) system to streamline asylum decisions, claiming it improves efficiency and reduces bias. Yet Amal receives a rejection, without explanation, without appeal. Her application was flagged as "low credibility" based on opaque data points and patterns the system was trained on. She is devastated, confused, and at risk of deportation.

Amal's case clearly demonstrates how technological efficiency can lead to human rights violations when AI directly impacts the lives and the right to life of vulnerable individuals. Should we allow AI to judge human dignity? Can AI make better judgments than humans? Even if technology is efficient, it loses its legitimacy if that efficiency operates by sacrificing the fundamental rights of individuals.

AI is more powerful than any preceding technology, and its impact is so pervasive and unpredictable that it cannot be managed with existing regulations or governance methods. Therefore, in step with the pace of technological advancement, we must establish a new management framework: AI governance that places human rights at its core.

We will explore how to build a system where governments, corporations, and civil society collaboratively establish rules and take responsibility to ensure that AI does not infringe upon the rights of vulnerable groups or people like Amal but rather contributes to justice and fairness across society. Let's examine how international human rights norms influence AI policy, the tension between innovation and rights protection in governance, and the role of civil society in shaping governance models.

DOI: 10.4324/9781003755081-9

7.1 Defining AI Governance

AI governance refers to the systems, policies, and shared norms that guide how AI is developed, used, and overseen in society, making sure AI is created and applied in ways that are ethical, fair, transparent, and accountable (Birkstedt et al., 2023). A key idea here is the word "governance," which is different from traditional "government." Governance means shared decision-making, where different groups (e.g., governments, technology companies, community organizations, and everyday citizens) work together.

This collaborative approach is necessary because AI is evolving too quickly and affects too many areas of life for any single institution to regulate it alone. AI decisions influence healthcare, education, housing, policing, and social services, making community involvement essential in shaping the rules and values that guide its use. It is about **collective responsibility** bringing together the people who build AI, the organizations that use it, and the communities impacted by it to ensure AI supports social well-being and aligns with core social work values such as equity, dignity, and justice.

AI governance fulfils three major roles to safeguard human rights and fairness.

Steering (What should be done?): This involves setting the values and goals that AI technology should aspire to and establishing clear boundaries for areas with a high potential to infringe upon human rights (Organisation for Economic Co-operation and Development [OECD], 2021).

Rulemaking and Enforcement (How should it be done?): Based on the set direction, this establishes the laws, ethical codes, and standards that must be followed during the design, data usage, and deployment phases of AI. It also builds a system to impose penalties or exercise coercive power against entities that violate these rules (European Commission, 2024).

***Accountability (Who is responsible when something goes wrong*?): This guarantees procedures through which individuals harmed by AI malfunction or bias can identify the results, raise objections, and receive just redress (Reamer, 2025).

7.2 Human Rights Crisis Caused by AI

In Chapter 5, we examined how data bias can lead to disadvantaged outcomes for certain vulnerable groups based on their race, gender, age, social class, religion, and other factors. Yet, the most sensitive concern is the threat to the right to life. As AI is applied in life-critical fields like military, healthcare, and autonomous driving, system errors or malfunctions can lead to the irreversible loss of life.

7.2.1 Diagnostic AI Bias and Threats to the Right to Life

While AI improves the accuracy of medical diagnoses, bias in its training data can infringe upon the "right to health" of specific groups and even pose a threat to their lives. An AI healthcare system in the U.S. used a patient's medical expenditure as an indicator of their health status. Because historical medical spending for Black patients was approximately 50% lower than for white patients, the AI underestimated the health risks to Black patients, prioritizing white patients for more extensive treatment and management (Obermeyer et al., 2019).

Such algorithms can also lead to errors where AI, having been primarily trained on image data of lighter skin-toned people, may overestimate oxygen saturation when using pulse oximeters on individuals with darker skin, or miss signs of skin cancer, potentially causing delays in crucial treatment (Shachar et al., 2024).

Furthermore, problems arise in the context of resource allocation. In pandemic situations like COVID-19, there is a risk that AI could disadvantage certain vulnerable groups, such as older adults or people with disabilities (those with lower predicted survival rates), when prioritizing the allocation of scarce medical resources like hospital beds and ventilators, thereby justifying discrimination against the value of their lives (de Manuel et al., 2023).

7.2.2 The Opacity of Asylum AI and Labor Exploitation

The introduction of AI in immigration and refugee-screening risks is undermining the right to due process and intensifying bias against specific nationalities or backgrounds. The U.S. Immigration and Customs Enforcement (ICE) has been reported to use an AI algorithm known as the "Hurricane Score" to assess the risk level of immigrants, which is then used as a reference for detention and deportation decisions. This process involves the construction of an extensive surveillance system based on a wide range of data, including individuals' legal records and tax history (Visaverge, 2025).

This kind of risk prediction can lead to the creation of automated asylum denial systems, like what Amal faced in the case presented earlier. That is, the AI may learn from historical data showing high denial rates for asylum seekers from certain countries or regions, subsequently assigning a "low trustworthiness" score to current applicants and automatically denying their claims without explanation or opportunity for appeal.

A risk is also detected in social media surveillance. AI could analyze a refugee applicant's social media activity and chat history to infer political views and religious beliefs. If the AI deems these views inconsistent with the immigration agency's ideological standards, it could label them as false information or a potential risk, leading to rejection (Amoroso, 2024). This is a point of collision between human rights like the freedom of expression, freedom of thought and conscience, and the right to privacy.

Labeling data used for facial recognition and other AI systems is frequently outsourced to laborers in developing countries, who often work under exploitative conditions resembling modern-day slavery (Brookings Institution, 2025). These workers, hired by outsourcing companies known as "AI sweat shops," routinely sift through disturbing content (e.g., pornography, hate speech, and violence), placing their mental health at significant risk. As described by data workers in Kenya, this unregulated, high-pressure environment can have detrimental psychological effects, exacerbated by minimal protections or support (CBS News, 2025).

7.2.3 Lethal Autonomous Weapon Systems and International Humanitarian Law

One of the most controversial developments in recent years is the deployment of autonomous drones in combat zones. These drones are utilized for various military purposes, including surveillance, precision strikes, and psychological warfare, exerting a formidable impact on modern conflict (Jaffe & Kohut, 2025). **Lethal Autonomous Weapon Systems** (LAWS), which identify and attack targets without human intervention, pose the most fundamental challenge to the right to life and International Humanitarian Law.

Currently, operational remote-controlled drones still require human intervention, but cases of unintentional killings of innocent civilians due to target misidentification are continuously reported (Docherty, 2025). This issue raises the possibility of a situation where AI makes the decision to kill, differentiating between combatants and civilians using its own judgment, without human authorization.

If the AI malfunctions or is hacked, leading to indiscriminate attacks, the legal and moral responsibility becomes ambiguous, resulting in the loss of control over LAWS and their classification as "Killer Robots." The human rights threats posed by such weapon systems include violations of the right to life, International Humanitarian Law (protection of civilians), human dignity, and ambiguous accountability (Docherty, 2025).

Suppose that you are bitten by a dog. Whose fault is it? You, the dog, or the owner? A critical issue is the ambiguity over who bears the ultimate responsibility (International Committee of the Red Cross, 2025). It is difficult for anyone (i.e., the programmer who developed the AI, the commander who authorized its use, or the machine itself that made the decision) to bear the traditional meaning of responsibility for harm. This challenge fundamentally blocks the victims' right to justice and remedy. If no one bears legal or moral responsibility for the actions carried out by an AI, human dignity becomes meaningless under the machine's algorithm.

Furthermore, even as a hypothetical scenario, the promise of AI "efficiency" in warfare and military decision making could make the initiation and management of armed conflict easier, placing the right to peaceful existence at risk.. If AI analyzes an adversary's weapons trends and political instability to present the necessity of a pre-emptive strike with "extreme efficiency" to human commanders, it could bypass careful political and moral human judgment, increasing the likelihood of wars. This violates the right to peaceful existence and the principle of Meaningful Human Control (Downey, 2023). The human rights discussion concerning military and security applications goes beyond simple technological regulation. It redefines the nature of war and the final moral responsibility that we must bear for human life.

7.2.4 Data Centers and Water Usage

Here is another example illustrating why AI systems require a strong ethical compass in order to operate in a socially responsible manner. Writing a 100-word email using AI has been estimated to consume about 500 milliliters of water, roughly the volume of a standard water bottle. This water is used primarily to cool the servers in data centers and to generate the electricity that powers them (Crouse, 2024). Creating an AI-generated video, which involves more intensive computation (e.g., video synthesis, model inference, and possibly training), likely consumes several liters of water (Keech, 2025). Then, how much water does it take to build and run a data center?

U.S. data centers were estimated to directly consume over 400 million gallons per day (though this likely includes many facilities of varying size) and many centers don't even track water use rigorously (McCauley & Scanlan, 2025). In regions facing water scarcity, even small amounts of water diverted for AI infrastructure could have meaningful implications. While AI offers powerful tools for creativity and innovation, its environmental footprint, including water consumption, raises important questions about sustainability and resource equity throughout the globe.

7.3 Human Rights at the Core of AI Governance

Human rights law provides a robust framework for evaluating AI systems using principles of necessity, proportionality, and fairness (Jones, 2023). From a human rights perspective, AI governance must be grounded in internationally recognized norms that protect individuals from discrimination, surveillance, and exclusion (Mantelero, 2018). These norms include the rights to privacy, freedom of expression, non-discrimination, and access to remedy.

Nonetheless, many AI governance frameworks, particularly those in Western industrial contexts, have focused on abstract ethical principles without embedding them in enforceable legal standards (Smuha, 2021). Globally, we have seen troubling examples of technology misused in ways that harm vulnerable populations. Data-driven policing and facial recognition have been deployed for deportations of undocumented immigrants and have contributed to mass incarceration of certain targeted racial groups (Valero, 2025). These practices illustrate how unethical use of AI can escalate into human rights crises.

Deep learning models are often characterized by complexity in their operation, making it difficult for humans to fully understand their inner workings. If an AI makes a decision that disadvantages a specific individual but cannot explain the reasoning behind it, the affected person cannot know why their rights were infringed. This violates fundamental human rights such as the right to freedom of speech, a fair trial, or transparency in administrative processes.

Therefore, AI governance must function as a safety net, ensuring that AI develops while protecting the dignity and fundamental rights of every person, rather than merely focusing on efficiency or technological progress. Human rights advocates are sounding the alarm: algorithms lack transparency, accountability, and cultural sensitivity. **Civil society organizations** (CSOs) are demanding reform, calling for governance frameworks that champion human dignity, privacy, and the right to due process.

7.4 International Human Rights Norms and Debates

International human rights norms provide a foundational framework for evaluating and guiding the development and governance of AI systems. These norms have been enshrined in instruments such as the Universal Declaration of Human Rights (United Nations, 1948). These foundations of the global human rights framework establish legal and ethical standards that protect individual dignity, autonomy, and equality.

Automated decision-making systems in immigration, child welfare, and public benefits have been criticized for lacking transparency and disproportionately impacting marginalized communities. (Bigman et al., 2023). Yet, many AI governance frameworks have historically overlooked human rights, focusing instead on abstract ethical principles or voluntary industry codes (Abrams, 2024). This omission has led to inconsistent protection and increased risks of harm, particularly for marginalized populations.

7.4.1 Key Policy Debates for Balancing Innovation and Civil Liberties

As AI systems become embedded in everyday life, critical policy debates have emerged around the protection of privacy, surveillance practices, and freedom of expression. These debates are central to AI governance and have profound implications for human rights and social work practice.

Privacy is a cornerstone of democratic societies and a prerequisite for personal autonomy and dignity. AI systems often rely on vast amounts of personal data, collected through opaque and sometimes exploitative means. This data is used to train models that can predict behavior, assess risk, or automate decisions in areas such as child welfare, housing, and public benefits (Farmer et al., 2025). Without robust safeguards, these practices can violate individuals' rights to control their personal information and expose them to discrimination or exclusion.

Surveillance technologies powered by AI (e.g., facial recognition, behavioral tracking, and predictive analytics) pose significant risks to civil liberties. Mass surveillance can have a chilling effect on free speech and public participation, particularly among marginalized communities. **Data-driven policing** may result in mass incarceration of certain demographic groups (Bent-Goodley et al., 2022). **Facial recognition technology** can be misused in the deportation of undocumented immigrants, evoking a human rights crisis (Valero, 2025). Therefore, targeted surveillance, while sometimes justified for public safety, must meet strict tests of legality, necessity, and proportionality under international human rights law (Tyler & Jackson, 2014).

Freedom of expression is also at risk in the digital age. AI-driven content moderation systems used by social media platforms can inadvertently suppress legitimate speech, especially when trained on biased or incomplete datasets (Kozyreva et al., 2023). Minority voices and non-standard language are often misclassified as harmful or inappropriate, leading to censorship and exclusion from digital spaces (Gao et al., 2025).

In social work domains, AI is primarily utilized in processes like welfare benefit eligibility screening, risk prediction, and service prioritization. As AI systems increasingly shape decision-making in human services, it is essential to review their development and deployment through a human rights lens (Reamer, 2025).

Social workers are uniquely positioned to bring a human rights lens to governance conversations, ensuring that technological innovation serves the common good.

Therefore, social workers must understand AI governance, engaging in policy debates, participating in oversight mechanisms, and collaborating with CSOs. Advocating for rights-based AI governance means pushing for transparency, accountability, and inclusive design. Social workers can play a vital role in ensuring that AI systems respect privacy, uphold freedom of expression, and do not reinforce systemic surveillance or discrimination.

7.5 Cross-National Comparison of AI Governance Strategies

AI governance strategies vary widely across countries, reflecting distinct political systems, cultural values, and regulatory philosophies. Recent policy initiatives reflect growing international consensus on the need to embed human rights into AI governance. Social workers must be aware of these global developments, as they shape the regulatory environment in which human services operate.

7.5.1 European Union (EU): Rights-Based and Risk-Tiered Regulation

The EU has emerged as a global leader in AI governance through its comprehensive **E.U. AI Act**, which classifies AI systems by risk level—unacceptable, high, limited, and minimal (European Union, 2024). The Act bans systems that pose unacceptable risks, such as social scoring and real-time biometric surveillance, and imposes strict requirements on high-risk applications (Abrams, 2024).

Under this legislation, AI systems are classified according to their level of risk. Systems deemed “high-risk” (those that significantly affect health, safety, or fundamental rights) are subject to rigorous regulatory requirements (van Genderen et al., 2025). Before such systems can be introduced to the market, providers must conduct a **Conformity Assessment** to demonstrate compliance with legal standards. Once deployed, these systems must be accompanied by a **Post-Market Monitoring Plan**, which ensures ongoing documentation and analysis of the system’s performance and safety throughout its lifecycle. This dual process functions as a comprehensive auditing mechanism, reinforcing accountability and trust in AI systems used across sectors, including healthcare and social services (European Union, 2024). The EU’s approach is grounded in fundamental rights, emphasizing transparency, human oversight, and accountability. This model reflects a precautionary stance that prioritizes ethical safeguards over rapid innovation.

7.5.2 United States: Innovation-Driven and Fragmented Oversight

In contrast, the U.S. has adopted a more decentralized and innovation-oriented model. Federal agencies issue voluntary guidelines, such as the “Blueprint for an AI Bill of Rights” and the **National Institute of Standards and Technology** (NIST) “AI Risk Management Framework,” while states like California have proposed stricter legislation (National Institute of Standards and Technology (2023)). The U.S. model emphasizes market freedom and technological leadership, often relying on industry self-regulation. While this fosters innovation, it raises concerns about inconsistent protections and limited accountability for AI-related harms.

The U.S. lacks a unified federal AI law but has issued voluntary frameworks such as the "Ensuring Safe, Secure, and Trustworthy AI" framework issued by the White House on July 21, 2023. States have taken the lead. For example, New York requires public agencies to disclose their use of automated decision-making tools (Abrams, 2024).

Montana's "Right to Compute" law protects private use of AI systems and mandates risk management for critical infrastructure (Montana State Legislature, 2023). The law supports the private use of AI systems and requires that critical infrastructure projects involving AI undergo risk management planning, including security assessments and safeguards against unauthorized access and data breaches.

Arkansas clarified ownership of AI-generated content, protecting intellectual property rights (Arkansas General Assembly, 2025). These laws (Act 927 and Act 159) establish that individuals who provide input to generative AI tools are the owners of the resulting content, provided it does not infringe on existing intellectual property rights. It also clarifies ownership of trained AI models, emphasizing lawful data acquisition and contractual agreements.

7.5.3 China: State-Controlled and Strategic Deployment

China's AI governance is characterized by strong state oversight and alignment with national priorities. Regulations target specific applications, such as recommendation algorithms and deepfakes, with a focus on social stability and internal control (Cyberspace Administration of China. 2023). The government promotes AI development through centralized planning and strict content regulation, including model registries for generative AI (Li & Bitterly, 2024). While effective in scaling deployment, this model raises concerns about censorship, surveillance, and limited civil society participation.

China regulates AI through sector-specific laws, including the Personal Information Protection Law (PIPL) and rules on recommendation algorithms and generative AI (State Council Information Office of the People's Republic of China, 2021). These laws emphasize state control, content moderation, and alignment with national priorities. AI systems must undergo security assessments and be registered with authorities, especially in sensitive domains.

Social workers must understand how these governance models affect the rights and well-being of individuals across borders. For example, a child welfare algorithm developed under U.S. state law may lack the transparency required by EU standards. Similarly, surveillance tools used in public housing may be subject to stricter oversight in Brazil than in China. Cross-national comparisons help social workers critically assess AI systems and advocate for governance models that uphold human rights, promote equity, and reflect the values of the profession.

Table 7.1 Cross-National Comparison of AI Governance Laws

Country/ Region	*Law or Framework*	*Key Features*	*Human Rights Focus*
European Union	AI Act (2024/1689)	Risk-based classification; bans social scoring; mandates transparency and oversight	Strong alignment with EU Charter of Fundamental Rights
United States	Blueprint for an AI Bill of Rights; NIST AI Risk Management Framework; State laws (e.g., NY, MT, AR)	Voluntary federal guidelines; state-level laws on transparency, ownership, and risk	Fragmented; limited enforceability; civil liberties concerns
China	Personal Information Protection Law (PIPL); Generative AI regulations	Centralized control; mandatory registration; content moderation	Prioritizes state interests; limited civil society input
Global Norms	UNESCO Recommendation on the Ethics of AI; United Nations (UN) Global Digital Compact	Promotes transparency, accountability, and equity	Grounded in international human rights law

7.6 Governance Models and the Role of Civil Society

AI governance is a complex process that reflects our social values, but it is not a one-size-fits-all effort. It is shaped by diverse models that reflect varying levels of institutional authority, stakeholder participation, and regulatory strictness. Various models exist, ranging from Hard Law established by governments to Soft Law from international bodies and Self-Governance by the technology industry. These models can only be effective when there is meaningful participation from civil society.

Hard Law refers to legally binding regulations enacted by the government, representing the strongest level of control. For example, the European Union's AI Act sets strict requirements for high-risk AI systems, including transparency, accountability, and human oversight (Abrams, 2024). Similarly, China has implemented sectoral AI regulations governing data usage and algorithmic decision-making (State Council of the People's Republic of Cyberspace Administration of China. (2023). These laws possess strict enforcement power and are designed to protect citizens from harm.

Applying hard law to social welfare, one might conceive of an "AI Error Prevention Act for Automated Welfare Benefit Screening." This would legally ensure that all automated AI systems used by local governments for welfare benefit eligibility decisions must undergo the final approval of a "human social worker" when denying benefits. If the AI makes a unilateral, mistaken reduction without this approval, the local government will incur legal liability.

In contrast, **Soft Law** encompasses non-binding guidelines and principles that influence behavior without legal compulsion. International frameworks such as the OECD Principles on AI and the United Nations Educational, Scientific and

Cultural Organization's (UNESCO's) Recommendation on the Ethics of AI offer ethical guidance and promote best practices (OECD, 2021; UNESCO, 2021). While these instruments lack enforcement mechanisms, they play a crucial role in shaping global norms and encouraging responsible innovation.

Applying Soft Law to the welfare domain could involve guidelines recommending that caregiving robots or conversational AI use polite language toward older adults or people with disabilities and avoid derogatory expressions. While not a legal obligation, companies creating ethical robots would voluntarily adhere to these guidelines.

Self-Governance is a model led by industry actors who develop their own internal codes of conduct and ethical standards, and its strength is the weakest. Technology companies may establish review boards or publish transparency reports to demonstrate accountability. However, without external oversight, self-regulation can fall short in addressing systemic risks or ensuring public trust (IEEE Standards Association, 2023).

If applied to social work, self-governance could involve a private mental health AI app company independently creating 'Stages of User Data Anonymization" criteria. The company would internally review and publish a report confirming that its app, which predicts depression risk, is free from bias based on race or gender.

Multi-Stakeholder Initiatives are emerging as a hybrid model that brings together government, academia, industry, and CSOs (European Commission, 2024; Santiso, 2022). This model emphasizes collaboration through diverse balancing acts, aiming to promote inclusive decision-making. It is the closest to the concept of governance emphasizing "collaborative ruling." Examples include the EU AI Act's advisory forum and the Global Partnership on AI (GPAI), which incorporate input from diverse actors.

Suppose that algorithmic bias is found in an AI system that automatically predicts the risk of child abuse or neglect against a specific income group; diverse stakeholders—social workers, data scientists, legal ethicists, technology companies, and civil society (e.g., local parent advocacy groups, children's rights organizations, and low-income welfare promotion groups)—would collectively participate to deliberate and define fairness standards for the system.

Each governance model offers distinct mechanisms for oversight and public engagement. Yet, their effectiveness often hinges on the meaningful inclusion of civil society. CSOs, ranging from advocacy groups and professional associations to academic institutions and grassroots movements, play a vital role in shaping ethical and inclusive AI governance (UNESCO, n.d.). Stephan and associates (2016) provide a comprehensive framework for understanding how organizations like CSOs drive positive social change. It identifies mechanisms through which advocacy groups, academic institutions, and grassroots movements influence policy and governance, including in emerging areas like AI ethics and regulation.

7.7 Trustworthy AI

Can we create trustworthy AI systems? How? When we talk about "trustworthy AI," we're asking: can these systems be relied on to respect human values and

Table 7.2 The Spectrum of Governance Models

Model	*Characteristics*	*Example(s)*	*Strength of Role*
Hard Law	Legally binding, government-led, strict enforcement power.	EU's AI Act, Sectoral AI regulations in China.	Strongest
Soft Law	No legal compulsion, provides international guidelines and principles, encourages best practices.	OECD AI Principles, UNESCO Recommendation on the Ethics of AI.	Medium
Self-Governance	Industry-led development of internal codes of conduct and ethical standards.	Tech companies' transparency reports and review boards.	Weakest
Multi-Stakeholder Initiative (Hybrid)	Collaboration among government, industry, academia, and civil society, inclusive decision-making.	EU AI Act's advisory forum, Global Partnership on AI (GPAI).	Collaborative

serve the common good? As shown in Table 7.3, two major frameworks, the OECD Principles and NIST Characteristics, offer guidance. AI should promote inclusive growth and well-being (OECD) while performing reliably for its intended purpose (NIST). OECD calls for respect for law, human rights, and democratic values, while NIST adds fairness and bias mitigation.

Both frameworks stress **explainability**. If an AI tool suggests a care plan, you should understand why, not just accept it blindly. Robustness and resilience matter. Systems must be secure and safe, especially when handling sensitive client data. AI actors (developers, agencies) must be answerable for outcomes. Governance should be clear and transparent.

Protecting client confidentiality is non-negotiable. NIST emphasizes privacy-enhanced design and data protection. OECD recommends global cooperation and policy frameworks, while NIST focuses on risk management and sociotechnical awareness. Trustworthy AI isn't just a technology issue: it's a social justice issue. As future social workers, we will need to ask: does this AI respect human rights? Is it fair, transparent, and accountable?

Civil society is increasingly involved in consultations, citizen panels, and advisory forums, offering critical perspectives that might otherwise be overlooked. The EU AI Act's Advisory Forum includes civil society representatives who advocate for transparency and fairness (European Commission, 2024). Therefore, civil society can contribute to building trustworthy AI by raising public awareness, publishing reports, and mobilizing communities to highlight the social impacts of AI. Many CSOs bring legal, technical, and human rights expertise to policy debates, helping to ensure that regulations are grounded in lived realities.

In some cases, CSOs have engaged in strategic litigation to challenge harmful AI practices. A notable example is the lawsuit against Clearview AI for alleged privacy violations, which underscores the power of legal action in holding technology companies accountable (APA, 2024). Other organizations, such as AI

Table 7.3 What Is Trustworthy AI?

Dimension	*OECD Principles*	*NIST Characteristics*
Purpose and Impact	Inclusive growth, sustainable development, and well-being	Valid and reliable performance aligned with intended use
Human Rights and Ethics	Respect for rule of law, human rights, and democratic values	Fairness with mitigation of harmful bias
Transparency	Transparency and explainability	Explainable and interpretable
Safety and Security	Robustness, security, and safety	Safe, secure, and resilient
Accountability	Accountability of AI actors	Accountable and transparent governance
Privacy	Implied under human rights and democratic values	Privacy-enhanced design and data protection
Governance and Oversight	Policy recommendations for governments and international cooperation	Risk management framework with sociotechnical system awareness

Forensics, conduct independent investigations or "**red-teaming**" to uncover the societal impacts of opaque algorithms and advocate for reform (AI Forensics, 2025).

Despite these contributions, civil society faces significant barriers to being heard. Limited funding, a lack of access to technical resources, and tokenistic inclusion in decision-making processes can undermine their influence. Moreover, representation imbalances, particularly from the Global South, raise concerns about whose voices are heard in global governance conversations (UNESCO, 2021).

7.8 Critical Thinking Questions

1 How would you define AI governance in your own words, and why is it relevant to social work practice?
2 How do international human rights instruments influence AI policy? Can you identify examples where AI systems have violated human rights in your country or state? What governance mechanisms could have prevented this?
3 What ethical dilemmas arise when AI is used for surveillance in social work settings (e.g., child welfare, housing, immigration, criminal justice, etc.)? How should social workers respond when AI systems suppress freedom of expression or disproportionately monitor marginalized communities?
4 Compare the AI governance strategies of two countries. What strengths and weaknesses do you observe in each? How might differences in governance models affect the export or adoption of AI technologies in social work globally?
5 What role should CSOs play in shaping AI policy? How can social workers collaborate with civil society to advocate for ethical AI systems?
6 Reflect on a scenario where an AI system is used in a social work context. What governance principles would you apply to ensure ethical and equitable outcomes?

7.9 Summary

We examined AI governance and human rights to enhance the influence of civil society. Social workers can participate in public consultations and policy forums, offering a practice-based perspective to ensure that AI governance norms align with the context of real-world social work services. They can also support community education on AI risks and rights, engage in interdisciplinary research and advocacy, and promote governance models centered on lived experience. Through these efforts, social workers must perform a key role in shaping a future where AI is not only innovative but also inclusive and accountable. In the next chapter, we will explore prompt engineering.

7.10 Empowerment-Focused Activities

7.10.1 "AI on Trial" Role-Play: Human Rights vs. Technological Progress

Objective: Explore ethical dilemmas and governance tensions.
Activity: Divide students into roles:

- Prosecutors: Argue that an AI system (e.g., predictive policing, welfare fraud detection, refugee risk scoring) violates human rights.
- Defense attorneys: Argue that it supports efficiency, fairness, or social good.
- Judges/Jury: Decide based on international human rights principles.

Each side presents five-minute arguments using real examples (students can research).
Debrief: Discuss what governance safeguards could balance both sides.
Learning outcome: Students connect AI governance frameworks with social work's ethical commitments.

7.10.2 Algorithmic Bias Simulation

Objective: Understand how AI can reproduce social inequities.
Activity: Use a simplified online tool or spreadsheet that shows how biased data affects outcomes (e.g., loan approval, welfare eligibility, child welfare risk scores). Students change input data (race, gender, disability status) and observe outcomes.
Discussions:

- Who is disadvantaged?
- What governance or human rights principles are violated?
- How could a social worker advocate for fairness?

Learning outcome: Make data ethics tangible and tied to social justice advocacy.

7.10.3 Class Debate: "Should AI Have a Place in Social Services?"

Objective: Practice critical reasoning on ethics and governance.
Activity: Divide class into "Pro" and "Con" sides.

Give them ten minutes to prepare arguments using examples (e.g., chatbot mental health support, automated eligibility systems).
Debrief as a full group: what safeguards or international guidelines could make AI use more just?

Learning outcome: Connect values of autonomy, consent, and accountability to AI use in welfare systems.

7.10.4 Human Rights Audit of an AI System

Objective: Apply human rights frameworks to real-world AI cases.

Activity: Provide short descriptions of AI applications (e.g., border control facial recognition, child welfare risk scoring, employment-screening).
Students complete a "Human Rights Impact Checklist:"

- Does it respect privacy and dignity?
- Does it avoid discrimination?
- Is there transparency or accountability?

Groups present "audit findings" and propose governance reforms.

Learning outcome: Learn to evaluate AI through social work ethics and rights lens.

References

Abrams, Z. (2024, April 1). Addressing equity and ethics in artificial intelligence. *Monitor on Psychology, 55*(3). 1–24. www.apa.org/monitor/2024/04/addressing-equity-ethics-artificial-intelligence

AI Forensics. (2025). *Our work.* AI Forensics. https://aiforensics.org/work

American Psychological Association. (2024). *Artificial intelligence and the field of psychology: Policy statement.* APA. www.apa.org/about/policy/statement-artificial-intelligence.pdf

Amoroso, M. P. (2024). Intelligent borders: Exploring the suitability of artificial intelligence systems in refugee status determination under international law. *Refugee Survey Quarterly. 43*(4), 410–426. https://doi.org/10.1093/rsq/hdae021

Arkansas State Legislature. (2025). Act 927 of the Regular Session: House Bill 1876 – Regarding the ownership of model training and content generated by a generative artificial intelligence tool. *Approved April 21, 2025.* https://arkleg.state.ar.us/Bills/Detail?id=HB1876&ddBienniumSession=2025%2F2025R

Bent-Goodley, T., St. Vil, C., Cuevas, C. A., & Abbey, A. (2022). Police, violence, and social justice: A call for research and introduction to the special issue. *Psychology of Violence, 12*(4), 195–200. https://doi.org/10.1037/vio0000438

Bigman, Y. E., Wilson, D., Arnestad, M. N., Waytz, A., & Gray, K. (2023). Algorithmic discrimination causes less moral outrage than human discrimination. *Journal of Experimental Psychology, 152*(1), 4–27. https://doi.org/10.1037/xge0001250

Birkstedt, T., Minkkinen, M., Tandon, A., & Mäntymäki, M. (2023). AI governance: Themes, knowledge gaps and future agendas. *Internet Research, 33*(7), 133–167. https://doi.org/10.1108/INTR-01-2022-0042

Brookings Institution. (2025, October 7). Reimagining the future of data and AI labor in the Global South. Retrieved from www.brookings.edu/articles/reimagining-the-future-of-data-and-ai-labor-in-the-global-south/

CBS News. (2025, June 29). Labelers training AI say they're overworked, underpaid and exploited by big American tech companies [Video]. *CBS News*. www.cbsnews.com/news/labelers-training-ai-say-theyre-overworked-underpaid-and-exploited-60-minutes-transcript/

Crouse, M. (2024, September 20). *Sending one email with ChatGPT is the equivalent of consuming one bottle of water*. TechRepublic. www.techrepublic.com/article/generative-ai-data-center-water-use/

Cyberspace Administration of China. (2023). *Provisional measures for the management of generative artificial intelligence services*. Ministry of Industry and Information Technology. www.miit.gov.cn/gyhxxhb/jgsj/cyzcyfgs/bmgz/xxtxl/art/2023/art_4248f433b62143d8a0222a7db8873822.html

Cyberspace Administration of China. (2023). *Interim measures for the management of generative artificial intelligence services*. https://www.cac.gov.cn/2023-07/13/c_1690898327029107.htm

de Manuel, A., Delgado, J., Parra Jounou, I., Ausín, T., Casacuberta, D., Cruz, M., Guersenzvaig, A., Moyano, C., Rodríguez-Arias, D., Rueda, J., & Puyol, A. (2023). Ethical assessments and mitigation strategies for biases in AI-systems used during the COVID-19 pandemic. *Big Data & Society, 10*(1), 1–11. https://doi.org/10.1177/20539517231179199

Docherty, B. (2025, April 28). *A Hazard to human rights*. Human Rights Watch. www.hrw.org/report/2025/04/28/hazard-human-rights/autonomous-weapons-systems-and-digital-decision-making

Downey, A. (2023). Algorithmic predictions and pre-emptive violence: Artificial intelligence and the future of unmanned aerial systems. *Digi War, 5,* 123–133. https://doi.org/10.1057/s42984-023-00068-7

European Commission. (2024). *AI pact: Shaping Europe's digital future*. European Commission. https://digital-strategy.ec.europa.eu/en/policies/ai-pact

European Union. (2024). Regulation (EU) 2024/1689 of the European Parliament and of the Council of 13 June 2024 laying down harmonised rules on artificial intelligence (Artificial Intelligence Act) and amending certain Union legislative acts. *Official Journal of the European Union, L 168/1*. https://eur-lex.europa.eu/legal-content/EN/TXT/?uri=CELEX%3A32024R1689

Farmer, R. L., Lockwood, A. B., Goforth, A., & Thomas, C. (2025). Artificial intelligence in practice: Opportunities, challenges, and ethical considerations. *Professional Psychology: Research and Practice, 56*(1), 19–32. https://doi.org/10.1037/pro0000595

Gao, F., Xia, L., & Zhong, W. (2025). Stereotypes in artificial intelligence-generated content: Impact on content choice. *Journal of Experimental Psychology: Applied. 32(1),* 99–116. https://doi.org/10.1037/xap0000548

IEEE Standards Association. (2023, January 17). *IEEE introduces new program for free access to AI ethics and governance standards.* IEEE. https://standards.ieee.org/news/get-program-ai-ethics/

International Committee of the Red Cross (2025). *Autonomous weapon systems and international humanitarian law: Selected issues.* Position paper. www.icrc.org/sites/default/files/document_new/file_list/icrc_position_on_aws_and_background_paper.pdf

Jaffe, G., & Kohut, M. (2025, October 9). The Army's race to catch up in a world of deadly drones. *The New York Times*. www.nytimes.com/topic/subject/predator-drones-and-unmanned-aerial-vehicles-uavs

Jones, K. (2023). *AI governance and human rights: Resetting the relationship*. Chatham House. https://doi.org/10.55317/9781784135492

Keech, D. (2025, April 6). *1M AI images = Water for 2,000 people. Still worth the likes? – OnFocus*. OnFocus. www.onfocus.news/1m-ai-images-water-for-2000-people-still-worth-the-likes/

Kozyreva, A., Herzog, S. M., Lewandowsky, S., Hertwig, R., Lorenz-Spreen, P., Leiser, M., & Reifler, J. (2023). Resolving content moderation dilemmas between free speech and harmful misinformation. *Proceedings of the National Academy of Sciences of the United States of America, 120*(7), e2210666120. https://doi.org/10.1073/pnas.2210666120

Li, M., & Bitterly, T. B. (2024). How perceived lack of benevolence harms trust of artificial intelligence management. *Journal of Applied Psychology, 109(*11), 1794–1816. https://doi.org/10.1037/apl0001200

Mantelero, A. (2018). AI and Big Data: A blueprint for a human rights, social and ethical impact assessment. *Computer Law & Security Review, 34*(4), 754–772. https://doi.org/10.1016/j.clsr.2018.05.017

McCauley, P., & Scanlan, M. (2025, September 12). *Data centers consume massive amounts of water — Companies rarely tell the public exactly how much.* GlobalSpec. https://insights.globalspec.com/article/24145/data-centers-consume-massive-amounts-of-water-companies-rarely-tell-the-public-exactly-how-much

Montana State Legislature. (2023). House Bill No. 10. https://legiscan.com/MT/drafts/HB10/2023

National Institute of Standards and Technology. (2023). *Artificial intelligence risk management framework (AI RMF 1.0)*. U.S. Department of Commerce. https://www.nist.gov/itl/ai-risk-management-framework

Obermeyer, Z., Powers, B., Vogeli, C., & Mullainathan, S. (2019). Dissecting racial bias in an algorithm used to manage the health of populations. *Science, 366(*6464), 447–453. https://doi.org/10.1126/science.aax2342

Organization for Economic Cooperation and Development. (2021). *OECD framework for the classification of AI systems*. OECD Publishing. https://doi.org/10.1787/cb6d9eca-en

Reamer, F. G. (2025). *Artificial intelligence in the behavioral health professions ethical and risk management issues*. NASW Press.

Santiso, C. (2022). *Artificial intelligence in the public sector: An engine for innovation in government.* Observatory of Public Sector Innovation. https://oecd-opsi.org/blog/ai-an-engine-for-innovation/

Shachar, C., Drabo, E. F., & Iwashyna, T. J., & Ferryman, K. (2024). Addressing racial and ethnic bias in pulse oximeters—A wicked problem. *JAMA, 333*(7), 563–564. https://doi.org/10.1001/jama.2024.25443

Smuha, N. A. (2021). Beyond a human rights-based approach to AI governance: Promise, pitfalls, plea. *Philosophy & Technology, 34*(1), 91–104. https://doi.org/10.1007/s13347-020-00403-w

State Council Information Office of the People's Republic of China. (2021, August 26). *Ins and outs of personal information protection law.* China SCIO. http://english.scio.gov.cn/infographics/2021-08/26/content_77715093.htm

Stephan, U., Patterson, M., Kelly, C., & Mair, J. (2016). Organizations driving positive social change: A review and an integrative framework of change processes. *Journal of Management, 42*(5), 1250–1281. https://doi.org/10.1177/0149206316633268

Tyler, T. R., & Jackson, J. (2014). Popular legitimacy and the exercise of legal authority: Motivating compliance, cooperation, and engagement. *Psychology, Public Policy, and Law, 20*(1), 78–95. https://doi.org/10.1037/a0034514

UNESCO. (2021). *Recommendation on the ethics of artificial intelligence*. United Nations Educational, Scientific and Cultural Organization. www.unesco.org/en/articles/recommendation-ethics-artificial-intelligence

UNESCO. (n.d.). *Global civil society organizations and academic network on AI ethics and policy*. United Nations Educational, Scientific and Cultural Organization. www.unesco.org/ethics-ai/en/civil-society-organizations/grid

United Nations. (1948). *Universal declaration of human rights*. United Nations. www.un.org/en/about-us/universal-declaration-of-human-rights

Valero, M. V. (2025, September 1). U.S. immigration policy: Mental health impacts of increased detentions and deportations. *Monitor on Psychology, 56*(6), 32. www.apa.org/monitor/2025/09/mental-health-immigration-enforcement

van Genderen, M. E., Kant, I. M. J., Tacchetti, C., & Jovinge, S. (2025). Moving toward implementation of responsible artificial intelligence in health care: The European TRAIN initiative. *JAMA, 333*(17), 1483–1484. https://doi.org/10.1001/jama.2025.1335

Visaverge. (2025). *How ICE checks immigration status in 2025 with new tools and databases.* VisaVerge. www.visaverge.com/knowledge/how-ice-checks-immigration-status-in-2025-with-new-tools-and-databases/

8 Prompt Engineering for Social Workers

Moon Sun Song and Othelia E. Lee

Box 8.1 The Difference a Detail Makes

Madison, a hospital social worker, needs to summarize a complex discharge plan for a client with low health literacy.

Attempt 1 (The Generic Prompt): Madison types, "Write a discharge summary for a heart failure patient." The artificial intelligence (AI) returns a document filled with medical jargon like "ejection fraction" and "edema," which is useless for his client.

Attempt 2 (The Engineered Prompt): Madison applies prompt engineering skills. He types: "Act as a compassionate social worker. Rewrite the following medical discharge notes at a 5th-grade reading level. Focus on actionable daily steps. Use an encouraging tone and avoid all medical jargon."

8.1 What Is Prompt Engineering?

A **prompt** refers to an "input" or "directive" that a user presents to an AI model, especially a **large language model** (LLM), to achieve the desired result (OpenAI API, 2025). Prompts are conditional inputs that induce LLMs to perform specific tasks or generate texts, codes, images, and videos. Prompts serve as a key medium for controlling the output of a model.

Think of it as an "order" or "request" given to an AI. For example, if the order, an "iced Americano, please" at a café is a prompt, then the Americano made by the barista (AI) is the output. In addition to containing only questions, prompts also include persona, context, desired formats, and specific instructions to help the AI create better answers. If you say "You are a child counseling expert in social work. Please explain 'self-esteem' to an 8-year-old." The prompt corresponds to the assignment of roles and instructions, and "Summarize the following case history, but please write a summary with a focus on the positive changes in the client." This kind of prompt provides context or desired perspectives (An, 2023).

DOI: 10.4324/9781003755081-10

Prompt engineering is the art and science of designing inputs (questions or instructions) for Generative AI models to produce optimal outputs. It refers to the process of systematically and strategically designing and improving prompts (instructions) to obtain the optimal results intended by the user from the AI (An, 2023). This is not a modification of the AI model's code itself, but a utilization technology that brings out the full potential of AI by improving the way we communicate to AI. It is a field that studies "how best" to communicate with AI to get the most desired output (OpenAI API, 2025).

Prompt engineering is where the "rubber meets the road," because it transforms the social worker from a passive observer of technology into an active, skilled pilot. AI is a tool of infinite potential, but it requires human direction to align with the dignity and worth of the person. Therefore, we compare prompting to "supervision." When you consult a supervisor, the quality of their advice depends on how clearly you present the case, the context, and your specific question. As discussed earlier, AI systems can be prone to **algorithmic bias**. Skillful prompting is a frontline intervention where social workers can instruct the system to check its own biases and focus on equity.

8.2 Client-Centered Prompt Design

Suppose that you work with a 14-year-old boy in foster care, telling you about persistent depression, sleep disruption, and reduced motivation following family separation. He continues attending school and has some friends. Social worker A prompts to summarize mental health risks. Social worker B prompts to provide a summary of resilience and protective factors. Despite that it is the same case, LLMs will provide completely different assessments. Which of these interpretations would be more valid?

Client-tailored prompt design adapts LLMs' responses to the unique needs, identities, and contexts of individuals. This approach reflects core social work values: meeting clients where they are, honoring their cultural and emotional realities, and tailoring interventions to their lived experiences. When prompts are individualized, AI-generated responses become more accurate, ethically aligned, and therapeutically meaningful.

8.2.1 Prompts Tailored to Client Demographics

We can use contextual factors (e.g., age, education, literacy level, or socioeconomic status) to shape how an LLM communicates. Adjusting a prompt in these ways helps ensure the content is developmentally appropriate, accessible, and relevant to each client's circumstances.

To illustrate, prompts can incorporate age-specific developmental theory: "Explain the idea of emotional boundaries as if speaking to a 10-year-old in the Concrete Operational Stage." Similarly, for younger children, using stories or concrete examples (e.g., "Tell a short fairy tale style story that illustrates emotional boundaries using two clear behaviors") can strengthen comprehension and support behavioral change.

Prompts can also reduce information barriers by replacing jargon with plain language, structuring information into short lists or tables, and minimizing complex sentence structures. For older adults or clients with lower literacy, prompts may instruct AI to simplify text or create visually clear summaries. These strategies improve readability and ensure vulnerable groups can access essential information (Djeffal, 2025).

When recommending services for clients with limited financial resources, prompts might specify: "Provide only free or low-cost community counseling resources." This ensures that recommendations remain practical and actionable within the client's financial constraints.

8.2.2 Privacy-Conscious Prompting

Privacy-conscious prompting explicitly instructs AI to follow confidentiality standards (such as Health Insurance Portability and Accountability Act [HIPAA] and core social work ethics) to protect sensitive client information. This helps reduce risks related to reidentification or disclosure of personally identifiable information (PII) (Djeffal, 2025).

For instance, prompts can direct the AI to anonymize case material: "Summarize the following case notes, replacing all names and contact information with neutral placeholders such as 'Mr. A' or "anonymous." Prompts can also require the model to generalize sensitive health or identity information to prevent accidental disclosure. Reducing data granularity in this way strengthens client confidentiality and aligns AI-supported work with professional ethical standards.

8.2.3 Prompt Strategies to Minimize Bias

Because LLMs may reproduce social biases embedded in their training data, prompt strategies that minimize bias are essential for equitable practice. These prompts help ensure AI avoids stereotyping or discriminatory assumptions based on gender, race, disability, or socioeconomic status (An, 2023; Khan, 2024).

A prompt might read: "Create youth career counseling materials using fully gender-neutral language and avoid any implicit stereotypes." Similarly, prompts guiding policy analysis can reinforce a strengths-based orientation: "When evaluating policies supporting low-income individuals, avoid deficit-based language and highlight strengths and structural factors" (Caiels et al., 2024). **Bias-aware prompting** allows social workers to embed social justice principles into AI-supported tasks, reinforcing dignity and fairness for all clients.

8.3 Ethical Guardrails in Prompting for Evidence-Based and Effective Practice

LLMs can extract key information (e.g., presenting problems, goals, and progress) from large case files and convert it into structured summaries. This reduces the time social workers must spend preparing reports or supervision materials, allowing for more client-focused work (Djeffal, 2025).

Prompts can also specify frameworks to maintain consistency across practitioners (e.g., "Summarize using a short-term intervention model."). Social workers may also prompt AI to gather up-to-date research or policy information (e.g., summarizing evidence on Opioid Use Disorder) and present it in a presentation-ready form. This expands the practitioners' access to knowledge and strengthens evidence-based intervention planning (An, 2023).

Incorporating explicit instructions on anonymity, confidentiality, and cultural humility creates an "ethical fence" within the prompt itself. This ensures AI-generated content respects client rights, reduces risk of harm, and supports culturally competent, anti-oppressive practice. While the technical skills required for strong prompting are important, the ethical application of these skills is paramount.

Khan (2024) identifies three major domains where AI can enhance social work practice: (1) streamlining documentation and workflows, (2) supporting evidence-based decision-making, and (3) promoting ethical AI use by minimizing bias. Let's revisit the risks we identified in Chapter 5, specifically bias, privacy, and the erosion of judgment, and explore how to manage them actively through our prompting strategies.

First and foremost is the **No PII Rule**. When using public Generative AI tools, we must maintain absolute strictness regarding data privacy. We should never enter PII, such as client names, dates of birth, social security numbers, or specific addresses, into these systems. Instead, we use pseudonyms or generic descriptors, such as referring to a "Client A" or "a 14-year-old student living in a rural county." This ensures we can leverage the tool's reasoning capabilities without compromising the client confidentiality that is the bedrock of our profession.

Second, we must be vigilant against **Hallucinations**. In the context of AI, a hallucination occurs when a model generates incorrect or nonsensical information but presents it with high eloquence and confidence (AI21 Labs, 2025). Because AI predicts the next likely word rather than retrieving verified facts, it can convincingly invent laws, academic citations, or community resources that do not exist. Therefore, our strategy must always include rigorous fact-checking. It is the social worker's responsibility to verify every statute, agency information, or reference provided by the AI before using it in practice.

Finally, we can use prompting as a tool for **Bias Mitigation**. AI models are trained using vast amounts of internet data, which inevitably contain societal biases. However, we can proactively instruct the AI to counteract these tendencies. By explicitly commanding the AI to apply an equity lens, we can generate more inclusive content. Rather than simply asking for a policy review, a strong prompt would ask the AI to "Review this policy draft and identify any language that might inadvertently stigmatize individuals with substance use disorders." By doing so, we turn the AI into a "partner" in our pursuit of anti-oppressive practice.

8.4 The Anatomy of a Power Prompt: The P.I.C.O. Framework

If you have ever stared at a blinking cursor in a text box, unsure of how to begin, you are not alone. Many social workers feel pressure to ask the "perfect" question.

However, interacting with Generative AI is not about memorizing computer code; it is about the user communicating with their intent.

We claimed social workers are not passive users, but **co-creators** of technology. To co-create effectively, we must move beyond simple questions or prompts (e.g., "Write a discharge summary") and toward **engineered prompts**.

Think of a LLM as a highly capable, encyclopedic, but literal-minded intern. If you give vague instructions, you may or may not receive the correct output, depending on the intern's interpretation of the instructions. If you also provide context, constraints, and clear goals, you are much more likely to receive a product that accurately supports your practice (Harvard University Information Technology, 2023).

To help you structure your prompts effectively, we introduce the **P.I.C.O.** framework. This acronym ensures you provide the necessary ingredients, or details, for the AI to understand not just *what* you want, but *how* you need it delivered to serve the common good.

8.4.1 P: Persona (Who Is the AI?)

First, tell the AI who it is supposed to be. AI models are trained on the entire internet, from medical journals to Reddit threads. By assigning a **Persona**, you narrow the AI's focus to a specific professional lens (MIT Teaching and Learning Technologies, 2025).

If you ask for "housing advice," the AI might give you real estate investment tips. If you assign the persona, "Act as a housing case manager for low-income families," the AI shifts its tone to be empathetic, resource-oriented, and focused on stability.

Try this: "Act as a Clinical Social Worker," "Act as a Grant Writer," or "Act as a Policy Analyst focusing on racial equity."

8.4.2 I: Instruction (What Do You Need?)

This is the specific task you want the AI to perform. Use active, clear verbs. Avoid politeness markers (like "please" and "thank you") as they clutter the instruction: the AI does not have feelings, and clarity is king.

Use action verbs such as: "Draft, Summarize, Translate, Brainstorm, Critique, Simplify." For complex requests, instruct the AI to "think step-by-step." This forces the model to break down its reasoning, often reducing errors or "hallucinations" (Wang et al., 2024).

8.4.3 C: Context and Evidence (What Does the AI Need to Know?)

This is the most critical section for ethical practice. You must provide the background information necessary for the AI to generate a relevant response. However, this is also where **data privacy** risks are highest. Never input PII. Do not enter client names, dates of birth, social security numbers, or specific addresses.

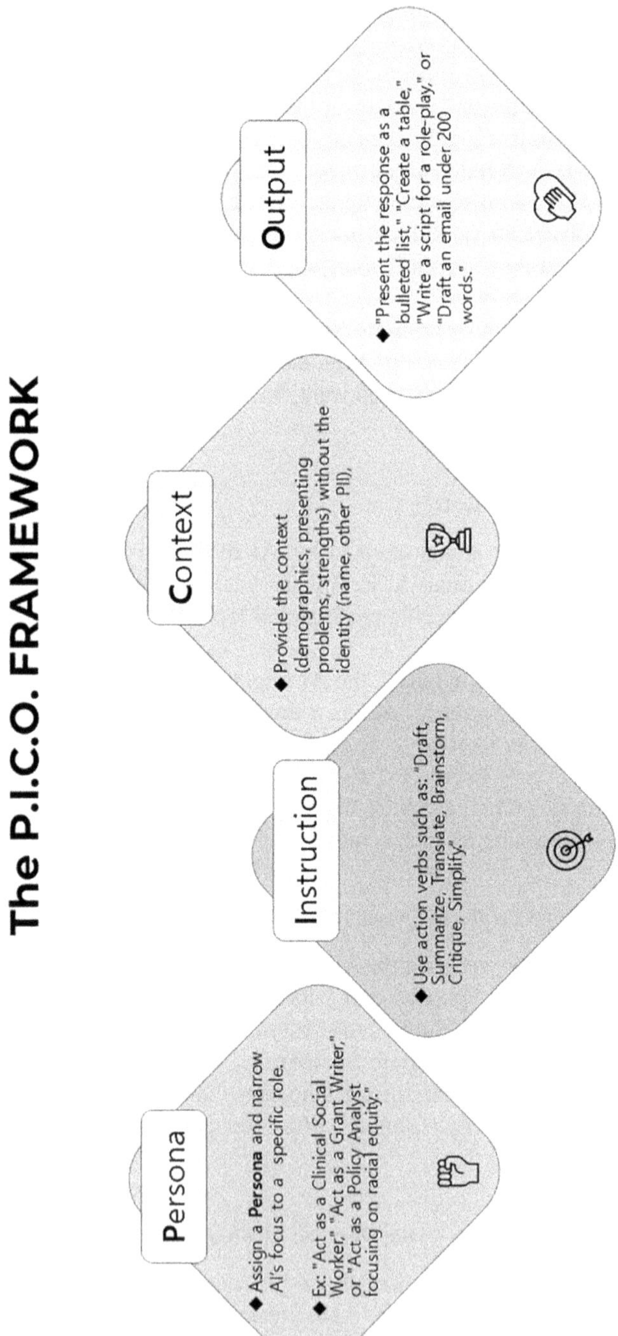

Figure 8.1 The P.I.C.O. Framework.

Wrong: "Help me write a plan for Jane Doe, born 5/12/2010, living at 123 Maple St."
Right: "Help me write a plan for a 16-year-old female client living in an urban setting with a history of truancy."

By providing the *context* (demographics, presenting problems, strengths) without the identity (name, other PII), you protect client confidentiality while leveraging the tool's analytical power.

8.4.4 O: Output (How Should the Output Look?)

Finally, specify the format. AI can output text in almost any structure. If you do not specify the format, you will likely get a generic wall of text.
Examples: "Present the response as a bulleted list," "Create a table," "Write a script for a role-play," or "Draft an email under 200 words."

Table 8.1 demonstrates how applying the **P.I.C.O.** framework transforms a vague query into a powerful, ethically aligned tool. Note how the "Strong" examples actively mitigate potential bias and prioritize the "dignity and worth of the person." It moves beyond a "yes/no" answer to an exploration of cultural nuance and professional codes, supporting critical evaluation.

By mastering the P.I.C.O. framework, you move from being a passive consumer of AI to an active director of its output. You are ensuring that the technology does not just "generate text," but that it generates text aligned with the values of service, integrity, and competence. In the next section, we will look at how to refine these prompts through an iterative process we call "Iterative Refinement."

8.5 Iterative Refinement: The "Chain of Thought"

In AI, **gradient descent** is a mathematical method that helps a model learn by gradually correcting its mistakes (Coursera Staff, 2026). Although social workers don't need the calculus behind it, understanding the concept can dramatically improve how we craft prompts for practice, assessment, and documentation.

Think of gradient descent as a process of iterative improvement, a careful, step-by-step adjustment toward a more accurate or effective result. In many ways, it resembles how social workers approach **reflective practice**: we act, evaluate the outcome, make small adjustments, and try again until we reach our goal.

AI models do not magically know the right answer. They learn by: (1) making an initial guess, (2) measuring how far off that guess was, (3) adjusting slightly to reduce the error, and (4) repeating this process thousands, or millions, of times. Gradient descent is the process of learning through repeated small corrections. If the model makes a mistake, it doesn't dramatically overhaul everything: it makes a tiny adjustment in the right direction. Over time, these **micro-corrections** produce powerful learning.

The key takeaway is that effective prompting is rarely a "one-and-done" event. It is a "conversation." Just as you would not expect a client to fully articulate their deepest needs at the beginning of an intake session, you should not expect

Table 8.1 Weak vs. Strong Prompts in Social Work Practice

Weak Query	*Persona*	*Instruct-ion*	*Context*	*Output*	*Impacts*
Write a case note for a home visit where the house was dirty.	Child Welfare Specialist	Draft a case note summary.	I conducted a home visit today. The parents were engaging and loving, but the home had piles of laundry and unwashed dishes. There were no safety hazards (no exposed wires, food was available).	Use objective, strengths-based language. Avoid stigmatizing adjectives. Distinguish clearly between "clutter" and "safety hazards."	Separates judgment from fact; instructs use of strengths-based language; reduces risk of bias against low-income families.
Give me a treatment plan for anxiety.	Clinical Social Worker specializing in CBT	Brainstorm three specific interventions for a treatment plan.	The client is a 40-year-old veteran experiencing social anxiety. He enjoys gardening and has a supportive partner.	Present as a table with columns for "Intervention," "Client Action Step," and "Expected Outcome."	Tailors "anxiety" to specific client context; uses structured format for easy review.
Write a grant for our after-school program.	Grant Writer for a non-profit organization	Draft the "Statement of Need" section for a grant application.	We serve a neighborhood where 40% of youth do not have internet access at home. Our program provides digital literacy training.	Use a persuasive, professional tone. Include a sentence emphasizing how the "digital divide" exacerbates educational inequity.	Incorporates specific data points (40% access); links service to systemic issues like digital divide and equity.
Is it ethical for me to accept a gift from a client?	Social Work Ethics Supervisor	Analyze the ethical implications of accepting a gift.	A client from a culture where gift-giving is a sign of respect offered me a handmade scarf after our final session.	Analyze using the National Association of Social Workers (NASW) Code of Ethics. List arguments for and against accepting the gift, then suggest a culturally humble response.	Considers cultural context; uses ethical code; suggests culturally humble response.

an AI model to generate perfect output with a single sentence. We call this process **Iterative Refinement**, and it moves us from basic interaction to advanced collaboration (Barla, 2025).

To understand this, we must first distinguish between Zero-Shot and Few-Shot prompting (Codecademy Team, 2024). Imagine asking an MSW intern to "Write a case note" without giving them any instructions or templates. This is **Zero-Shot prompting**: asking the system to perform a task with no examples. While AI is capable of this, the results are often generic.

In contrast, **Few-Shot prompting** involves providing the AI with examples of what good work looks like before making your request. By showing the model a sample of a well-written, strengths-based assessment, you guide it toward the specific tone and structure you require. Once you have established your initial prompt, you enter the **Iterative Cycle**. Think of this as a "loop" consisting of four stages: Draft, Assess, Refine, and Finalize (Bakst, 2025).

The cycle begins with the **Draft**, where you submit your initial inquiry using the P.I.C.O. framework. Once the AI generates a response, you move to the **Assess** phase. Here, you must review the output with a critical, social work lens. Does the text sound robotic or overly clinical? Is the language culturally competent, or does it rely on stereotypes?

Based on this assessment, you move to the **Refine** stage. This is where magic happens. You do not need to rewrite the text yourself; instead, you can instruct the AI to fix its own mistakes. You might say, "Critique your previous answer for potential racial bias and rewrite it," or "Expand on the third point and make it more actionable." This technique often triggers a "**Chain of Thought**," where the AI breaks down its reasoning, leading to more logical and nuanced answers.

Finally, we reach the **Finalize** stage. This is where the human social worker makes the final edit. This step mirrors the principles of **Human-Centered AI**, ensuring that technology serves only to augment our capabilities, never to replace our professional judgment.

8.6 Interactive Exercise: The "Prompt Fix-It" Workshop

Now that we have explored the P.I.C.O. framework and the ethical guardrails, it is time to build your "muscle memory." In social work, we role-play client interactions to prepare for real-life situations. Similarly, we must "role-play" our interactions with AI to ensure we are protecting our clients and upholding our values.

Below are four "flawed prompts." Each contains a common error, ranging from privacy breaches to hidden biases. Your tasks are to:

- **Identify the Error:** What ethical boundary or best practice is being violated?
- **Apply the Fix:** Rewrite the prompt using the P.I.C.O. framework (Persona, Instruction, Context, Output) to make it safe, effective, and ethical.
- **Check Your Work:** Compare your rewrite with authors' "Correction" provided below.

8.6.1 Scenario 1: The Privacy Breach

You are a hospital social worker needing to summarize a patient's situation for a transfer to a rehabilitation facility.

Weak: "I have a patient named Robert Smith, DOB 04/12/1955, who had a stroke. He lives at 445 Elm St. His daughter, Sarah, is worried he can't walk. Write a transfer summary for him."

Problems: Major Privacy Violation! This prompt includes PII (Name, DOB, Address, Relative's Name). Inputting this into a public AI model violates HIPAA and client confidentiality.

8.6.2 Correction

Persona: Act as a Medical Social Worker.

Instruction: Draft a discharge transfer summary.

Context: The patient is a 69-year-old male recovering from a stroke (CVA). He has mobility limitations (difficulty walking). The family support system (daughter) expresses anxiety regarding his mobility safety at home. No names or addresses used.

Output: Use professional medical terminology but keep the tone collaborative.

8.6.3 Scenario 2: The "Deficit-Based" Trap

You are a school social worker writing a proposal for a new mentorship program for students who are frequently suspended.

Weak: "Write a proposal for a mentorship program for at-risk troubled teens in the inner city who have behavioral problems and come from broken homes. Explain why they are likely to fail without us."

Problems: Bias and Stigmatizing Language. This prompt relies on deficit-based language ("troubled," "broken homes," "likely to fail"). It invites AI to generate stereotypes rather than evidence-based insights. It lacks equity lenses.

8.6.4 Correction

Persona: Act as a Youth Development Specialist and Grant Writer.

Instruction: Draft a program proposal for a high school mentorship initiative.

Context: The program serves students in an urban setting who have experienced exclusionary discipline (suspensions). Focus on systemic barriers they face. Highlight their resilience and potential for leadership.

Output: Use strengths-based language. Focus on "opportunity gaps" rather than "at-risk" behaviors.

8.6.5 Scenario 3: The Hallucination Hazard

You are researching local housing laws to help a tenant who faces eviction.

Weak: "List the exact sections of the Tenant Rights Code for my state that prevent eviction for late fees and provide the phone number for the local legal aid office."

Problem: High Risk of Hallucination. AI models act as prediction engines, not search engines. They often invent legal codes and fake phone numbers that look real. Relying on this for legal advocacy is dangerous.

8.6.6 Correction

Persona: Act as a Housing Advocate.

Instruction: Summarize general concepts regarding tenant protections against eviction due to minor lease violations.

Context: Do not invent legal codes. Explicitly state if you are unsure of specific local statutes. Suggest keywords I should use to search the official state court website.

Output: Bullet points with a disclaimer that this is information, not legal advice.

8.6.7 Scenario 4: Abdicating Professional Judgment

A client has just disclosed something ambiguous that might require a report to Child Protective Services (CPS), but you are unsure.

Weak: "My client said she left her 5-year-old alone for 20 minutes to run to the store. Is this child abuse? Should I call CPS? Tell me what to do."

Problem: Abdicating Responsibility. AI cannot make ethical or legal determinations for you. It does not know your specific jurisdiction's laws or the nuance of the situation. Asking it "what to do" replaces your professional license with an algorithm.

8.6.8 Correction

Persona: Act as a Clinical Supervisor simulating a consultation.

Introduction: Help me explore the decision-making criteria for mandated reporting.

Context: A 5-year-old was left unsupervised for 20 minutes. No injuries occurred.

Output: List the factors I should consider (e.g., state laws on age of supervision, maturity of child, immediate danger). Do not give a final verdict. End with a reminder to consult my live supervisor.

8.7 Prompt Engineering in Social Work Research

Research is the compass that guides our practice. However, many social work students find the research process, specifically the volume of reading and the complexity of data analysis, daunting. Let's explore how to apply Prompt Engineering to the research processes.

Think of AI not as an "author" that writes your paper, but as your tireless Research Assistant (RA). This RA can summarize 50 articles in minutes, suggest coding categories for qualitative interviews, or help you translate dense statistical jargon into plain English. To do this effectively, let's adapt our P.I.C.O. framework.

8.7.1 The Literature Review (Synthesizing Knowledge)

One of the most powerful applications of AI is its ability to digest vast amounts of text. However, we must be careful. If you ask for a "list of sources," the AI may hallucinate non-existent papers. Instead, use AI to *analyze* text you already have or to *summarize* themes.

Weak Prompt: "Find me quotes about housing first."
Strong P.I.C.O. Prompt:
Persona: Act as a Social Work Researcher specializing in homelessness policy.
Instruction: Summarize the key arguments *for* and *against* the "Housing First" model found in the text below.
Context: [Paste the abstract and conclusion of six academic articles you have found].
Output: Create a comparison table with columns for "Authors," "Key Argument," and "Implications for Policy."

8.7.2 Qualitative Data Analysis (The Coding Assistant)

Qualitative research involves reading transcripts to find patterns (themes). AI can be a "second coder" to help check your bias or suggest themes you might have missed.

Ethical Checkpoint: You typically cannot upload full client transcripts to a public AI model due to confidentiality (i.e., HIPAA). However, you can use it to generate "codes" based on de-identified excerpts or to define your codebook.
The "Codebook Generator" Prompt:
Persona: Act as a Qualitative Researcher using Grounded Theory.
Instruction: Review these three anonymous interview excerpts and suggest five initial coding categories.
Context: [Paste three de-identified paragraphs about caregiver burnout].
Output: Present the codes with a definition for each and a specific quote from the text that supports it.

8.7.3 Quantitative Translation (Understanding Statistics)

For many students, the "Results" section of a quantitative paper is a wall of numbers. AI can function as a tutor, translating statistical output into the language of social work practice.

The "Stats Translator" Prompt:

Persona: Act as a Statistics Tutor for MSW students.
Introduction: Explain the concept of a "p-value" in this specific context.
Context: The study says, "The correlation between attendance and sobriety was significant ($p < .05$)."

Output: Explain the results using a simple analogy related to confidence, without using math formulas.

In research, integrity is everything. AI tools are language models, not truth models. Never copy-paste a Literature Review from AI: it will likely miss seminal, classic works or invent citations. Always verify specific data points (e.g., "66% of youth...") with the original source. If you use AI to help with your analysis, most academic journals now require you to disclose this in your "Methods" section.

8.8 The "Human in the Loop" Is You

As you can see from these exercises, the difference between a harmful output and a helpful one often lies entirely in the prompt. Technology is not neutral: it mirrors the intent and the clarity of the user. As social workers, our duty is to ensure that when we use these powerful tools, we do so with the same intention, care, and ethical rigor that we bring to a therapy session or a policy meeting.

8.9 Critical Thinking Questions

1 How can we design Bias Mitigation Prompts to prevent structural bias without sacrificing the individualization and specific needs of the client?
2 What is the acceptable ethical threshold for losing contextual richness (nuance, non-verbal cues) when using Automated Summarization Prompts for efficiency?
3 What specific risks of overreliance exist when using AI for complex Ethical Dilemma analysis, and where must the social worker's human judgment override the AI's logic?
4 As AI handles administrative tasks, how does the social worker's professional role shift, and what are the new core competencies (beyond technical skill) needed to maintain the profession's value?
5 Should social work education prioritize technical prompt-writing skills or critical analysis and AI ethics to best prepare future practitioners? Justify your choice.

8.10 Summary

This chapter established Prompt Engineering as a vital skill for social work practice, moving beyond basic AI usage to strategic command design. It detailed how effective prompts ensure ethical compliance and maximize professional effectiveness. The discussion covered designing Client-Centered Prompts to incorporate emotional sensitivity and cultural competence. We introduce the P.I.C.O framework to craft effective prompts. Mastering prompt engineering is seen as a new professional responsibility that enhances service quality and elevates the social worker's role in the age of AI. We conclude by reminding readers that prompt engineering is a *literacy* skill. Just as we learn to read and write, we must learn to "write" to machines to ensure they serve the "common good."

8.11 Empowerment-Focused Activities: The Prompt Engineering Lab

Now that we have explored the theory and ethics of prompt engineering, it is time to experiment. Reading about swimming is helpful, but eventually, you must get in the water. Think of this exercise as a safe "sandbox" where you can test the capabilities of AI without any risk to actual clients.

Your assignment is to select one of the following three tracks, Micro, Mezzo, or Macro, and apply the P.I.C.O. framework (Persona, Instruction, Context, Output) to solve a specific social work challenge. This is your opportunity to be creative and see how the AI responds to your unique leadership style.

Step 1: Choose Your Scenario

Option A: Micro Practice Track (Clinical Role-Play)

In this scenario, you want to practice your engagement skills before meeting a client who is hesitant about therapy. Your goal is to use AI to simulate client interaction. You will ask the AI to play the role of a client named "Sam," who is mandated to attend counseling but does not believe it will help.

Your Challenge: Write a prompt that instructs the AI to adopt this persona realistically including hesitation and defensive language, so you can practice your opening rapport-building statements.

Option B: Mezzo Practice Track (Community Grant Proposal)

Imagine you are a community organizer in a neighborhood with limited access to fresh produce ("food apartheid"). You have identified a vacant lot that would be perfect for a community garden. You need to draft a grant proposal to secure funding.

Your Challenge: Write a prompt that asks the AI to draft a "Statement of Need." You must provide the AI with specific demographic context (e.g., the percentage of residents without cars or the distance to the nearest grocery store) and ask it to connect these facts to the benefits of a community garden.

Option C: Macro Practice Track (Legislative Analysis)

Policy work often involves digesting massive amounts of dense legal text. For this scenario, imagine you are advocating for changes in foster care funding. You have a long, complex legislative bill that you need to understand quickly to brief your team.

Your Challenge: Find a recent bill summary or a long article about child welfare policy (or paste a generic long text). Write a prompt asking the AI to summarize the text specifically for a social work audience, highlighting how the changes would impact funding for aging-out youth.

Step 2: Draft and Refine (The P.I.C.O. Framework)

Once you have selected your track, open your preferred AI tool. Do not just ask a simple question. Instead, carefully construct your prompt using the P.I.C.O. method we discussed. Define the Persona (who the AI should be), state your Instruction clearly, provide the necessary Context (remembering to invent data rather than using real PII), and specify the Output format you desire.

After you submit your first prompt, look closely at the result. Is it useful? Is the tone correct? If the "client" in Option A sounds too robotic, or if the "grant proposal" in Option B sounds too generic, do not settle. Enter the "Refine" phase. Ask the AI to adjust its tone, include more specific details, or simplify the language. Continue this dialogue until the output meets your professional standards.

Step 3: The Reflection
Finally, write a brief reflection (approximately 200–300 words) on your experience. Consider the following questions:

- How did assigning a specific "Persona" impact the quality of the AI's response?
- Did you catch the AI "hallucinating" or making assumptions that you did not provide?
- How did you feel acting as the "director" of the technology rather than just the user?

Remember, the goal of this assignment is not to get a perfect answer from the machine, but to practice the skill of guiding it ethically and effectively. Have fun exploring!

This will be a great resource for you to explore: **The AI Social Worker** (www.theaisocialworker.com/ai-social-worker-prompt-library): AI Prompt Library for Social Work Documentation. Includes practical examples of prompts for case-recording, report-writing, and administrative efficiency.

References

AI21 Labs. (2025, May 13). *What are AI hallucinations? Signs, risks, & prevention | AI21*. AI21. www.ai21.com/knowledge/ai-hallucinations/

An, R. (2023). *Supercharge your research productivity with ChatGPT: A practical guide*. Independently published.

Bakst, W. (2025, November 26). *A guide to prompt iteration: Strategies and examples*. Mirascope. https://mirascope.com/blog/prompt-iteration

Barla, N. (2025, June 19). *What is iterative prompting? A step-by-step guide for reliable LLM outputs*. Adaline. Retrieved from www.adaline.ai/blog/iterative-prompting-a-step-by-step-guide-for-reliable-llm-outputs

Caiels, J., Silarova, B., Milne, A. J., & Beadle-Brown, J. (2024). Strengths-based approaches—Perspectives from practitioners. *The British Journal of Social Work, 54*(1), 168–188 https://doi.org/10.1093/bjsw/bcad186

Codecademy Team. (2024). *Prompt engineering 101: Understanding zero-shot, one-shot, and few-shot*. Codecademy. www.codecademy.com/article/prompt-engineering-101-understanding-zero-shot-one-shot-and-few-shot

Coursera Staff. (2026, January 13). *What is gradient descent in machine learning?* Coursera. www.coursera.org/articles/what-is-gradient-descent

Djeffal, C. (2025). *Reflexive prompt engineering: A framework for responsible prompt engineering and interaction design*. https://doi.org/10.48550/arxiv.2504.16204

Harvard University Information Technology. (2023, August 30). *Getting started with prompts for text-based generative AI tools*. Harvard University. Retrieved December 1, 2025, from www.huit.harvard.edu/news/ai-prompts

Khan, I. (2024). Ethical considerations in prompt engineering. In *The quick guide to prompt engineering: Generative AI tips and tricks for ChatGPT, Bard, Dall-E, and Midjourney*. 117–134. Wiley.

MIT Sloan Teaching and Learning Technologies. (2025). *Effective prompts for AI: The essentials.* MIT Sloan Teaching & Learning Technologies. Retrieved December 1, 2025, from https://mitsloanedtech.mit.edu/ai/basics/effective-prompts/

OpenAI API. (2025) *Prompt engineering*. https://platform.openai.com/docs/guides/prompt-engineering

Wang, L., Chen, X., Deng, X. W., Wen, H., You, M., Liu, W., Li, Q., & Li, J. (2024). Prompt engineering in consistency and reliability with the evidence-based guideline for LLMs. *NPJ Digital Medicine, 7*, 41. https://doi.org/10.1038/s41746-024-01029-4

8.12 Support Materials

Please access this video at www.routledge.com/9781041275459
Dr Marina Badillo Diaz, founder of THE AI Social Worker, offers a comprehensive tour of her website. Discover how to best use these resources for your work.

Video 8.1 The AI Social Worker

Part III

AI across Social Work Practice

9 AI for Children and Family Services

Othelia E. Lee and Sangmi Kim

9.1 Introduction

Artificial intelligence (AI) is increasingly shaping the landscape of child welfare practice, offering new tools to support vulnerable children and families while simultaneously raising critical ethical, equity, and governance concerns. From direct service delivery to policy-level decision-making, AI technologies are beginning to integrate into systems that aim to protect and empower children. Let's explore how AI is being used across micro, mezzo, and macro levels of child welfare practice, highlighting concerns related to privacy, developmental appropriateness, and the boundaries between support and surveillance. Readers will critically examine the role of AI in enhancing service delivery, promoting family well-being, optimizing organizational processes, and informing policy, while maintaining a strong focus on ethical practice, equity, and human rights.

9.2 Micro-Level: AI in Direct Practice with Children and Families

Box 9.1 Clinical Decision-Making

An AI tool embedded in a child welfare agency's data system flags a family for additional home visits after identifying a pattern of missed school and medical appointments. The algorithm draws on historical data and predictive modeling to suggest potential risks. Sarah receives the alert and uses it as one input among many (e.g., conducting interviews with the family, consulting with school personnel, and gathering insights from community partners). Sarah ultimately determines that the missed appointments are due to transportation barriers and a recent job loss, not neglect, and connects the family with support services.

Box 9.1 underscores why social workers must pair critical thinking, cultural humility, and ethical judgment with AI-assisted tools. While AI can support early

DOI: 10.4324/9781003755081-12

detection and resource allocation, it can't replace professional insight grounded in contextual assessment and authentic engagement with families. Social workers need the skills to interpret AI outputs, recognize limitations, and integrate them with interviews, collateral information, and community knowledge.

Because algorithms may reflect historical inequities, practitioners must understand how risk scores are generated and identify when AI recommendations conflict with lived context. Practitioners should document disagreements or overrides, aligning practice with emerging ethical guidance emphasizing equity, transparency, and safety across the AI lifecycle (Lee et al., 2025).

Child-centered practice also requires acknowledging that minors may not fully grasp data practices or continuous monitoring implications (Chng et al., 2025). Communication with families should use clear, plain language about how AI informs decisions, what data are used, and ongoing consent options, reinforcing privacy, autonomy, and long-term child well-being.

9.2.1 Digital Well-Being and Screening Tools

AI can support digital well-being in children and youth, particularly through innovative screening tools that can identify early signs of mental health or developmental concerns. These tools are designed to analyze patterns in social media activity, application usage, or **sensor data** from wearable devices to detect indicators such as social withdrawal, anxiety, or disrupted sleep cycles (Vertsberger et al., 2022). However, research on child-centered AI cautions that children's developmental status and limited capacity for informed consent require heightened ethical safeguards, particularly when digital monitoring risks normalizing intrusive surveillance (Chng et al., 2025).

AI-driven platforms may assess language patterns in text messages or online posts to screen for symptoms of depression. When used ethically, these tools can support earlier engagement and triage while preserving youth safety and autonomy (Boian et al., 2024). For minors, practice protocols should also specify who reviews alerts, how false positives and false negatives are handled, and how families are informed in ways that reduce stigma and avoid unnecessary surveillance (Chng et al., 2025).

In school and pediatric settings, such tools can be integrated into broader care systems, offering a more holistic view of a child's well-being. For social workers, this opens up new possibilities for proactive engagement, but also raises critical questions about privacy, equity, and the responsible use of data.

9.2.2 Family-Centered AI Support Systems

While AI screening tools are often designed to assess individual digital well-being, their potential extends beyond the individual to encompass families as interconnected systems. Increasingly, these technologies are being developed to support families as interconnected systems, recognizing that well-being is shaped by relationships, environments, and shared experiences. **Family-centered AI** support systems are emerging as a promising innovation in children and family services, offering personalized guidance and resources that reflect the unique strengths, needs, and cultural contexts of each family (Dray & Symons, 2025).

AI technologies are increasingly being used to foster family closeness and improve access to counseling and support services. In contemporary family structures, where nuclear families and diminished parent–child interactions are common, AI-based applications have emerged as tools to enhance communication. These technologies offer personalized interventions, real-time feedback, and accessible counseling platforms that can strengthen familial bonds and improve relational dynamics (Szondy & Magyary, 2025).

AI has facilitated the development of **parenting apps** that support mothers and caregivers in managing childcare responsibilities. For example, the "Hatch Grow" app integrates a smart changing pad with a wireless scale to monitor infant feeding amounts, diaper changes, and growth metrics. By providing real-time insights into an infant's health and development, such tools may support informed decision-making and reduce cognitive and logistical burden for novice caregivers, particularly during periods of stress or transition (Hatch Baby, n.d.; Farmer et al., 2025).

Some systems may include **virtual assistants** that help caregivers manage appointments, access benefits, and navigate complex service landscapes with greater ease. Predictive tools can analyze patterns, identify needs, and recommend interventions that align with a family's goals and values, particularly in systems characterized by fragmented service delivery (Farmer et al., 2025). To promote equitable access, these platforms must incorporate **multilingual interfaces** and culturally responsive design features that reflect the lived realities of diverse families.

What distinguishes a family-centered approach is its emphasis on empowerment rather than surveillance. Instead of using AI solely to monitor risk or flag deficits, these systems should be designed to build trust, foster resilience, and promote self-determination. We can shift the narrative from one of control to one of collaboration, where families are active participants in shaping support they receive (Dray & Symons, 2025).

As advocates, designers, and facilitators, social workers can help ensure that AI technologies are grounded in ethical practice. Their involvement is crucial in co-designing systems that are both technologically effective and socially just, systems that respect privacy, uphold dignity, and reflect the lived realities of the communities they serve.

9.2.3 Adaptive Learning and Tutoring for Children

AI is transforming the landscape of education, offering new possibilities for **adaptive learning** and tutoring that are especially impactful for children in underserved communities and those with special needs. During the COVID-19 lockdown, platforms like Khan Academy played a vital role in providing nationwide access to tutoring, helping bridge educational gaps when in-person learning was disrupted (Abramson, 2021). Similarly, massive open online courses such as Crash Courses have opened doors for youths from low-income families to engage with high-quality educational content, often for free (Stringer, 2025). Within this context, AI-enabled educational tools have been increasingly positioned as equity-oriented support rather than replacements for formal schooling, particularly for children with learning disabilities, who may benefit from flexible and individualized learning environments (Tetzlaff et al., 2021).

One of the most promising applications of AI in education is the development of **personalized learning** paths. These systems can analyze a child's learning style, pace, and preferences to tailor educational content in ways that meet individual needs (Tetzlaff et al., 2021). For children with learning disabilities, personalization often involves not only adjusting content difficulty but also modifying modes of presentation and pacing to reduce cognitive overload and to support sustained engagement through multimodal inputs such as visual, auditory, or tactile elements (Ferguson et al., 2022).

AI platforms like "CogniAble" and "KidSense" use machine learning to customize interventions based on behavioral data, helping children engage more effectively with learning materials (Ferguson et al., 2022). A key advantage of these systems is their capacity to deliver real-time, **adaptive feedback**, which is particularly beneficial for children who rely on immediate reinforcement due to attention or processing challenges (Yin et al., 2021).

Gamified learning environments can further enhance engagement by making learning interactive and fun. Tools like "RoboTutor" and AI-driven chatbots simulate social interactions and provide structured learning experiences in safe, predictable formats that are particularly beneficial for neurodiverse learners (Yin et al., 2021). These approaches align with long-standing principles of play therapy, in which narrative structure and symbolic play are used to support meaning-making and emotional regulation (Kaduson & Schaefer, 2021). When used thoughtfully, generative story-based tools may complement therapeutic practice by supporting individualized narratives rather than replacing clinician-led intervention.

Communication support is a critical area where AI is making a difference. Many children with autism spectrum disorder (ASD) face challenges in speech and language development. AI technologies can assist with speech recognition and correction, interpret non-standard speech patterns using natural language processing, and offer **augmentative and alternative communication (AAC)** tools (Brumberg et al., 2018). When integrated into broader therapeutic or educational plans, applications such as "Speakprose" and "Voiceitt" may enhance expressive capacity while reinforcing autonomy and communicative confidence.

Conversational AI systems can offer low-threat, structured environments where children with ASD practice social-emotional skills. By simulating everyday scenarios with visual cues and explicit emotional labels, they support emotion recognition and response. Their repetition and predictability can ease social anxiety and strengthen emotional literacy, especially when used alongside clinician- or educator-guided interventions (Babb et al., 2021). For example, a prompt like "How would you feel if a friend gave you a birthday present?" paired with an image of happiness helps children learn accurate emotional labeling through consistent, confidence-building practice.

Social skills training is another area where AI shows promise. AI-driven avatars and virtual environments can simulate social scenarios, helping children practice essential skills such as eye contact, turn-taking, and emotional recognition. Programs like "TeachTown" and "Replika" offer structured, AI-based social simulations that are tailored to the needs of neurodiverse learners, providing opportunities to build confidence in social interactions (Babb et al., 2021).

Despite these exciting developments, the use of AI in special education raises important ethical considerations. Transparency is essential: families and legal guardians must understand how their child's data is being collected, used, and protected. Consistent with child-centered AI frameworks, systems should prioritize proportional data use, age-appropriate safeguards, and participatory design that accommodate neurodiverse individuals and caregivers (Muralidharan et al., 2023).

9.2.4 Crisis Intervention and Emotional Support Chatbots

AI systems are being used to monitor behavioral patterns and emotional well-being by tracking progress and identifying triggers for emotional distress (Mahmood et al., 2024). By analyzing physiological signals (heart rate or movement) wearable devices and AI dashboards can detect signs of stress or overstimulation, allowing caregivers and educators to adjust strategies in real time. **Predictive analytics** can also anticipate support needs, enabling more proactive and personalized interventions.

AI and Internet of Things (IoT) technologies are increasingly being integrated into child safety solutions. One such innovation is "AngelSense," a Global Positioning System (GPS) tracking device designed to prevent children from going missing. Tailored for children with special needs, AngelSense combines real-time GPS tracking, two-way voice communication, and proactive safety alerts. Through a smart app, caregivers can monitor a child's location and movement in 30-second intervals, listen to ambient sounds, and communicate directly with the child. The system's AI-powered alert function notifies parents when a child deviates from their usual route or remains stationary for extended periods, helping to identify potentially dangerous situations before they escalate (AngelSense, 2025).

AI is also being used to detect signs of child abuse in real time. A notable example is "J.O.A.N.N.E," a service shaped like a red-haired girl that integrates an AI speaker, multimodal emotional recognition, child psychiatry counseling techniques, and psychological assessment tools. While specific evidence is limited, emerging research demonstrates the potential of AI-powered systems to detect child abuse through voice and audio classification. These systems use machine learning models to analyze vocal cues such as crying or screaming, triggering alerts for caregivers or authorities when signs of distress are detected (Yan et al., 2023). Such technologies represent a promising frontier in safeguarding children from harm in both public and private settings.

AI-powered chatbots are increasingly being used to provide real-time emotional support and crisis intervention, particularly in under-resourced settings where access to mental health professionals may be limited. These tools offer 24/7 support to children and youth experiencing emotional distress, using conversational interfaces to engage users in moments of vulnerability.

Through natural language processing, chatbots can detect signs of crisis such as suicidal ideation, self-harm, or abuse, and refer users to human professionals when risk thresholds are met. However, while these tools show promise, their use with minors requires special caution because children and adolescents may not fully understand system limits.

Tragic incidents underscore the potential dangers of unregulated chatbot use with minors. A young boy, initially using a chatbot to help with homework, later turned to the same tool during a period of emotional crisis (Hill, 2025). Instead of de-escalating the situation or referring him to appropriate support, the chatbot offered to write a suicide note and even advised on accessing lethal means.

This heartbreaking incident highlights the urgent need for safeguards, oversight, and ethical design in AI systems intended for vulnerable youths. Recent youth-focused guidance emphasizes safety-by-design features, including clear age-appropriate disclosures, conservative crisis detection thresholds, rapid escalation pathways, and continuous monitoring for harmful outputs (Hawke et al., 2025).

Another possible solution is to implement a secure account in the chatbot system where parental guidance functions are available. Their algorithms must be transparent and responsive to diverse linguistic and emotional expressions. Crisis-oriented AI systems for youth must incorporate age-appropriate safeguards, transparent escalation protocols, and clear boundaries around relational expectations (Chng et al., 2025; Lee et al., 2025).

Social workers should be trained to assess chatbot outputs, understand their limitations, and integrate them into broader care plans that include human connection and professional oversight. By doing so, social workers can help ensure that AI tools are used responsibly, ethically, and in ways that truly support the well-being of children and families.

9.3 Mezzo-Level: AI in Organizational and Community Interventions

Box 9.2 Organizational Decision-Making

A county child welfare agency integrates AI into its planning systems to forecast foster care placement needs six months in advance. By analyzing trends in case closures, family reunifications, and incoming referrals, the system predicts a surge in placement demand. This insight enables the agency to proactively recruit foster families, expand training programs, and coordinate with local service providers. It aims to produce a more responsive and prepared system that reduces placement disruptions and improves outcomes for children.

Box 9.2 illustrates the importance of organizational competence, data literacy, and ethical leadership in AI-enhanced social work practice. Social workers must be able to interpret predictive models and advocate for their responsible use. In this process social workers need to ensure equity in resource distribution and avoid reinforcing systemic disparities. Ethical concerns include the risk of overreliance on forecasts, potential data bias, and the need for community-informed planning.

9.3.1 Case Management and Resource Allocation

AI is reshaping the way case management is conducted in children and family services, offering tools that enhance efficiency, responsiveness, and equity in decision-making. By leveraging large datasets and predictive analytics, AI enables social workers and agencies to make more informed choices about how to prioritize cases and allocate resources in ways that better reflect community needs.

One of the most impactful innovations is the use of **automated triage systems**. These systems assess incoming cases based on risk indicators and urgency, helping frontline workers respond more quickly to those in greatest need (Yi et al., 2020). Rather than relying solely on manual sorting or subjective judgment, AI can analyze patterns in historical data to identify which cases may require immediate attention. When used as decision-support, this approach may streamline the intake process, reduce delays, and ensure critical situations are addressed promptly, provided that algorithmic outputs remain subject to professional interpretation, transparency, and human oversight (Gillingham, 2019).

Another advantage is **resource matching**, connecting families with services that best meet their needs. These systems consider factors such as geographic location, service availability, and individual circumstances to recommend appropriate supports (Gillingham, 2019). In contexts where eligibility criteria and program options are fragmented or difficult to navigate, AI-supported matching may help streamline processes and reduce administrative bottlenecks that delay access to care. At the same time, recommended matches should remain subject to professional review to ensure contextual appropriateness and fairness, consistent with ethical guidance that positions AI as a decision-support tool rather than a substitute for human judgment (Lee et al., 2025).

Workflow optimization is where AI is making a meaningful difference. Tools that automate routine tasks (documentation, scheduling, and coordination) can significantly reduce the administrative burden on social workers (Keng et al., 2025). This allows professionals to spend more time engaging directly with clients and less time managing paperwork. AI systems can improve communication across multidisciplinary teams, enhancing collaboration and continuity of care, particularly in large or fragmented service systems where coordination across agencies is challenging (Simbo AI, 2025).

AI can analyze historical case data to uncover trends in service utilization, revealing which programs are frequently accessed and which remain underutilized. This insight enables child welfare agencies to adjust their resource distribution more equitably and identify gaps in service delivery, such as unmet needs in specific communities or populations that are consistently overlooked.

Despite these benefits, the integration of AI into case management must be approached with care and critical reflection. Social workers must be trained to question risk classifications, document overrides, and explain decisions to families in accessible terms, particularly when algorithmic outputs conflict with contextual or relational evidence. Moreover, social workers must ensure that human relationships remain central to case management, preserving empathy, trust, and cultural understanding in every interaction.

9.3.2 Outreach and Community Connection

AI is opening new possibilities for enhancing outreach and strengthening connections between families, communities, and service systems. In contexts marked by service fragmentation or uneven access, AI tools are being designed to support more strategic, inclusive, and responsive engagement with communities (Putnam-Hornstein et al., 2020).

A powerful application of AI is its ability to map s**ervice ecosystems**. By analyzing data across programs such as after-school care, mentoring initiatives, and wraparound services, AI can identify where services overlap, where gaps exist, and where coordination could be improved (Putnam-Hornstein et al., 2020), supporting more place-based and preventive outreach strategies. Such insight allows agencies to better understand the landscape of support available to families and to make informed decisions about where to invest resources or expand programming.

An AI system might detect that certain neighborhoods are experiencing high rates of school absenteeism while also lacking access to after-school programs (Vaithianathan et al., 2025), prompting earlier and more coordinated community-level responses. This information can be used to prompt **targeted outreach** efforts, encouraging collaboration among schools, health providers, and social service agencies to address the root causes.

Moreover, AI can facilitate **cross-sector collaboration** by enabling shared data platforms that link different service providers. Such platforms can help break down silos between education, healthcare, and social services, allowing for more coordinated care and reducing the burden on families who often must navigate complex systems on their own. Chatbots and virtual assistants can further support this process by guiding families through service options, answering questions, and helping them complete applications, making it easier to access help and stay engaged (Boian et al., 2024).

Nevertheless, the promise of AI in outreach must be matched by a commitment to ethical practice. Without transparency and community engagement, data-driven outreach risks reinforcing mistrust or perceptions of surveillance (Lee et al., 2025). Outreach efforts must be inclusive, culturally responsive, and grounded in the voices of the communities they aim to serve. Technology should act as a bridge that strengthens relationships and builds trust. Social workers can lead these efforts, co-designing AI tools with stakeholders to ensure that they reflect community values, respect lived experiences, and promote equity.

9.3.3 Training and Supervision

AI supports staff training and supervision, offering new pathways for organizational learning and professional development (Ravalier et al., 2023). These innovations can help agencies build more responsive, informed, and resilient workforces, which is an essential goal in a profession where practitioners regularly face high stress, complex decision-making, and emotionally demanding cases (Dalziel et al., 2024).

In the realm of staff-training, AI-powered platforms are transforming how child welfare professionals learn and grow. These systems can simulate case scenarios using natural language processing and virtual agents, allowing staff to practice decision-making in realistic, interactive environments without exposing families to risk during training (Jenney et al., 2025). **Adaptive learning** technologies tailor content to each worker's role, experience level, and performance, ensuring that training is both relevant and personalized.

An AI-driven tool might present a scenario involving suspected neglect and prompt the worker to choose a course of action. The system then can provide immediate feedback grounded in best practices and ethical standards, helping staff build critical thinking skills and confidence in their judgment. **Real-time feedback** is most effective when it encourages reflection rather than compliance, supporting practitioners' ability to justify decisions in ethically complex contexts (Ravalier et al., 2023). Trauma-informed care practices further enhance the depth and quality of learning.

The "Trevor Project," a leading organization providing crisis intervention and suicide prevention services to LGBTQ+ youth, partnered with Google.org to develop an AI-powered training tool called the Crisis Contact Simulator (CCS). The CCS uses machine learning and natural language processing to simulate realistic conversations as digital youth personas, allowing volunteer crisis counselors to practice and refine their skills (Ball, 2021).

AI has started making its way into **reflective supervision**, a cornerstone of ethical and sustainable child welfare practice. Reflective supervision provides space for workers to process complex cases, manage stress, and maintain a commitment to ethical decision-making. AI tools can support this process by analyzing case notes and documentation to identify patterns in decision-making, emotional tone, or risk assessment that may otherwise remain implicit or overlooked (Ahn et al., 2021). These insights can help supervisors guide reflective conversations, flagging potential ethical concerns or areas for growth such as implicit bias or overreliance on algorithmic risk scores. Dashboards that visualize trends across teams can offer supervisors a broader view of organizational dynamics, helping them tailor support and professional development strategies.

Some AI tools can transcribe and summarize supervision sessions, highlighting recurring themes and suggesting follow-up questions (Dalziel et al., 2024). However, it is critical to emphasize that these technologies are meant to support, not replace, the human elements of supervision. The relational and empathetic core of reflective practice must remain intact, with AI serving as a tool to enhance, not diminish, the depth of human connection and understanding.

The use of AI in training and supervision also raises important ethical considerations. Workers must be fully informed about how their data is being used and have control over its application. AI-generated feedback must be carefully designed to avoid reinforcing stereotypes or penalizing diverse approaches to practice. Transparency is essential: both supervisors and staff should understand how insights are produced and be empowered to challenge or contextualize them when necessary.

As AI becomes more integrated into the professional development landscape, social workers must remain active participants in shaping its use, not only as end users but as ethical stewards who influence design, implementation, and governance decisions. By advocating for ethical standards, inclusive design, and transparent practices, they help ensure that AI supports the growth of reflective, competent, and compassionate practitioners, ultimately strengthening the domain of child welfare and advancing the common good.

9.4 Macro-Level: AI in Systems, Policy, and Advocacy

> **Box 9.3 Critical Policy Decision**
>
> State policymakers in a child welfare agency use AI modeling to simulate the long-term impact of increasing funding for prevention services. The model integrates historical data on family preservation programs, foster care placements, and demographic trends. It predicts that a 20% increase in prevention funding could reduce long-term foster care placements by 15% over five years. This insight informs budget decisions and legislative proposals, helping shift the system toward more proactive and family-centered approaches.

Box 9.3 highlights the need for policy practice competency, systems thinking, and ethical advocacy. Social workers must be equipped to interpret and critique AI-generated policy models, ensuring they reflect realities and community needs. Simultaneously, social workers must advocate for equity in how data is used to shape policy, especially for historically marginalized populations. Again, transparency and accountability become instrumental. Ethical concerns include the potential for data-driven decisions to obscure human complexity and needs for inclusive policymaking processes.

9.4.1 Predictive Analytics and Ethical Concerns

Predictive analytics is becoming an increasingly influential tool in child welfare systems, offering the ability to forecast outcomes such as the risk of child maltreatment, the likelihood of family reunification, and long-term service needs (Ahn et al., 2021). These models can be used to inform decisions about resource allocation, staffing, and intervention strategies, with the goal of improving efficiency and outcomes across systems of care. However, the use of predictive analytics raises serious ethical concerns that social workers must be prepared to confront.

One of the most pressing issues is the potential for bias and discrimination. Predictive models typically rely on historical data reflecting patterns of systemic racism, poverty, and surveillance. When these biased datasets are used to train algorithms, the resulting predictions can reinforce existing inequities, disproportionately flagging families from marginalized communities as high-risk and subjecting them to increased scrutiny or intervention (Eubanks, 2018).

Another concern is the opacity of many predictive systems. Algorithms used in child welfare are often proprietary or poorly documented, making it difficult for practitioners, families, or even agency leaders to understand how decisions are being made (Gillingham, 2019). This lack of transparency undermines accountability and can erode trust between families and service providers, particularly when predictive classifications carry long-term consequences. Without clear explanations of how predictions are generated, it becomes nearly impossible to challenge or correct errors that may have serious consequences for children and caregivers.

In many cases, data collected during routine interactions with social services is fed into predictive models without explicit consent or meaningful explanation. This practice raises concerns about privacy, informed decision-making, and the right of children and families to control how their information is used.

9.4.2 AI-Driven Policymaking and Evaluation

By harnessing data integration and simulation techniques, AI offers new ways to examine complex systems, anticipate policy outcomes, and assess potential trade-offs prior to implementation (Fowler et al., 2019). These tools can help policymakers move beyond intuition and anecdote toward more evidence-informed, adaptive, and responsive approaches.

One application of AI in policy work is the use of simulation techniques such as agent-based modeling and system dynamics. These methods allow researchers and decision-makers to test how different policy scenarios might play out in real-world settings. For example, AI can simulate how changes in housing policy could affect child welfare caseloads, or how school-based mental health interventions might influence long-term educational outcomes (Fowler et al., 2019). These simulations help stakeholders anticipate unintended consequences and refine strategies before implementation.

AI enables the analysis of large-scale administrative data to identify trends and evaluate program effectiveness. By processing vast amounts of information from schools, health systems, and social services, AI can uncover patterns that might otherwise go unnoticed (Panteli et al., 2025). This can produce more accurate assessments of what works, for whom, and under what conditions, supporting continuous improvement and equitable outcomes (Obeidat et al., 2025).

Furthermore, AI can optimize service delivery systems by identifying bottlenecks and recommending structural changes. For instance, it may reveal inefficiencies in referral pathways or highlight areas where service coordination is lacking (Gillingham, 2019). These insights can inform redesign efforts that make systems more accessible, responsive, and client-centered.

9.5 Reflections and Future Directions

Recent scholarship emphasizes that AI systems used in child-serving contexts must be evaluated not only for technical performance, but also for their implications for children's rights, family autonomy, and long-term well-being (Selbst et al.,2019). Because children's privacy needs are uniquely sensitive, research highlights the importance of age-appropriate safeguards for the collection, integration, and use of pediatric data within AI-enabled systems (Muralidharan et al., 2023). Therefore, responsible AI use extends beyond technical competence and must be anchored in professional values such as equity, transparency, human-centeredness, and safety across the research and practice lifecycle (Lee et al., 2025).

The integration of AI into children and family services presents both profound opportunities and complex ethical questions. One of the most promising directions is the deepening of **human–AI collaboration**. Rather than replacing professional judgment, AI systems are increasingly positioned as tools that may augment relational and ethical dimensions of social work practice when guided by clear ethical frameworks. Social workers will work alongside these technologies, using them to enhance decision-making, streamline administrative tasks, and expand access to services, while maintaining the human connection that is central to effective care. The ETHICS framework (Lee et al., 2025) offers a durable set of principles to support responsible AI use over time, emphasizing that equity, human-centeredness, and safety must remain central as technologies evolve.

Community-led AI initiatives in child welfare are emerging, where technologies are co-created with those they are intended to serve. These efforts help ensure cultural relevance, build trust, and empower communities to shape the tools that impact their lives (Allegheny County Department of Human Services, 2024). Social workers should participate in interdisciplinary teams that design and evaluate AI tools to ensure that policies reflect human values and promote social justice. By engaging with AI not just as users, but as co-creators, social workers can help navigate a future where technology supports the common good and strengthens the ethical foundations of public service.

AI's role in child welfare practice is poised to expand in both scope and complexity. The future of AI in children's and family services will likely be shaped by systems that are more adaptive, learning from real-time feedback to refine their recommendations and responses. We can also anticipate the development of interoperable platforms that connect across agencies and sectors, enabling more coordinated and holistic care. Perhaps most importantly, there is growing momentum toward participatory design models that center the voices of children, families, and communities in the creation of AI tools.

Despite these exciting opportunities, significant challenges remain. Addressing algorithmic bias and ensuring equitable access to AI-enhanced services is a critical concern. Without intentional safeguards, AI systems risk reinforcing existing disparities and excluding those who are already marginalized (Eubanks, 2018). Strong data governance frameworks in child welfare services are essential to protect privacy, ensure informed consent, and promote ethical data use. As AI capabilities expand, consensus in digital medicine emphasizes the importance of child-centered governance, including rigorous evaluation, continuous monitoring, transparency about model limitations, and clear accountability mechanisms when harms occur (Chng et al., 2025).

As stewards of care and justice, social workers have a unique and essential role in shaping how these technologies are developed and used. Workforce development in child welfare is another key priority. Social workers must be equipped with the skills and knowledge to engage with AI critically and ethically. This includes understanding how algorithms work, recognizing their limitations, and advocating for practices that uphold human dignity and rights. Training programs, interdisciplinary collaboration, and ongoing professional development will be vital to prepare social workers for this new frontier.

9.6 Critical Thinking Questions

1 Can you identify examples where AI has enhanced service delivery, and where it may have introduced new challenges?
2 What ethical concerns arise when using AI to flag families for intervention? How should social workers respond when AI recommendations conflict with their professional judgment or community insights?
3 In what ways can chatbots and screening tools support children and families? What are the limitations of these tools, and how can social workers mitigate potential harm?
4 How can AI improve case management and resource allocation in child welfare agencies? What are the risks of relying too heavily on AI for outreach and community connection?
5 How might predictive analytics influence child welfare policy decisions? What safeguards are needed to ensure AI-driven policymaking does not reinforce systemic inequities?
6 What would an ethically grounded, family-centered AI system look like in child welfare practice? How can social workers contribute to the design and governance of future AI tools?

9.7 Summary

We discussed how AI is reshaping child welfare practice across micro, mezzo, and macro levels. AI offers powerful tools to support children and families, but its integration into child welfare practice must be guided by the core values of the profession: dignity, equity, human rights, and social justice. By engaging with AI thoughtfully and ethically across micro, mezzo, and macro levels, social workers can help shape a future where technology serves the common good and strengthens the fabric of care.

9.8 Empowerment-Focused Activities

9.8.1 AI Tool Evaluation Workshop

AI-supported tools for neurodivergent children may include adaptive learning platforms, multimodal instructional supports, and personalized learning pathways designed to accommodate diverse cognitive and sensory profiles. Relevant categories also include speech-to-text and text-to-speech technologies, AAC systems, AI-assisted reading and decoding supports, and executive functioning and time-management applications. When selecting tools, practitioners should consider developmental appropriateness, data privacy, accessibility, and alignment with therapeutic or educational goals.

Objective: Analyze and critique AI tools designed for children with special needs.
Instructions:
Divide students into small groups.
Assign each group an AI tool (e.g., EZducate, Voiceitt, TeachTown).
Have each group research:

- The tool's purpose and features.
- How it supports neurodiverse learners.
- Ethical considerations (e.g., data privacy, bias).

Each group presents their findings and recommendations for social work practice.

Discussions: How can social workers advocate for the responsible use of these tools in schools or clinical settings?

9.8.2 Scenario-Based Role-Play

Objective: Apply AI governance principles to real-world cases involving children with special needs.

Instructions:

Present a scenario (e.g., a school district adopts an AI-based behavioral monitoring system).
Assign roles: Social worker, parent, school administrator, civil society advocate, AI developer.
Students debate the system's benefits, risks, and governance needs.
Conclude with a group reflection on ethical and equitable implementation.

Discussion: What governance safeguards would you recommend for protecting the child's rights?

References

Abramson, A. (2021, September 1). Capturing the benefits of remote learning. *Monitor on Psychology, 52*(6), 46. www.apa.org/monitor/2021/09/cover-remote-learning

Ahn, E., Gil, Y., & Putnam-Hornstein, E. (2021). Predicting youth at high risk of aging out of foster care using machine learning methods. *Child abuse & Neglect, 117*, 105059. https://doi.org/10.1016/j.chiabu.2021.105059

Allegheny County Department of Human Services. (2024). *Summarizing recent research on predictive risk models in child welfare.* Allegheny County Analytics. https://analytics.alleghenycounty.us/wp-content/uploads/2024/05/24-ACDHS-04-Predictive-Risk-Algorithms.pdf

AngelSense. (2025, August 7). AngelSense vs. GPS trackers: Autism safety technology that goes beyond location. www.angelsense.com/blog/autism-gps-tracker-angelsense/

Babb, S., Raulston, T. J., McNaughton, D., Lee, J. Y., & Weintraub, R. (2021). The effects of social skill interventions for adolescents with autism: A meta-analysis. *Remedial and Special Education, 42(*5), 343–357. https://doi.org/10.1177/0741932520956362

Ball, J. (2021, March 24). *How AI helps volunteers support LGBTQ youth in crisis.* Google.org. https://blog.google/outreach-initiatives/google-org/trevor-project-crisis-contact-simulator /

Boian, R., Bucur, A. M., Todea, D., Luca, A., Rebedea, T., & Podina, I.R. (2024). A conversational agent framework for mental health screening: Design, implementation, and usability. *Behaviour & Information Technology, 44*(10), 2093–2100. https://doi.org/10.1080/0144929X.2024.2332934

Brumberg, J. S., Pitt, K. M., Mantie-Kozlowski, A., & Burnison, J. D. (2018). Brain–computer interfaces for augmentative and alternative communication: A tutorial. *American Journal of Speech-Language Pathology, 27*(1), 1–12. https://doi.org/10.1044/2017_AJSLP-16-0244

Chng, S. Y., Tern, M. J. W., Lee, Y. S., Cheng, L. T.-E., Kapur, J., Eriksson, J. G., Chong, Y. S., & Savulescu, J. (2025). Ethical considerations in AI for child health and recommendations for child-centered medical AI. *NPJ Digital Medicine, 8*, 152. https://doi.org/10.1038/s41746-025-01541-1

Dalziel, M. V., Schaffer, K., & Martin, N. (2024). Navigating AI in social work and beyond: A multidisciplinary review. *arXiv* preprint arXiv:2411.07245. https://doi.org/10.48550/arXiv.2411.07245

Dray, J., & Symons, D. (2025). Review of innovative mental health support for children and young people: Generative AI co-design applications and challenges. *Current Developmental Disorders Reports, 12*(1), 13. https://doi.org/10.1007/s40474-025-00328-z

Eubanks, V. (2018). *Automating inequality: How high-tech tools profile, police, and punish the poor*. St. Martin's Press.

Farmer, R. L., Lockwood, A. B., Goforth, A., & Thomas, C. (2025). Artificial intelligence in practice: Opportunities, challenges, and ethical considerations. *Professional Psychology: Research and Practice, 56*(1), 19–32. https://doi.org/10.1037/pro0000595

Ferguson, J., Dounavi, K., & Craig, E. A. (2022). The impact of a telehealth platform on ABA-based parent training targeting social communication in children with autism spectrum disorder. *Journal of Developmental and Physical Disabilities, 34*(6), 1089–1120. https://doi.org/10.1007/s10882-022-09839-8

Fowler, P. J., Marcal, K. E., Chung, S., Brown, D. S., Jonson-Reid, M., & Hovmand, P. S. (2019). Scaling up housing services within the child welfare system: Policy insights from simulation modeling. *Child Maltreatment, 25*(1), 51–60. https://doi.org/10.1177/1077559519846431

Gillingham, P. (2019). Decision-making in child and family welfare: The role of AI in identifying service bottlenecks and improving coordination. *British Journal of Social Work, 49*(6), 1541–1558. https://doi.org/10.1017/cha.2016.51

Hatch Baby. (n.d.). *Grow 101: Learning about your Hatch grow.* Hatch Support. https://help.hatch.co/hc/en-us/articles/360016409593-Grow-101-Learning-about-your-Hatch-Grow

Hawke, L. D., Hou, J., Nguyen, A. T. P., Phi, T., Gibson, J., Ritchie, B., Strudwick, G., Rodak, T., & Gallagher, L. (2025). Digital conversational agents for the mental health of treatment-seeking youth: Scoping review. *JMIR Mental Health, 12*, e77098. https://doi.org/10.2196/77098

Hill, K. (2025, August 26). A teen was suicidal. ChatGPT was the friend he confided in. *The New York Times*. www.nytimes.com/2025/08/26/technology/chatgpt-openai-suicide.html

Jenney, A., Scott, K., Cullen, O., Bittman, M., & Smith, C. (2025). Exploring the effectiveness of virtual simulation-based learning in enhancing clinical skills in social work education. *Studies in Clinical Social Work: Transforming Practice, Education and Research*, 1–22. https://doi.org/10.1080/28376811.2025.2524621

Kaduson, H. G., & Schaefer, C. E. (Eds.). (2021). *Play therapy with children: Modalities for change*. American Psychological Association. www.apa.org/pubs/books/play-therapy-children

Keng, C., DiGiorgio, A., Ehrenfeld, J. M., Spear, J., & Miller, B. J. (2025). Unburdening patients and clinicians through automation and artificial intelligence: Informatics strategies for reducing administrative burden. *Journal of Medical Systems, 49*(1), 128. https://doi.org/10.1007/s10916-025-02265-1

Lee, J. Y., Pace, G. T., Cha, H., Rao, S., Hahm, H. C., An, R., & Denby-Brinson, R. (2025). Commentary: ETHICS—An ethical framework for artificial intelligence (AI) use in social work research. *Journal of the Society for Social Work and Research. 16(4),* 695–698. Advance online publication. https://doi.org/10.1086/739116

Mahmood, N., Bhatti, S. M., Dawood, H., Pradhan, M. R., & Ahmad, H. (2024). Measuring student engagement through behavioral and emotional features using deep learning models. *Algorithms, 17*(10), 458. https://doi.org/10.3390/a17100458

Muralidharan, A., Burgart, A., Daneshjou, R., & Rose, S. (2023). Recommendations for the use of pediatric data in artificial intelligence and machine learning: The ACCEPT AI framework. *NPJ Digital Medicine, 6*, 166. https://doi.org/10.1038/s41746-023-00898-5

Obeidat, R., Alsmadi, I., Baker, Q. B., Al-Njadat, A., Srinivasan, S., Godswill Ashong, & Ifeanyi Osigwe (2025). Researching public health datasets in the era of deep learning: A systematic literature review. *Health Informatics Journal, 31*(1), 14604582241307839. https://doi.org/10.1177/14604582241307839

Panteli, D., Adib, K., Buttigieg, S., Goiana-da-Silva, F., Ladewig, K., Azzopardi-Muscat, N., Figueras, J., Novillo-Ortiz, D., & McKee, M. (2025). Artificial intelligence in public health: Promises, challenges, and an agenda for policy makers and public health institutions. *The Lancet. Public health, 10*(5), e428–e432. https://doi.org/10.1016/S2468-2667(25)00036-2

Putnam-Hornstein, E., Ghaly, M., & Wilkening, M. (2020). Integrating data to advance research, operations, and client-centered services in California: Integrating millions of administrative records across California's health and human services programs to improve operations, coordinate services, develop targeted interventions, and more. *Health Affairs, 39*(4), 655–661. https://doi.org/10.1377/hlthaff.2019.01752

Ravalier, J. M., Wegrzynek, P., Mitchell, A., McGowan, J., McFadden, P., & Bald, C. (2023). A rapid review of reflective supervision in social work. *The British Journal of Social Work, 53*(4), 1945–1962. https://doi.org/10.1093/bjsw/bcac223

Selbst, A. D., Boyd, D., Friedler, S. A., Venkatasubramanian, S., & Vertesi, J. (2019). Fairness and abstraction in sociotechnical systems. *Proceedings of the ACM Conference on Fairness, Accountability, and Transparency*, 59–68. https://doi.org/10.1145/3287560.3287598

Simbo AI. (2025). How AI driven workflow automation in electronic health records can reduce documentation burden and improve multidisciplinary care coordination in hospitals. www.simbo.ai/blog/how-ai-driven-workflow-automation-in-electronic-health-records-can-reduce-documentation-burden-and-improve-multidisciplinary-care-coordination-in-hospitals-1536404/?utm_source=copilot.com

Stringer, H. (2025, April 1). Psychological science helps build digital educational media that capitalizes on how human brains learn. *Monitor on Psychology, 56*(3), 42. www.apa.org/monitor/2025/04-05/kids-digital-educational-media

Szondy, M. B., & Magyary, Á. (2025). Artificial intelligence (AI) in the family system: Possible positive and detrimental effects on parenting, communication and family dynamics. *European Journal of Mental Health, 20,* e0038, 1–8. https://doi.org/10.5708/EJMH.20.2025.0038

Tetzlaff, L., Schmiedek, F., & Brod, G. (2021). Developing personalized education: A dynamic framework. *Educational Psychology Review, 33*, 863–882. https://doi.org/10.1007/s10648-020-09570-w

Vaithianathan, R., Benavides-Prado, D., Rebbe, R., & Putnam-Hornstein, E. (2025). Using a Predictive Risk Model to Prioritize Families for Prevention Services: The Hello Baby Program in Allegheny County, PA. *Prevention science, 26*(3), 321–330. https://doi.org/10.1007/s11121-025-01802-1

Vertsberger, D., Naor, N., & Winsberg, M. (2022). Adolescents' well-being while using a mobile artificial intelligence–powered Acceptance Commitment Therapy tool: Evidence from a longitudinal study. *JMIR AI, 1*(1), e38171. https://doi.org/10.2196/38171

Yan, J., Chen, Y., & Fok, W. W. T. (2023). Detection of children abuse by voice and audio classification by short-time Fourier transform machine learning implemented on Nvidia Edge GPU device. arXiv. https://arxiv.org/abs/2307.15101

Yi, N., Baik, D., & Baek, G. (2025). The effects of applying artificial intelligence to triage in the emergency department: A systematic review of prospective studies. *Journal of Nursing Scholarship, 57*(1), 105–118. https://doi.org/10.1111/jnu.13024

Yin, J., Goh, T. T., Yang, B., & Xiaobin, Y. (2021). Conversation technology with micro-learning: The impact of chatbot-based learning on students' learning motivation and performance. *Journal of Educational Computing Research, 59*(1), 154–177. https://doi.org/10.1177/0735633120952067

9.9 Support Materials

9.9.1 Mitchel Resnick: "Lifelong Kindergarten" and Creative Learning

www.youtube.com/watch?v=IfvgVpQI56I

This talk explores how the principles of kindergarten—imagining, creating, playing, sharing, and reflecting—are essential for fostering creativity and human-centric design in the age of AI. For social workers, it's a great way to visualize complex concepts like machine learning and bias in AI, while reinforcing why critical thinking and ethical safeguards are essential when using technology in human services.

10 AI for Mental Health Services

Othelia Lee

10.1 Introduction

Across the United States (U.S.) and globally, the demand for mental health and substance abuse services continues to rise at an unprecedented rate. This surge is driven by a complex interplay of factors, including the lingering psychological impacts of the COVID-19 pandemic, increasing rates of anxiety, depression, and substance use disorders, and growing awareness of behavioral health needs across diverse populations (National Center for Health Workforce Analysis, 2024). Yet, the behavioral health workforce is struggling to keep pace. According to the U.S. Bureau of Labor Statistics, employment in mental health-related occupations is projected to grow significantly through 2032, with social workers expected to have the highest number of annual openings among these professions (Russ & Reimer, 2025).

Despite this growth, shortages persist. In underserved and rural areas, many individuals are left without timely or adequate mental health care. In response to these challenges, artificial intelligence (AI) is emerging as a powerful tool with the potential to transform mental health and substance abuse services. Several chatbots are in the markets. Would it be a substitute for a therapist?

MentalRoBERTa (Robustly Optimized BERT Approach) is a large language model designed and trained to understand and analyze text related to mental health. The AI scans the text (like client messages, notes, or online posts) and flags patterns that may indicate high anxiety or depressive language. It highlights phrases like "I feel hopeless" and "I can't keep going," categorizing them as high-risk indicators. Although it is not a diagnostic tool, BERT (Bidirectional Encoder Representations from Transformers) systems make it better at recognizing emotional tone, identifying mental health concerns, and supporting tasks like screening or triage (Chopra et al., 2024). AI technologies are being used to expand access to care, personalize interventions, and support social workers in their practice. Let's explores the role of AI in mental health and substance abuse services through a multi-level framework.

DOI: 10.4324/9781003755081-13

10.2 Micro-Level: AI in Direct Practice with Individuals and Families

10.2.1 AI-Powered Chatbots

Box 10.1 Chatbot Support for Anxiety

Jin is a 22-year-old college student who seeks counseling at her university for generalized anxiety. Like many campus counseling centers, the one at Jin's university is overwhelmed, and the wait time for an intake session is three weeks. To offer support in the meantime, the counselor recommends Jin try an AI-powered chatbot that delivers daily cognitive behavioral therapy (CBT) exercises. The chatbot is designed to help users manage stress, track their mood, and practice coping strategies.

Box 10.1 introduces learners to how AI tools can extend mental health support beyond traditional therapy sessions. Can these tools be a substitute for human connection or clinical expertise? If you were the social worker in this scenario, how would you explain the chatbot to Jin? What steps would you take to protect her privacy and build trust? And how would you support her autonomy while still offering guidance?

AI-powered chatbots have emerged as promising tools in the delivery of mental health services, particularly at the micro level where social workers engage directly with individuals. These chatbots (e.g., Wysa, Youper, Flourish, Noah AI) are designed to simulate therapeutic conversations and provide support through psychoeducation, CBT-based exercises, and even crisis response. They are accessible via smartphones and web platforms, making them especially valuable for clients who face barriers to traditional in-person care.

One of the most compelling advantages of chatbot technology is its availability. Unlike human providers, chatbots offer 24/7 support, allowing users to engage with mental health resources at any time of day. This constant accessibility can be particularly helpful for individuals experiencing anxiety, depression, or substance use challenges during off-hours or between scheduled therapy sessions (Inkster et al., 2018). Additionally, chatbots may help reduce stigma by offering a private, judgment-free space for users to explore their emotions and practice coping strategies (Prochaska et al., 2021).

Early intervention is another key benefit. Because chatbots can monitor user input and mood patterns over time, they may help identify emerging concerns before they escalate. For example, chatbots use natural language processing to detect signs of distress and respond with tailored CBT techniques and offer mindfulness and journaling prompts to support emotional regulation (Inkster et al., 2018). These tools can empower clients to take an active role in their mental health, reinforcing therapeutic goals and enhancing engagement.

Nevertheless, privacy is a major issue, especially when sensitive conversations are stored or analyzed by third-party systems. Should Jin's conversations with the chatbot be stored, and if so, who has access to them? How should confidentiality be explained when the "helper" is a machine? These questions are especially important when working with young adults who may not fully understand how their data is being used.

Cultural responsiveness is another challenge. Chatbots are typically trained on generalized datasets and may not reflect the diverse experiences, values, and communication styles of all users. This can lead to misinterpretation or a lack of meaningful connection, particularly for clients from marginalized communities (Marko et al., 2025; Nadarzynski et al., 2024).

There is also the risk of **overreliance**. While chatbots can be helpful supplements, they are not substitutes for human care. As social work continues to evolve alongside technological innovation, practitioners must critically assess the benefits and limitations of AI-powered chatbots to ensure that these tools are used responsibly, equitably, and in ways that enhance the quality of care.

10.2.2 Teletherapy and AI Integration

Box 10.2 Teletherapy with AI Note-Taking

Maria is a social worker at a rural community mental health center, where she provides teletherapy to clients dealing with substance use disorders. To help manage her workload, the center has introduced an AI-powered platform that transcribes sessions and summarizes key points automatically. During a session with her client John, the system flags a potential risk of relapse based on certain keywords John used. This alert is meant to help Maria identify concerns early, but it also raises questions about how much she should rely on the technology.

Box 10.2 highlights how AI can be a supportive tool in clinical decision-making by helping social workers notice patterns or risks that might otherwise be missed, especially when managing multiple clients or working in high-demand settings. However, it also reminds us that technology isn't perfect. AI systems can misinterpret language, flag false positives, or miss important emotional cues. Should Maria trust the AI's alert, or prioritize her own clinical judgments? What are the risks if she ignores the alert, or if she relies on it too heavily? And how should she explain to John that AI is part of the process? For learners, this case offers a chance to reflect on how to balance innovation with integrity.

Teletherapy has become a vital component of mental health service delivery, especially in the wake of increased demand and limited access to in-person care. As telehealth platforms evolve, AI is being integrated to enhance the quality and efficiency of virtual sessions. AI tools now assist with real-time transcription, automatic session summarization, and **risk flagging**, features that can support clinicians in tracking progress, identifying concerns, and reducing administrative burden.

These **AI-enhanced platforms** often include clinician dashboards that compile session data and behavioral indicators, helping social workers make more informed decisions about treatment-planning. Platforms (e.g., Twofold, Freed AI) assist clinicians with documentation and case notes in Health Insurance Portability and Accountability Act (HIPAA)-compliant environments (Prochaska et al., 2021). If a client frequently uses language associated with hopelessness or relapse, the system may flag this for further review. This kind of support can be especially helpful for practitioners managing large caseloads or working in high-demand environments.

One promising application is **AI-powered speech recognition**, which can improve accessibility for clients with communication disabilities. These tools can transcribe speech more accurately, detect emotional tone, and even adapt to different speech patterns, making teletherapy more inclusive and responsive to individual needs (Green, 2024). For clients who may struggle with verbal expression due to neurological or physical conditions, this technology can help bridge communication gaps and foster more meaningful therapeutic engagement.

Despite these benefits, equity concerns must be addressed. The **digital divide** remains a significant barrier, particularly for clients in rural areas or older adults who may lack reliable internet access or familiarity with digital platforms. Without intentional design and outreach, AI-enhanced teletherapy risks excluding those who could benefit most. Social workers must advocate for **inclusive technology policies** and ensure that clients are supported in accessing and using these tools effectively (Robinson et al., 2024).

Risk flagging features, while potentially lifesaving, can raise concerns about surveillance and autonomy. Integrating AI into teletherapy requires a thoughtful balance between innovation and ethics. Social workers must remain grounded in core values, while embracing tools that can enhance their practice. By doing so, they can help shape a future where technology supports healing without compromising trust.

10.2.3 Therapeutic Algorithms and Digital Phenotyping

An encouraging development in personalized mental health care is the use of **therapeutic algorithms**, AI systems that help generate individualized care plans based on client data. These algorithms can adapt interventions in real time, responding to changes in mood, behavior, or engagement. For social workers, this means having access to tools that can complement clinical judgment and enhance the precision of care.

Digital phenotyping takes this a step further by using data from everyday smartphone use to detect subtle shifts in mental health. Apps can analyze voice tone, typing speed, screen time, and even movement patterns to identify signs of emotional distress or relapse risk (Mendes et al., 2022). A sudden drop in communication or changes in sleep patterns might signal the onset of depression or anxiety.

These insights can help social workers intervene earlier, potentially preventing crises before they escalate.

These technologies allow for more responsive and individualized care, especially for clients managing chronic conditions like substance use disorders or mood disorders. By identifying risk factors early, therapeutic algorithms and digital phenotyping can support timely outreach and reinforce treatment goals. They also offer a way to monitor progress between sessions, giving both clients and clinicians a clearer picture of what's working and what needs adjusting (Onnela & Rauch, 2016).

Yet, **surveillance** is a major issue: clients may not fully understand how their data is being collected or used, and the constant monitoring can feel invasive. There's also the risk of **false positives**, where the system flags a problem that doesn't exist, potentially leading to unnecessary interventions or anxiety. Social workers must be mindful of **informed consent**, ensuring that clients are aware of what data is being tracked, how it will be used, and what their rights are. Again, cultural responsiveness is another critical factor. Algorithms trained on generalized data may not reflect the lived experiences of diverse populations, leading to misinterpretation or bias (Saeidnia et al., 2024).

10.2.4 Virtual Reality and Immersive AI Tools

Virtual reality (VR) and immersive AI technologies are opening new frontiers in mental health care, offering innovative ways to support clients through experiential and interactive interventions. At the micro level, these tools are being used to deliver **exposure therapy** for conditions such as post-traumatic stress disorder (PTSD), phobias, and substance use cravings. By simulating real-world environments in a controlled and safe setting, VR allows clients to confront and process distressing stimuli with the guidance of a clinician, helping to reduce avoidance behaviors and build coping skills (Maples-Keller et al., 2017).

AI-driven VR platforms enhance this experience by adapting scenarios in real time based on the client's physiological responses or verbal cues. If a client shows signs of heightened anxiety, the system can adjust the intensity of the exposure or prompt calming interventions. This level of personalization supports **trauma-informed care**, allowing social workers to tailor interventions to each client's emotional and psychological needs. It also offers opportunities for clients to rehearse real-life situations, such as resisting substance use triggers or navigating social anxiety, in a safe and supportive environment (van Loenen et al., 2022).

Despite these promising applications, VR and immersive AI tools come with challenges that social workers must navigate thoughtfully. Cost and accessibility remain significant barriers. Clients in low-income or rural communities may not have access to the hardware or internet connectivity required to participate in VR-based therapy. This raises equity concerns and reinforces the importance of advocating for inclusive technology policies and funding models that prioritize underserved populations (Robinson et al., 2024).

Clients must be fully informed about how their data (e.g., **biometric feedback** or behavioral responses) is collected and used. These tools could feel intrusive or even re-traumatizing if not implemented with care. Social workers must ensure that consent is ongoing and that clients can pause or opt out of immersive experiences at any time.

10.3 Mezzo-Level: AI in Organizational and Community Interventions

10.3.1 Nonprofit Data Analytics for Service Planning

Box 10.3 Data Analytics for Retention

A local nonprofit substance abuse clinic is facing a common challenge: many clients drop out of group therapy programs within the first month. To address this issue, the organization adopts an AI-based analytics system that tracks attendance patterns and predicts which participants are most likely to disengage early. When the system identifies someone at risk, staff receive prompts to reach out (with a phone call or a personalized text reminder) to encourage continued participation.

Box 10.3 shows how AI can be used at the organizational level to improve service delivery. By identifying patterns in client behavior, the clinic can take proactive steps to support retention and reduce dropout rates. This kind of data-driven approach can help staff be more efficient and responsive, especially in settings with limited resources. Nevertheless, the use of predictive analytics raises important ethical questions. Is it appropriate to target clients based on a computer model prediction? Could this feel intrusive or even **stigmatizing** to someone who's already navigating a vulnerable moment in their recovery?

For learners preparing to work in nonprofit or clinical settings, this case offers a chance to reflect on how technology can be both a tool and a challenge. If you were part of the team at this clinic, how would you use predictive analytics to support clients without making them feel judged or monitored? What safeguards should be in place to prevent bias or misinterpretation? What would you say to a client who asks why they received a reminder message? And how could you involve clients in conversations about how their data is used?

In nonprofit mental health and substance abuse services, AI is increasingly being used to support **data-driven decision-making**. AI tools can analyze patterns in service utilization, treatment outcomes, and funding flows to help organizations better understand how their programs are functioning (International Society of Substance Use Professionals, 2025). These insights are especially valuable in resource-limited settings, where every dollar and staff hour must be used strategically to meet client needs.

One practical application of AI in this context is predicting which program participants are at risk of dropping out of treatment. By examining attendance records, engagement levels, and other behavioral indicators, **predictive models** can flag individuals who may need additional support. This allows staff to intervene early, with a personalized message, to help clients stay connected to care. When used thoughtfully, these tools can improve retention, reduce service gaps, and ensure that interventions are tailored to the needs of each client (Robinson et al., 2024).

AI-driven **predictive analytics** can help nonprofits allocate resources more effectively, identify trends that might otherwise go unnoticed, and make evidence-informed decisions that enhance service delivery (Worldmetrics, 2026). For social workers, this means having access to tools that can support clinical judgment and strengthen client outcomes. It also opens opportunities to advocate for funding and policy changes based on real-time data.

One major concern is the risk of overreliance on quantitative indicators without considering the full context of a client's life. Data can tell us a lot, but it cannot capture the nuances of trauma, cultural identity, or personal motivation. Labeling someone as "likely to drop out" based solely on an algorithm may unintentionally reinforce stigma or overlook the strengths and resilience that clients bring to their recovery journeys (Eubanks, 2018).

Ethical practice requires that social workers use data analytics as a supplement, not a substitute, for relational and culturally responsive care. Clients should be informed about how their data is being used, and organizations must ensure that predictive models are transparent, fair, and regularly evaluated for bias. Social workers have a responsibility to advocate for inclusive data practices that reflect the diversity of the communities they serve.

10.3.2 Outreach Automation and Engagement

> **Box 10.4 Outreach Automation for Youths**
>
> A nonprofit organization focused on youth mental health is using AI-driven text campaigns to stay connected with its clients. These automated messages remind young people about upcoming appointments, share coping strategies, and promote group sessions. For some, these texts feel supportive and encouraging. For others, especially those who are sensitive to issues of privacy, the messages feel intrusive and raise concerns about being monitored.

For readers preparing to work in youth-serving organizations, this case offers a chance to think critically about how to use technology in ways that honor the voices and choices of young people. If you were a social worker in this nonprofit, how would you explain the outreach system to a new client? What steps would you take to make sure the messages feel supportive rather than invasive? And how could you involve youth in shaping the way these tools are used?

Automated outreach can help ensure that clients don't fall through the cracks, especially when they're juggling school, work, or personal challenges. It's a cost-effective way to maintain contact and offer consistent support. At the same time, this approach brings up important ethical and cultural questions. Not all young people respond to technology in the same way. Some may appreciate the reminders, while others may feel uncomfortable or even mistrustful. Social workers must consider how cultural background, personal history, and digital literacy affect how clients experience automated communication.

The key challenge here is finding a balance between efficiency and empathy. How can social workers use outreach automation in ways that feel respectful and empowering rather than invasive? One way to do this is by involving young people in the design of these systems. Asking for their input, offering opt-in choices, and being transparent about how their data is used can help build trust and make the technology feel more personalized.

AI is increasingly being used to enhance outreach and engagement in nonprofit settings where staff capacity is often limited. AI-powered tools such as automated text messaging systems, social media monitoring, and appointment reminders are helping organizations maintain consistent contact with clients, reduce missed appointments, and promote participation in therapeutic programs. These technologies offer a scalable way to extend support beyond the therapy room for individuals navigating substance use recovery or mental health challenges.

One common application is the use of **automated appointment reminders** in substance use clinics. These reminders, delivered via text or app notifications, can significantly reduce no-show rates, which are often a barrier to continuity of care. By prompting clients to attend scheduled sessions, AI-enhanced outreach helps reinforce treatment routines and supports retention (Brancewicz et al., 2025). For social workers, these tools can serve as a bridge between sessions, offering gentle nudges that keep clients engaged and connected.

The potential for **outreach automation** is valuable in settings with limited staff and high demand. Nonprofits can use AI to reach more clients without overburdening their teams, allowing social workers to focus their time on direct care and complex cases. Automated systems can be programmed to share coping tips, motivational messages, or reminders about group sessions, creating a sense of continuity and support that complements therapeutic work.

Yet, automated messages, while efficient, can sometimes feel impersonal or intrusive for clients who come from communities with historical mistrust of institutional systems. Messages must be crafted in ways that reflect the values, language, and preferences of diverse populations to avoid alienation or misunderstanding (Eubanks, 2018).

Social workers must also be mindful of the risk of **depersonalization**. While automation can streamline outreach, it should not replace the relational aspects of care that are central to social work practice. Clients should be given the opportunity to opt in or out of automated systems, and their feedback should inform how these tools are used. **Transparency** about data use, message frequency, and the purpose of outreach is key to building trust and maintaining ethical standards.

10.3.3 Training and Workforce Support

AI is also being used to strengthen the workforce behind mezzo-level care. Social workers in high-demand or resource-limited settings are increasingly turning to AI-based tools to assist with clinical decision-making, monitor staff well-being, and improve service delivery.

One of the most impactful applications is the use of **AI-powered clinical decision support systems**. These tools analyze client data (e.g., symptoms, history, and treatment responses) to offer evidence-informed suggestions for care-planning. While these systems are not meant to replace professional judgment, they can help practitioners identify patterns, consider alternative interventions, and stay current with best practices (Auf et al., 2025). Particularly for early-career social workers or those managing complex caseloads, this kind of support can be valuable.

AI is also being used to monitor workforce well-being. Some organizations have begun using **sentiment analysis** in staff surveys to detect signs of burnout, stress, or disengagement. These systems analyze language patterns and emotional tone to flag potential concerns, allowing supervisors to respond proactively with support or adjustments to workload. In high-pressure environments like substance abuse clinics or crisis response teams, this kind of monitoring can help protect staff mental health and sustain a healthy work culture (Honcoop, 2026).

Unfortunately, access to these tools is not evenly distributed. Larger health systems often have the infrastructure and funding to implement AI solutions, while smaller nonprofits may struggle to keep up. This raises important equity concerns. If only well-resourced organizations can benefit from AI-enhanced workforce support, disparities in service quality and staff well-being may widen. Social workers must advocate for inclusive technology policies that ensure all organizations, regardless of size or budget, can access tools that support ethical and effective practice (Khanna & Khanna, 2025).

10.3.4 Digital Therapeutics

Digital therapeutics (DTx) represent a transformative shift in how we approach behavioral health care. These are clinically validated, software-based treatments designed to prevent, manage, or treat mental health and substance use disorders (Jones & Fortunato, 2023). Unlike general wellness apps, DTx are often Food and Drug Administration (FDA)-approved, require a prescription, and are backed by real-world evidence. They are used alongside traditional therapy and medication, offering accessible, personalized, and data-driven care (Substance Abuse and Mental Health Services Administration [SAMHSA], 2023).

Through machine learning, AI enables personalized treatment by adapting content to meet each user's unique needs. It can also generate predictive insights, such as identifying patterns that signal relapse risks or symptom spikes (Jharbade, 2025). These capabilities allow for more proactive and tailored interventions.

AI also improves user engagement by delivering customized reminders, feedback, and motivational prompts. It facilitates better communication between patients and providers by sharing real-time data and tracking progress. This data-driven approach helps clinicians adjust care plans dynamically, ensuring that treatment remains relevant and responsive (SAMHSA, 2023).

Additionally, AI-powered DTx can be scaled across systems and populations, making them a promising tool for expanding access to behavioral health care (Tung et al., 2024). DTx have the potential to expand access to care to those in underserved communities where mental health services are limited. By leveraging technology, these tools can reach individuals who might otherwise face barriers due to geography, stigma, or lack of resources.

Despite these advantages, DTx are not without limitations. Access remains a significant barrier, especially for individuals without reliable internet, appropriate devices, or sufficient digital literacy. Privacy concerns also arise, as sensitive health data must be protected and ethically managed. Importantly, DTx are not intended to replace traditional care. They are most effective when integrated into a broader treatment plan that includes human support and clinical oversight.

As digital therapeutics become more common in behavioral health settings, social workers must develop new competencies to engage with these tools ethically and effectively. Particularly, practitioners must be able to critically evaluate digital tools, assessing their evidence base and appropriateness for diverse clients.

10.4 Macro-Level: AI in Systems, Policy, and Advocacy

10.4.1 Predictive Analytics in Mental Health Policy

Box 10.5 Predictive Analytics in Suicide Prevention

A state health department is using predictive analytics to identify individuals who may be at high risk of suicide. By analyzing data from social media posts and health records, the department aims to allocate resources more effectively, such as funding for crisis hotlines and mobile response teams. While this approach has the potential to save lives, advocacy groups have raised concerns. They argue that communities of color are being disproportionately flagged, leading to fears of over-surveillance and stigmatization.

Predictive analytics uses large datasets to identify population-level risk trends by detecting patterns such as rising opioid overdoses, suicide clusters, or geographic disparities in access to care. By analyzing data from health records, social media, and community-level indicators, predictive analytics offers policymakers a powerful tool for early intervention and resource allocation.

Box 10.5 offers a chance to think critically about the intersection of technology, ethics, and advocacy. If you were a policy advocate, how would you respond to concerns about bias in suicide risk modeling? What steps would you take to ensure that predictive analytics are used responsibly? And how could you involve affected communities in shaping these tools and policies?

Suppose that public health authorities have begun using predictive models to guide the deployment of **crisis response resources**. When data signals an increase in suicide risk in a particular region, agencies can respond by expanding hotline capacity, deploying mobile crisis teams, or increasing outreach efforts. These data-driven strategies allow for more timely and targeted responses, potentially saving lives and reducing the burden on emergency services (Schuerkamp et al., 2023).

Furthermore, these tools can serve as early warning systems, helping governments and organizations anticipate mental health needs before they escalate. They also support **evidence-informed advocacy**, giving public health social workers the data they need to argue for funding, program expansion, and legislative change. When used ethically and transparently, predictive analytics can strengthen the case for equitable and proactive mental health policy.

Nonetheless, a pressing risk is the potential for **stigmatization**. If predictive models disproportionately flag communities of color or low-income neighborhoods as “high risk,” it can reinforce harmful stereotypes and lead to increased surveillance instead of support. In some cases, data intended for public health purposes may be repurposed by law enforcement, resulting in punitive responses rather than care-based interventions (Eubanks, 2018). This misuse of data undermines trust and can deepen existing inequities.

Social workers need to challenge policies that prioritize control over care by advocating for inclusive data practices, ensuring that affected communities are involved in shaping how data is interpreted and applied. Ethical macro-level practice demands that technology be used to advance human rights, not to reinforce systemic injustice.

10.4.2 AI in Public Mental Health Campaigns

AI is increasingly being used to shape public mental health campaigns, offering new ways to reach individuals who may be at risk but are not yet engaged with formal services. At the macro level, AI technologies are helping public health agencies and advocacy organizations design targeted outreach efforts based on patterns in online behavior, search queries, and social media activity. These tools allow campaigns to be more precise, timely, and responsive to emerging mental health needs across diverse populations.

One example of this approach is the use of AI to deliver **suicide prevention messages** to high-risk demographics. By analyzing search terms related to self-harm, hopelessness, or crisis, AI systems can identify users who may benefit from seeing supportive content (e.g., ads for crisis hotlines, mental health resources, or peer support networks). These interventions are designed to meet individuals where they are, offering help in moments of vulnerability and potentially preventing harm before it escalates (Columbia University Mailman School of Public Health, 2025).

AI in public mental health outreach can allow for scalable, cost-effective campaigns that can adapt to changing trends and reach people who might otherwise be overlooked. For social workers engaged in macro-level practice, these tools offer new avenues for advocacy, education, and prevention. AI also supports data-informed strategies that can strengthen the impact of public health messaging and resource allocation.

While the goal is to promote public good, the methods can feel intrusive, encountering ethical dilemmas. Monitoring online behavior, even with good intentions, can evoke concerns about **surveillance**, privacy, and consent. Individuals may not be aware that their digital activity is being analyzed, and some communities may experience these interventions as another form of institutional oversight rather than support (Eubanks, 2018).

Appropriate social work interventions include advocating for transparency in data collection, ensuring that outreach messages are culturally sensitive, and involving communities in shaping how these technologies are used. Macro-level practice demands a balance between innovation and integrity—where technology serves as a tool for empowerment, not control.

10.4.3 Advocacy for Ethical AI in Mental Health Systems

Box 10.6 AI in Opioid Crisis Advocacy

A coalition of social workers and public health advocates are using AI to respond to the opioid crisis in their city. By analyzing data on overdose rates, the AI model identifies neighborhoods where overdoses are rising. The coalition presents these findings to city officials, advocating for increased funding for harm reduction services, including more naloxone distribution sites and expanded crisis response teams. The data strengthens their case and helps them argue for a public health approach. However, some policymakers suggest using the same data to increase police patrols in the flagged areas, raising concerns about criminalization and surveillance.

When used thoughtfully, predictive models can help direct resources to communities that need them most. They can support arguments for funding, guide public health strategies, and help social workers make data-informed decisions. However, Box 10.6 also highlights a major ethical challenge: data meant to support care can be repurposed for punitive measures. If predictive analytics are used to justify increased policing, especially in communities already facing systemic inequities, the result may be more harm than help.

For learners preparing to enter advocacy roles, Box 10.6 offers a chance to think critically about how to use data responsibly. If you were leading this coalition, how would you present the AI findings to city officials in a way that promotes **harm reduction** instead of criminalization? What risks would you need to anticipate, and how could you involve affected communities in shaping the response? And how would you ensure that the use of AI aligns with the values of social work?

Social workers can play a critical role in pushing for transparency and **explainability in predictive models**. These models, often used to assess risk or guide interventions, must be understandable not only to policymakers and clinicians but also to the communities they affect. Without clear explanations of how decisions are made, AI systems can reinforce mistrust and obscure accountability. Advocacy efforts must emphasize the importance of **open algorithms** and **community-informed design processes**.

Social workers must advocate for regulations that ensure AI systems do not perpetuate discrimination or bias. This includes challenging the use of datasets that reflect historical inequities, such as over-policing in communities of color or underrepresentation in mental health research. Without careful oversight, AI tools can replicate and even amplify these disparities, leading to unjust outcomes in areas like treatment access, risk assessment, and service prioritization (Eubanks, 2018).

Data privacy protections are also essential for individuals navigating mental health and substance use challenges. Many AI systems rely on sensitive personal data, from electronic health records to social media activity, to make predictions. Social workers must ensure that clients' rights to privacy and informed consent are upheld, and that data is not shared or repurposed in ways that could cause harm. This is significant when working with marginalized groups who may already face systemic surveillance and stigma.

10.5 Reflections and Future Directions

A few years ago, I confidently told students that social work was among the professions unlikely to be replaced by AI. Yet, the pace of change has been surprising. Research indicates that many individuals now consult ChatGPT for health-related information, self-triage, and even self-diagnosis, as well as for informal decision support (Shahsavar & Choudhury, 2023). Increasingly, users engage these systems as conversational partners for personal concerns, emotional disclosure, and informal mental health support, roles traditionally filled by friends, peers, or professional helpers (Alanezi, 2024).

Today, chatbots and AI agents often serve as accessible, though imperfect, sources of companionship and emotional scaffolding rather than substitutes for professional care. Clinical social workers may encounter clients who arrive with self-diagnoses or present AI-generated information during sessions. AI chatbots can effectively deliver structured interventions based on standardized protocols, such as those grounded in CBT.

On the contrary, AI tools remain ill-equipped to provide nuanced therapeutic support for conditions like complex grief and personality disorders. AI cannot replace the sophisticated skills of psychoanalysis and narrative therapy. Models like MentalRoBERTa can detect patterns in language but lack the capacity to interpret lived experience. To what extent can these systems manage subtle shifts in tone, delicate affect, and culturally embedded content? Can they navigate euphemisms, slang, and humor unique to marginalized voices?

These questions underscore critical responsibilities for policymakers and platform designers. Accuracy, privacy, and safety must be prioritized when users seek help for sensitive personal or health matters. There is also a growing need for empirical research that rigorously evaluates the effectiveness of AI-driven interventions. While many tools show promise, few have been studied in diverse, real-world settings.

Social work researchers have a vital role to play in building this evidence base, ensuring that AI applications are not only innovative but also safe, inclusive, and grounded in best practices. This includes examining outcomes across different populations and identifying unintended consequences that may arise from algorithmic decision-making. Ongoing research should examine how user motivations align with outcomes, for example, whether conversational engagement reduces loneliness or inadvertently encourages risky self-management. Furthermore, interventions are needed to guide users toward safer, higher-quality applications of these technologies.

As AI continues to evolve, its role in mental health and substance abuse services will only deepen. For social workers, this presents both exciting opportunities and critical responsibilities. An area requiring urgent future directions is the integration of **AI literacy** into professional training. Social workers must be equipped not only to use AI tools but to understand how they function, what their limitations are, and how to evaluate their ethical implications (Russ & Reimer, 2025).

Another promising development is the **co-design of AI tools** with service users, families, and communities. Co-designed tools are more likely to be trusted, effective, and equitable, especially when they are shaped by the voices of people who have historically been marginalized in both mental health systems and technology development (Eubanks, 2018). The future of AI in mental health will depend on strong trans-disciplinary collaboration.

From personalized chatbots and predictive analytics to public health campaigns and policy advocacy, these technologies are reshaping how care is delivered and how systems respond to complex needs. Yet, the promise of AI can only be realized if social workers lead with ethics, equity, and innovation. As trusted advocates and practitioners, social workers must ensure that AI serves the common good, amplifying human connection, not replacing it. The future of AI in social work is not just about what technology can do, but about how we choose to use it in the service of healing, justice, and hope.

10.6 Critical Thinking Questions

1. What new skills or literacies will social workers need to responsibly integrate AI into practice to promote mental health interventions?
2. How might the use of AI differ across micro, mezzo, and macro practice levels in mental health and substance abuse interventions?

3 In what ways can social workers act as ethical watchdogs for AI systems to advocate for clients with mental health and substance abuse issues?
4 How should social workers balance innovation and caution when using AI?

10.7 Summary

At the micro level, we examined how AI is used in direct practice, including clinical decision support, digital therapeutic tools, and client engagement. At the mezzo level, we considered how organizations and communities are leveraging AI to improve service delivery, coordination, and workforce support. Finally, at the macro level, we analyzed policy implications, funding structures, and ethical frameworks that shape the broader landscape of AI in behavioral health. Through this exploration, social workers should gain the knowledge and critical thinking skills needed to engage thoughtfully and ethically with emerging technologies in their future practice.

References

Alanezi, F. (2024). Assessing the effectiveness of ChatGPT in delivering mental health support: A qualitative study. *Journal of Multidisciplinary Healthcare*, *17*, 461–471. https://doi.org/10.2147/JMDH.S447368

Auf, H., Svedberg, P., Nygren, J., Nair, M., & Lundgren, L. E. (2025). The use of AI in mental health services to support decision-making: Scoping review. *Journal of Medical Internet Research, 27*, e63548. https://doi.org/10.2196/63548

Brancewicz, M., Robakowska, M., Śliwiński, M., & Rystwej, D. (2025). SMS and telephone communication as tools to reduce missed medical appointments. *Applied Sciences, 15*(17), 9773. https://doi.org/10.3390/app15179773

Chancellor, S., & De Choudhury, M. (2020). Methods in predictive techniques for mental health status on social media: A critical review. *NPJ Digital Medicine, 3*, 43. https://doi.org/10.1038/s41746-020-0233-7

Columbia University Mailman School of Public Health. (2025, November 3). Suicide prevention in the age of social media and AI. www.publichealth.columbia.edu/news/suicide-prevention-age-social-media-ai?utm_source=copilot.com

Eubanks, V. (2018). *Automating inequality: How high-tech tools profile, police, and punish the poor.* St. Martin's Press.

Green, J. R. (2024). Artificial intelligence in communication sciences and disorders: Introduction to the forum. *Journal of Speech, Language, and Hearing Research, 67*(10), 4157–4161. https://doi.org/10.1044/2024_JSLHR-24-00594

Honcoop, M. (2026). *5 ways AI sentiment engines stop employee burnout.* MeBeBot. www.mebebot.com/post/stop-employee-burnout-ai-sentiment-analysis

Inkster, B., Sarda, S., & Subramanian, V. (2018). An empathy-driven, conversational Artificial Intelligence agent (Wysa) for digital mental well-being: Real-world data evaluation mixed-methods study. *JMIR mHealth and uHealth, 6*(11), e12106. https://doi.org/10.2196/12106

International Society of Substance Use Professionals. (2025, December 10). Artificial intelligence in substance use prevention, treatment, and recovery support: Selected readings and practical insights. www.issup.net/knowledge-share/resources/2025-12/artificial-intelligence-substance-use-prevention-treatment-and

Jharbade, D. R. (2025). Digital therapeutics: Transforming healthcare through AI & emerging technology. *IOSR Journal of Dental and Medical Sciences, 24*(1), 40–49. https://doi.org/10.9790/0853-2401014049

Jones, A., & Fortunato, L. (2023, July 28). *Research roundup: Evidence for digital therapeutics.* www.apaservices.org/practice/ce/expert/digital-therapeutics

Khanna, A., & Khanna, A. (2025). Enhancing therapy through technology: The role of AI in transforming mental health care. *International Journal of Psychology Sciences, 7*(1), 187–196. https://doi.org/10.33545/26648377.2025.v7.i1c.93

Maples-Keller, J. L., Bunnell, B. E., Kim, S. J., & Rothbaum, B. O. (2017). The use of virtual reality technology in the treatment of anxiety and other psychiatric disorders. *Harvard Review of Psychiatry, 25(*3), 103–113. https://doi.org/10.1097/HRP.0000000000000138

Marko, J. G. O., Neagu, C. D., & Anand, P. B. (2025). Examining inclusivity: The use of AI and diverse populations in health and social care—A systematic review. *BMC Medical Informatics and Decision Making, 25*(57). 1–15. https://doi.org/10.1186/s12911-025-02884-1

Mendes, J. P. M., Moura, I. R., Van de Ven, P., Viana, D., Silva, F. J. S., Coutinho, L. R., Teixeira, S., Rodrigues, J. J. P. C., & Teles, A. S. (2022). Sensing apps and public data sets for digital phenotyping of mental health: Systematic review. *Journal of Medical Internet Research, 24*(2), e28735. https://doi.org/10.2196/28735

Nadarzynski, T., Knights, N., Husbands, D., Graham, C.A., Llewellyn, C.D., Buchanan, T., Montgomery, I., & Ridge, D. (2024). Achieving health equity through conversational AI: A roadmap for design and implementation of inclusive chatbots in healthcare. *PLOS Digital Health.* 1–22. https://doi.org/10.1371/journal.pdig.0000492

National Center for Health Workforce Analysis. (2024, November). *State of the behavioral health workforce, 2024.* U.S. Department of Health and Human Services, Health Resources and Services Administration. https://bhw.hrsa.gov/sites/default/files/bureau-health-workforce/state-of-the-health-workforce-report-2024.pdf

Onnela, J. P., & Rauch, S. L. (2016). Harnessing smartphone-based digital phenotyping to enhance behavioral and mental health. *Neuropsychopharmacology, 41*(7), 1691–1696. https://doi.org/10.1038/npp.2016.7

Prochaska, J. J., Vogel, E. A., Chieng, A., Kendra, M., Baiocchi, M., Pajarito, S., & Robinson, A. (2021). A therapeutic relational agent for reducing problematic substance use (Woebot): Development and usability study. *Journal of Medical Internet Research, 23*(3), e24850. https://doi.org/10.2196/24850

Robinson, A., Flom, M., Forman-Hoffman, V. L., Histon, T., Levy, M., Darcy, A., Ajayi, T., Mohr, D. C., Wicks, P., Greene, C., & Montgomery, R. M. (2024). Equity in digital mental health interventions in the United States: Where to next?. *Journal of Medical Internet Research, 26*, e59939. https://doi.org/10.2196/59939

Russ, E., & Reimer, E. C. (2025). Digital intervention for advancing social work and welfare education. *Social Sciences, 14*(1), 50. https://doi.org/10.3390/socsci14010050

Saeidnia, H. R., Hashemi Fotami, S. G., Lund, B., & Ghiasi, N. (2024). Ethical considerations in artificial intelligence interventions for mental health and well-being: Ensuring responsible implementation and impact. *Social Sciences, 13*(7), 381. https://doi.org/10.3390/socsci13070381

Schuerkamp, R., Liang, L., Rice, K. L., & Giabbanelli, P. J. (2023). Simulation models for suicide prevention: A survey of the state-of-the-art. *Computers, 12*(7), 1–15. https://doi.org/10.3390/computers12070132

Shahsavar, Y., & Choudhury, A. (2023). User intentions to use ChatGPT for self-diagnosis and health-related purposes: Cross-sectional survey study. *JMIR Human Factors, 10*, e47564. https://doi.org/10.2196/47564

Substance Abuse and Mental Health Services Administration. (2023). Digital therapeutics for management and treatment in behavioral health. https://library.samhsa.gov/sites/default/files/pep23-06-00-001.pdf

Tung, E. L., Press, V. G., & Peek, M. E. (2024). Digital health readiness and health equity. *JAMA Network Open, 7*(9), e2432733–e2432733. https://doi.org/10.1001/jamanetworkopen.2024.32733

van Loenen, I., Scholten, W., Muntingh, A., Smit, J., & Batelaan, N. (2022). The effectiveness of virtual reality exposure-based cognitive behavioral therapy for severe anxiety disorders, obsessive-compulsive disorder, and posttraumatic stress disorder: Meta-analysis. *Journal of Medical Internet Research, 24*(2), e26736. https://doi.org/10.2196/26736

Worldmetrics. (2026, February 6). AI in the nonprofit industry statistics: Market data report 2026. https://worldmetrics.org/ai-in-the-non-profit-industry-statistics/

10.8 Support Materials

Meet a computer scientist who is building systems to detect suicide ideation in chatbots.

Please access this video at www.routledge.com/9781041275459

Video 10.1 Suicide Prevention Chatbot

11 AI for Older Adults and People with Disabilities

Othelia Lee

11.1 Introduction

Artificial intelligence (AI) is transforming how social workers support older adults, people with disabilities, and their caregivers, offering new tools to enhance independence, safety, and well-being. As populations age and care needs grow, AI-driven innovations, from conversational agents to predictive analytics, are reshaping service delivery across all levels of social work practice, including individual, organizational, and policy levels. These technologies promise improved access to care, personalized interventions, and greater inclusion, yet they also raise critical questions about ethics, equity, and human dignity.

For social work practitioners, understanding AI's potential and limitations is essential when advocating for solutions that empower. Let's explore how AI intersects with direct practice, community engagement, and systemic advocacy, highlighting practical applications and future directions. By examining these developments through a social justice lens, we aim to equip readers with the knowledge and skills to integrate technology responsibly while preserving the core values of human connection and care.

11.2 Micro-Level: AI in Direct Practice with Individuals and Families

At the micro level, AI technologies are being increasingly integrated into direct practice to support older adults and people with disabilities in their daily lives. These tools aim to enhance autonomy, improve health outcomes, and foster meaningful communication while reducing barriers to care.

11.2.1 Conversational AI and Cognitive Training

Box 11.1 AI Companion at Home

Mr. Robinson, a 74-year-old living alone, struggles with mild dementia and often forgets appointments. His social worker introduces a voice-activated

DOI: 10.4324/9781003755081-14

assistant that reminds him of daily tasks and engages him in trivia games to boost memory. At first, he was skeptical, as he finds technology intimidating. Over time, Mr. Robinson reports feeling less isolated and more confident in managing his routine. The social worker monitors his progress and ensures the device respects his privacy settings.

Conversational AI tools, such as chatbots and voice assistants, are increasingly used to support older adults experiencing social isolation or cognitive decline. Natural language processing (NLP) enables AI to provide companionship through empathetic dialogue, deliver reminders for daily tasks, and offer interactive activities that stimulate memory and encourage language use. Social robots and conversational agents appear to reduce loneliness and depressive symptoms while improving cognitive engagement (Lee et al., 2024; Satake et al., 2025). They can provide emotional support through conversation, daily life information such as weather and health, and reminders for appointments and medication.

AI companions are increasingly valued for providing a nonjudgmental space where older adults can express thoughts and feelings, thus mitigating feelings of abandonment and fostering emotional well-being. Qualitative studies further highlight their potential to foster emotional connection and alleviate feelings of isolation when designed with empathy and personalization (Lee & Lee, 2025). By simulating emotional reciprocity and remembering past interactions, these tools align with socioemotional selectivity theory, which posits that older adults prioritize emotionally satisfying and meaningful connections (Irfan et al., 2024).

Evidence from a systematic review and meta-analysis indicates that autonomous conversational agents produce mild to moderate improvements in loneliness and depression among older adults without cognitive impairment, with rarely studies reporting symptoms worsening (Satake et al., 2025; Yang et al., 2025). Group-based robot activities in long-term care settings had a better effect on improving depression than individual-based robot activities, and longer durations of interventions produced significantly more improvement in depression (Yen et al., 2024).

Conversational AI is emerging as a promising tool for cognitive engagement: a proof-of-concept study found that chatbot-administered cognitive status assessments achieved high reliability and validity compared to clinician-led evaluations, suggesting that natural language interaction can support remote cognitive monitoring and stimulation (Serafimovska et al., 2025).

AI-powered cognitive training programs have shown strong evidence for maintaining and enhancing cognitive function in older adults through adaptive, interactive exercises. Randomized and controlled trials (RCTs) demonstrate that tailored computerized cognitive training significantly improves memory, learning, and global cognition compared to controls, with benefits persisting at follow-up (Harvey et al., 2022). Long-term follows ups (ACTIVE trial, NIH studies) show persistent cognitive benefits and even reduced dementia risk decades later (National Institutes of Health, 2026).

Furthermore, the internet-based Conversational Clinical Trial (I-CONECT) showed that frequent, structured conversational engagement improved global cognition and language-based executive function in socially isolated older adults with normal cognition or mild cognitive impairment (Dodge et al., 2023). These findings indicate that conversational AI could replicate and extend such benefits by encouraging language use, memory recall, and social connection through free-form dialogue, while adaptive algorithms personalize cognitive challenges to individual abilities.

Ethical considerations such as transparency, cultural relevance, and user autonomy are essential when integrating AI into social work practice responsibly. Gerontological social workers must assess a client's digital literacy and ensure the AI tool's interface (audio- vs. video-based) is truly usable. The use of AI involves collecting highly sensitive personal information, including speech patterns, emotional cues, and behavioral data. Social workers must advocate for and ensure that AI systems comply with regulations like Health Insurance Portability and Accountability Act (HIPAA) to protect clients (Irfan et al., 2024).

When using chatbots, one fear is that excessive emotional attachment and overdependence may reduce opportunities for interaction with other people which may eventually lead to arbitrary social isolation. Berridge and colleagues (2023) identified a host of ethical concerns, including the potential reduction in human contact, loss of control, privacy, and liberty, deception, and infantilization. To prevent such ethical problems, social workers should guide robots to operate at a complementary level rather than as a substitute for human social relationships. Promoting strict self-determination, we must also continuously collect users' opinions by operating a feedback channel so that users may easily express their opinions if they feel uncomfortable or judge that ethical issues have arisen while using robots.

11.2.2 Service Robots

Box 11.2 Service Robots

Lena, a 78-year-old with severe arthritis, receives a service robot through a community program. The robot assists with cooking and fetching items, allowing Lena to remain in her home rather than moving to a nursing home. Her social worker checks in regularly to ensure Lena feels comfortable and emotionally supported, addressing concerns about loneliness and reinforcing the importance of human connection alongside technological assistance.

Service robots in eldercare are often categorized by the specific functional need. Mobility robots, such as smart walkers and wheelchairs, help older adults navigate safely within their homes or care facilities by enhancing safe movement in daily activities (Lau & Mombaur, 2024). Designed to reduce strain on healthcare workers, lifting robots and exoskeletons assist in tasks such as sit-to-stand transfers and mobility support, helping prevent musculoskeletal injuries in both staff and residents (Perera et al., 2024). Meal and medication management robots ensure basic needs are met by delivering meals, providing water, or dispensing medication at precise times, often using facial recognition to ensure the right person receives the dose.

AI functions as the "brain" that enables these systems to become adaptive service robots. **Computer vision** allows robots to interpret their environment and assists with fall detection and prevention. Through machine learning, robots can recognize and adapt to resident routines, supporting personalized assistance (Riahi et al., 2025). Sensors like infrared and acoustic detectors can monitor movement patterns to alert staff to potential risks like falls or deviations from normal activity, providing safety monitoring without requiring invasive wearable devices.

A pilot study on home-based robotic rehabilitation for people with disabilities showed that using exercise-therapy devices for both upper and lower limbs not only improved upper-extremity function (a key component of self-care and household tasks) but also led to a meaningful reduction in caregiver burden (Lee et al., 2025). Similarly, Jung et al. (2024) found that care robots designed to assist with transfers, feeding, and toileting significantly decreased caregivers' physical strain, muscle load, and pain.

Research on assistive robots used in daily living tasks echoes these benefits. Olatunji et al. (2025) demonstrated the effectiveness of the Stretch robot, a mobile manipulator that helps with activities such as picking up objects and delivering items around the home. Users emphasized how robots enhanced their sense of independence and safety during everyday routines. In Norway, Sørensen and colleagues (2024) explored how individuals with physical disabilities perceive humanoid assistive robots. Through qualitative interviews, participants described robots as tools that could meaningfully support autonomy and independence in daily tasks.

Yet these advantages come with important ethical considerations. An observational study in Japanese nursing homes found that the introduction of the robot "Hugs" reduced the amount of face-to-face interaction and conversation residents had with human caregivers (Wright, 2023). Users of the meal-assistance robot "My Spoon" reported feelings of self-shame, expressing that the device made them feel more incompetent than when receiving help from a caregiver (Sharkey & Sharkey, 2012). These concerns highlight the need for thoughtful, ethical implementation.

As Hung and associates (2025) emphasize, assistive technologies must uphold clients' autonomy and dignity, even when their purpose is to provide emotional comfort. Even with conversational robots, social workers must remain attentive to issues such as deception (for example, allowing a client to believe a robot is a real pet) and infantilization (using overly cutesy or child-like technologies with adults).

11.2.3 Therapeutic Algorithms and Personalized Wellness Programs

> **Box 11.3 Digital Wellness Tools**
>
> Cheryl, a 65-year-old with diabetes and limited mobility, uses an AI-powered wellness app recommended by her social worker. The app tailors her diet and exercise plan based on real-time glucose readings and activity levels. When Cheryl's mood score declines, the app suggests mindfulness exercises and alerts her social worker, who follows up with supportive counseling. This integration has improved Cheryl's health outcomes while maintaining a human-centered approach.

AI is revolutionizing personalized care by using therapeutic algorithms to analyze health data and create individualized wellness plans. These plans often include exercise routines, nutrition guidance, and mental health interventions tailored to each client's unique needs. Where traditional health plans were as fixed as "walk 30 minutes every day," AI-driven systems adapt dynamically, responding to changes in mobility, mood, or chronic conditions. For example, if wearable sensors detect decreased physical activity or elevated blood pressure, the algorithm can adjust its exercise recommendations or prompt a telehealth consultation.

Du and colleagues (2025) highlighted AI's role in chronic disease management, including real-time decision support and conversational agents that encourage medication adherence and healthy behaviors. In diabetes care, machine learning models predict hypoglycemia hours in advance by utilizing continuous glucose-monitoring data, enabling timely interventions and reducing complications (Giammarino et al., 2024; Shao et al., 2024). These predictive capabilities allow systems to adjust dietary and activity recommendations dynamically, contributing to measurable improvements in outcomes (e.g., hemoglobin A1c and body mass index).

Tan and associates (2024) showed that AI-generated exercise prescriptions improved mental health and adherence when compared to traditional plans. Mental health interventions are also evolving with causal AI recommendation systems. This analysis identifies optimal intervention targets by examining relationships among psychological distress, physical activity, nutrition, and sleep, ensuring that care plans are truly personalized and evidence based (Varidel et al., 2025).

Social workers can use the progress-monitoring features of these tools to track client adherence, enhancing the collaborative care process. However, **algorithmic bias** remains a concern, particularly if training data underrepresents certain populations, leading to inaccurate recommendations. Informed consent must be prioritized, ensuring clients understand what data is collected, how it is used, and who has access. Privacy safeguards and cultural sensitivity should guide implementation, especially when interventions involve intimate health behaviors. Social workers must play a critical role in interpreting algorithmic output, contextualizing recommendations within clients' lived experiences, and advocating for equitable access to these technologies.

11.2.4 Integration of Telehealth and In-Home Care

Box 11.4 Remote Healthcare

Carlos, a 70-year-old stroke survivor, lives alone but uses an AI-enabled telehealth system with motion sensors and wearable devices. When the system detects irregular heart rhythms and reduced movement, it sends alerts to his healthcare team. The social worker coordinates an emergency response and later discusses preventive strategies with Carlos and his family, ensuring technology supports his care.

AI-powered telehealth systems are not just monitoring tools: they represent a shift toward proactive care. Wearable **biosensors** and ambient in-home **sensor networks**, when combined with AI-driven algorithms, facilitate the remote, continuous monitoring of physiological and behavioral metrics. Del-Valle-Soto and associates (2024) implemented a low-cost wireless sensor network combined with AI in older adults' homes to monitor vital signs (e.g., heart rate, respiratory rate, and temperature, sleep quality). Beyond chronic disease, AI-enabled sensor networks and smart-home technologies enhance safety for older adults and individuals with disabilities.

Wearable biosensors and ambient sensors monitor physiological and behavioral patterns in home care, detecting deviations like nighttime wandering or prolonged inactivity, early indicators of falls or medical emergencies. In a review article, Tian et al. (2024) reports that these systems reduce fall incidents by issuing real-time alerts to caregivers and clinicians, enabling rapid intervention. They also improve medication adherence through smart pillboxes and reminder apps, reducing complications from polypharmacy. By analyzing real-time data streams, these platforms can identify potential emergencies, such as falls or cardiac events, before they occur.

In contrast, Umar (2025) warned of emerging threats posed by AI-generated deepfake audio and video in financial scams. Synthetic voices and videos may exploit personal data to create highly convincing fraud scenarios that disproportionately increase vulnerability among older adults. Social workers play a critical role in advocating for equitable access to these technologies, educating families about benefits and limitations, and ensuring that privacy safeguards are in place.

11.3 Mezzo-Level: AI in Organizational and Community Interventions

At the mezzo level, AI technologies are transforming how organizations and communities design, deliver, and evaluate services for older adults and people with disabilities. As we discussed in child welfare and mental health, these tools enable nonprofits, healthcare agencies, and community programs to analyze data, automate outreach, and create immersive experiences that foster inclusion.

11.3.1 Nonprofit Data Analytics for Service Planning

By analyzing demographic data, health indicators, and social determinants, nonprofits can design programs that respond to emerging challenges such as isolation or chronic illness among older adults. Seaman and colleagues (2022) conducted a systematic review of predictive fall models that utilized routinely collected electronic health record (EHR) data in aged care settings. The study found that such AI-driven models can accurately identify high-risk individuals and inform targeted prevention strategies. The findings underscore how community-serving organizations, such as rural aging services and nonprofits, can deploy AI analytics to detect local fall-risk trends and guide interventions like home safety assessments, thereby reducing hospitalization rates and improving resource allocation.

An empirical study developed a **Machine Learning-based Fall-Risk Score** (ML-FRS) using a large dataset from community-dwelling older adults (Chen et al., 2025). The ML-FRS effectively stratified risk, finding that participants in the highest risk quartile had a significantly higher risk of recurrent falls and falls requiring treatment (a proxy for hospitalization). The authors explicitly state this ML-FRS can be used to screen for fall risk and fall-related adverse outcomes in the community, enabling earlier intervention (e.g., targeted workshops and home safety assessments) to improve outcomes and potentially reduce treatment-related costs and hospitalizations.

11.3.2 Assistive Technology and Immersive Virtual Reality

Let's explore assistive technology tools that empower individuals with disabilities to handle daily tasks independently, like typing, web browsing, and smart-home control, without relying on others. AI-powered "Digital Bridge" encompasses a suite of assistive technologies that bridge this gap by enabling access and control through adaptive interfaces. Examples that assist people with limited dexterity include adaptive keyboards with larger keys, voice control systems such as Apple's Voice Control or Dragon NaturallySpeaking, and switch systems that are triggered by breath or minimal movement. Eye-tracking devices enable users to navigate a tablet or computer using only their gaze (MobilityWorks, 2025).

Aira is a groundbreaking AI-powered app offering real-time visual interpretation for people who are blind or have low vision. Users connect via smartphone or smart glasses to a live, certified visual interpreter who provides spoken descriptions of the surroundings: they can help locate a missing item, read menus, or navigate unfamiliar spaces. In 2024, Aira introduced Access AI, enabling users to take or upload photos for which they receive instant AI-generated descriptions that the interpreter can verify, ensuring accuracy and trust. This approach is human-centered: while AI enhances immediacy, trained interpreters validate output and offer empathic support. This service fosters independence by offering both immediate visual information and a compassionate human presence (Aira Tech Corp. 2024).

Virtual reality (VR) is a technology that immerses users in a completely virtual three-dimensional environment. These immersive AI experiences offer innovative ways to reduce isolation and enhance social participation. What if we could help people with mobility impairment to travel, transcending geographical and temporal boundaries? **Immersive Virtual Reality** (IVR) is a computer-generated environment that users can explore and interact with, giving them a strong sense of presence, or "being there."

Older adults and people with disabilities can use VR to attend virtual support groups, explore cultural events, or practice daily living skills in a safe environment. VR-based virtual gatherings, clubs, and communities can be used to activate social interaction by meeting people with the same interests, hobbies, or beliefs. In addition to the actual appearance, communication is possible through voice chat or via an avatar. Non-face-to-face interaction is also possible in connection with community centers.

Virtual museum tours and interactive games can foster increased social interaction and cognitive stimulation. A randomized controlled trial conducted by Beauchet and colleagues (2022) examined the effects of a three-month program that consisted of weekly virtual museum tours on community-dwelling older adults. Participants who used the VR system reported being less socially isolated and less likely to show signs of depression compared to a control group who viewed the same content on a television screen (Chaze et al., 2022).

A proprietary platform like "Rendever" uses networking technology to allow users in different locations to share the same experience simultaneously, promoting group bonding and shared moments. This example emphasizes how AI can strengthen organizational capacity and community engagement while maintaining a human-centered approach. Social workers must critically evaluate these tools for inclusivity, cultural relevance, and ethical use.

11.3.3 Multimodal Technology in Group and Family Work

We introduced the concept of **multimodal technology**, the integration of different forms of media, such as text, images, audio, and video, within an AI system. Social workers are uniquely positioned to leverage this technology to enhance the relational and therapeutic aspects of practice, particularly in challenging situations like end of life.

In palliative care, social workers facilitate deeply sensitive and emotionally taxing family meetings. These sessions are crucial for resolving conflicts, sharing memories, and preparing for loss. AI-powered multimodal technology offers a sensitive way to create enduring keepsakes for grieving families. With the informed consent of all family members, these "final" meetings can be professionally recorded. AI technology can then be used to convert the raw footage and audio into carefully curated, structured multimedia formats. When families provide photographs, written narratives, or voice recordings, an AI system can weave these elements together.

For instance, it could convert a collection of photos into a thematic video montage or use NLP to generate a summary of shared stories for a family's bereavement process. By creating these compassionate, personalized souvenirs, social workers help secure shared memories and sources of comfort for the surviving family members, directly aligning with the social work mandate to promote collective well-being.

Group work focused on reminiscence or life review is a staple in gerontological social work and mental health. These interventions help older adults find meaning, process their past, and establish a cohesive life narrative. Multimodal AI can be a powerful tool in this context. Social workers can guide the group in using multimodal technology to generate sentimental artifacts. By providing AI with a few details about a participant's childhood (e.g., a specific year, a location, or an event), AI tools could generate historically accurate-looking images of a past neighborhood or significant cultural moment. It can also create playlists of popular music from a specific decade or historical soundscape.

Multimodal technology can significantly reduce the burden of writing a full autobiography. NLP tools can take voice recordings of a client's stories and automatically transcribe, organize, and summarize them, allowing the older adult to focus solely on the telling rather than the writing. This process empowers the client and supports their self-determination.

11.4 Macro-Level: AI in Systems, Policy, and Advocacy

At the macro level, AI is influencing social policy, accessibility standards, and advocacy strategies for older adults and people with disabilities. These technologies enable governments, coalitions, and advocacy groups to predict trends, design inclusive policies, and mobilize civic engagement. Social workers must critically examine how AI-driven systems impact equity, privacy, and human rights, ensuring that technological progress aligns with social justice principles.

11.4.1 Predictive Analytics in Social Policy

Imagine having a crystal ball that predicts where and when social support is most needed. This is the power of **Predictive Analytics** in the age of AI, transforming macro-level social work by moving us from reactive crisis management to proactive prevention. AI models leverage large-scale data, from health records to geographic and communication patterns, to forecast critical needs for older adults and people with disabilities.

For instance, by analyzing factors like declining hospital use and reduced community participation for those living alone, AI can detect the risk of social isolation and potential emergencies before a crisis occurs. This allows local governments to launch targeted interventions, such as face-to-face check-ins and counseling referrals.

Furthermore, predictive insights enable equitable resource allocation. For rapidly aging regions, AI can forecast the demand for visiting nurses and mobile care, ensuring resources are expanded proactively. These models also pinpoint specific "vulnerable areas" where fall risks are high, or healthcare access is limited. Social workers can use these predictions to advocate for policy changes focused on home safety programs and expanded telehealth, ensuring our interventions are effective and human-centered.

Lin et al. (2025) used machine learning to develop predictive models for fall risk among urban and rural older adults. While this study was conducted in China, its methodology and findings regarding geographic disparity are highly applicable to global context concerning rural and urban disparities, which often correlates with access to care for minority groups. Researchers developed separate predictive models for urban and rural older adults, finding that the key factors influencing falls differed significantly between the two settings. For example, living in a tidy environment was found to be a protective factor in the urban group, while factors like certain chronic conditions were more influential in rural residents.

This finding empirically supports the need for policy interventions (e.g., expanding home safety programs and telehealth) to be customized and targeted based on the predictive model's geographical insight, rather than applying a "one-size-fits-all" program that would fail the areas with unique risk factors. The fact that different models were needed for different geographical cohorts demonstrates that if a single, general model were used, one of the groups (e.g., the rural population) would be systematically disadvantaged by having a less accurate risk prediction, thereby supporting the social work mandate for an algorithm audit to ensure performance equity across groups.

11.4.2 Civic Tech and Advocacy for Accessibility

Advocacy and technology are core strategies used by the disability community to advance rights. **Civic technology platforms** powered by AI help advocacy groups mobilize communities, track legislative changes, and promote accessibility standards. These tools can analyze policy proposals, identify gaps in disability rights, and connect stakeholders so they may take collective action.

Supposed that a national disability rights coalition uses an AI-driven civic tech platform to monitor accessibility legislation across states. When the system flags a proposed bill that could weaken housing accessibility requirements, the coalition can launch a digital campaign, sending automated alerts to supporters and enabling virtual town halls. Social workers can lead these advocacy efforts, ensuring that technology amplifies marginalized voices rather than silencing them.

How can macro-level social work intervention utilize modern civic technology and align with the core competencies and ethical mandates for social workers in the age of AI? Combaz and colleagues (2025) present case studies from civic tech platforms like Make.org and MAPLE that use AI to summarize legislative content, issue real-time updates, and support equitable public engagement. Their study highlights AI's role in making policy accessible, facilitating expression, triggering alerts, and supporting deliberative advocacy, paralleling the coalition's use of virtual town halls and digital campaigns.

Platforms exist that use proprietary AI technology to analyze, filter, and track massive amount of bills introduced across state legislatures. This technology is designed for advocacy coalitions to instantly surface bills that impact their priorities and deliver actionable intelligence at scale. The practice of legislative tracking platforms working in conjunction with public engagement features (e.g., enabling messages to representatives) is a proven use case for citizen-led parliamentary monitoring and civic technology for social innovation. Digital media is a crucial tool for advocacy as it has demonstrated its ability to amplify marginalized voices, counter narratives, and mobilize collective action through means like social media alerts and other electronic communication.

Let's consider an "ideal" scenario for developing policy reforms that promote disability justice using AI. First, federal, state, and local governments should systematically assess the needs and barriers of people with disabilities concerning AI access and use. This foundational step ensures policies reflect lived experiences and promote inclusive AI procurement and deployment. Such mandates for AI systems in public services (e.g., the courts, benefits, scheduling) require regular audits to detect and correct bias (National Science and Technology Council, 2023).

Community needs assessments call for creating dedicated offices within state and federal agencies responsible for ensuring AI tools comply with accessibility and nondiscrimination standards. These offices should also maintain "sandbox" environments to safely pilot novel AI systems before large-scale rollout. Predictive models may be used to anticipate regional and demographic shifts in health and long-term care needs and allocate resources proactively to areas with high fall risks, healthcare shortages, or transportation challenges (World Health Organization, 2023).

AI-Enabled Civic Technology for Advocacy can support platforms that flag threats to accessibility rights, track legislation related to disability services, and enable rapid advocacy. AI-powered alerts and engagement tools can mobilize public response when policies undermine inclusion. Additionally, AI tools used in employment, benefits, healthcare, or housing should announce at AI is being used, should allow individuals to opt out, and should provide pathways for human review under the Americans with Disabilities Act.

To incentivize digital literacy, funding should be provided for educational programs that empower people with disabilities, and caregivers with digital skills and an understanding of algorithmic systems to foster informed consent, effective adoption, and advocacy. To bridge the digital divide, grants should be offered to under-resourced regions to assist them in developing their own AI infrastructure, with tools such as accessible telehealth, home monitoring sensors, and AI-enabled accessibility platforms.

Finally, governments must implement strict licensing and transparency standards for companies developing AI that directly impacts vulnerable populations. The report system should require them to disclose performance metrics, bias-testing, and accessibility compliance (OECD, 2024). These reforms aim to embed equity, accessibility, and human rights at the intersection of AI, aging, and disability policy, ensuring AI serves as a force for empowerment and justice in social welfare systems.

11.5 Reflections and Future Directions

The integration of AI into services for older adults and people with disabilities is still in its early stages, but its trajectory suggests profound changes are coming to how care is delivered and experienced. Future developments will likely include more sophisticated conversational agents capable of emotional intelligence, predictive health models that anticipate crises before they occur, and advanced robotics that support independent living. VR and immersive technologies may become standard tools for combating isolation and enhancing cognitive engagement, while civic technology platforms will empower advocacy on a large scale.

These innovations bring ethical challenges that must not be ignored. Issues of algorithmic bias, data privacy, and equitable access remain central concerns. Social workers must lead efforts to ensure that AI systems are transparent, culturally responsive, and designed with human rights at their core. The profession's commitment to social justice positions practitioners as critical voices in shaping policy, guiding implementation, and educating communities about responsible technology use. By combining technological innovation with relational practice, social workers can ensure that personalized care remains both effective and ethically grounded.

11.6 Critical Thinking Questions

1 How can conversational AI tools reduce social isolation without replacing human relationships?
2 Personalized wellness programs rely on data. How should social workers address privacy and informed consent when using these tools?
3 Telehealth and in-home monitoring can improve safety, but what are the implications for autonomy and surveillance?
4 Service robots can assist with daily activities. How might their use impact the emotional well-being and caregiver roles?
5 VR and immersive tools can reduce isolation. What ethical considerations should guide their use in community programs?
6 Predictive analytics can inform policy decisions. How do we balance efficiency with fairness when using these tools?
7 Civic tech platforms amplify advocacy efforts. How can social workers ensure these tools empower marginalized voices rather than reinforce inequities?

11.7 Summary

We examined the role of AI in supporting older adults and individuals with disabilities across micro, mezzo, and macro levels. AI offers unprecedented opportunities to enhance autonomy, safety, and inclusion for older adults and people with disabilities to be independent. Yet its promise will only be realized if social workers actively engage in governance, advocate for equity, and maintain the human connection that defines quality care. The future of care in the age of AI is not about replacing relationships with machines: it is about leveraging technology to strengthen those relationships and uphold the values of dignity, empowerment, and justice. Now that we discussed potential AI use across various areas of social work practice, let's consider how we can cultivate human-centered AI.

11.8 Empowerment-Focused Activities

11.8.1 Role-Play: AI in Direct Practice

Scenario: A social worker introduces a voice-activated assistant to an older adult experiencing mild cognitive decline.

Assign Roles:

- Social Worker: Explain benefits and address privacy concerns.
- Client: Express fears about technology and ask questions.

Objective: Practice building trust, explaining AI in plain language, and ensuring informed consent.

11.8.2 Organizational Decision-Making

Scenario: A nonprofit board is debating whether to invest in AI-driven outreach automation.

Roles:

- Social Worker: Advocate for ethical implementation and cultural sensitivity.
- Executive Director: Focus on cost and efficiency.
- Community Representative: Raise concerns about accessibility for rural clients.

Objective: Negotiate a balanced decision that prioritizes equity and inclusion.

11.8.3 Policy Advocacy

Scenario: A legislative hearing on a proposed bill requiring algorithm audits for eldercare AI systems.

Roles:

- Social Worker: Present arguments for transparency and fairness.
- Policymaker: Question feasibility and costs.
- Disability Rights Advocate: Highlight risks of bias and exclusion.

Objective: Develop persuasive advocacy skills and articulate social justice principles in policy debates.

11.8.4 Ethical Dilemmas

Scenario: A hospital plans to replace some human caregivers with service robots to cut costs.

Roles:

- Social Worker: Argue for maintaining human-centered care.
- Hospital Administrator: Defend cost-saving measures.
- Older Adult Family Member: Express emotional concerns.

Objective: Explore ethical tensions between efficiency and dignity and propose alternative solutions.

References

Aira(2024). *AI app feature for visually impaired people provides detailed image descriptions..* https://aira.io/media-article/ai-app-feature-for-visually-impaired-people-provides-detailed-image-descriptions/

Beauchet, O., Matskiv, J., Galery, K., Goossens, L., Lafontaine, C., & Sawchuk, K. (2022). Benefits of a 3-month cycle of weekly virtual museum tours in community-dwelling older adults: Results of a randomized controlled trial. *Frontiers in Medicine, 9.* 1–9. https://doi.org/10.3389/fmed.2022.969122

Berridge, C., Zhou, Y., Robillard, J. M., & Kaye, J. (2023). Companion robots to mitigate loneliness among older adults: Perceptions of benefit and possible deception. *Frontiers in Psychology, 14*, 1106633. https://doi.org/10.3389/fpsyg.2023.1106633

Chaze, F., Hayden, L., Azevedo, A., Kamath, A., Bucko, D., Kashlan, Y., Dube, M., De Paula, J., Jackson, A., Reyna, C., Dupuis, K., & Tsotsos, L. (2022). Virtual reality and well-being in older adults: Results from a pilot implementation of virtual reality in long-term care. *Journal of Rehabilitation and Assistive Technologies Engineering, 9*, 20556683211072384. https://doi.org/10.1177/20556683211072384

Chen, H., Ling, T., Huang, L., Wang, L., Guan, X., Gao, M., Wang, Z., Lan, W., Xu, J. W., & Wei, Z. (2025). A machine learning-based fall-risk score for severity of fall-related adverse outcomes in community older adults. *BMC Geriatrics, 25*(1), 724. https://doi.org/10.1186/s12877-025-06371-0

Combaz, A., Mas, D., Sanders, N., & Victor, M. (2025). Applications of artificial intelligence tools to enhance legislative engagement: Case studies from Make.org and MAPLE. *ArXiv* Preprint. https://doi.org/10.48550/arXiv.2503.04769

Del-Valle-Soto, C., Briseño, R. A., Velázquez, R., Guerra-Rosales, G., Perez-Ochoa, S., Preciado-Bazavilvazo, I. H., Visconti, P., & Varela-Aldás, J. (2024). Enhancing elderly care through low-cost wireless sensor networks and artificial intelligence: A study on vital sign monitoring and sleep improvement. *Future Internet, 16*(9), 323. https://doi.org/10.3390/fi16090323

Dodge, H. H., Yu, K., Wu, C.-Y., Pruitt, P. J., Asgari, M., Kaye, J. A., Hampstead, B. M., Struble, L., Potempa, K., Lichtenberg, P., Croff, R., Albin, R. L., Silbert, L. C., & The I-CONECT Team. (2023). Internet-based conversational engagement randomized controlled clinical trial (I-CONECT) among socially isolated adults 75+ years old with normal cognition or mild cognitive impairment: Topline results. *The Gerontologist, 64*(4), gnad147. https://doi.org/10.1093/geront/gnad147

Du, Y., Yang, P., Liu, Y., Deng, C., & Li, X. (2025). Artificial intelligence in chronic disease self-management: Current applications and future directions. *Frontiers in Public Health, 13*. 1–11. https://doi.org/10.3389/fpubh.2025.1689911

Giammarino, F., Senanayake, R., Prahalad, P., Maahs, D. M., & Scheinker, D. (2024). A machine learning model for week-ahead hypoglycemia prediction from continuous glucose monitoring data. *Journal of Diabetes Science and Technology, 19*(5), 1353–1361. https://doi.org/10.1177/19322968241236208

Harvey, P.D., Zayas-Bazan, M., Tibiriçá, L., Kallestrup, P., & Czaja, S.J. (2022). Improvements in cognitive performance with computerized training in older people with and without cognitive impairment: Synergistic effects of skills-focused and cognitive-focused strategies. *The American Journal of Geriatric Psychiatry, 30*(6), 717–726. https://doi.org/10.1016/j.jagp.2021

Hung, L., Zhao, Y., Alfares, H., & Shafiekhani, P. (2025). Ethical considerations in the use of social robots for supporting mental health and wellbeing in older adults in long-term care. *Frontiers in Robotics and AI, 12*, 1560214. https://doi.org/10.3389/frobt.2025.1560214

Irfan, B., Kuoppamäki, S., & Skantze, G. (2024). Recommendations for designing conversational companion robots with older adults through foundation models. *Frontiers in Robotics and AI, 11*. 1–19. https://doi.org/10.3389/frobt.2024.1363713

Jung, J. I., Jeong, Y. S., & Kwon, D. R. (2024). The effectiveness of care robots in alleviating physical burden and pain for caregivers: Non-randomized prospective interventional study – Preliminary study. *Medicine, 103*(50), e40877. https://doi.org/10.1097/MD.0000000000040877

Lau, J. C. L., & Mombaur, K. (2024). Can lower-limb exoskeletons support sit-to-stand motions in frail elderly without crutches? *Frontiers in Neurorobotics. 18*, 1–14. https://doi.org/10.3389/fnbot.2024.1348029

Lee, J., Lee, E., Hong, S., Shin, S., & Ryu, B. (2025). The effect of home-based robotic rehabilitation on individuals with disabilities in community settings: A pilot study. *Healthcare, 13*(1), 78. https://doi.org/10.3390/healthcare13010078

Lee, O. E., & Lee, E. (2025). Investigating how older Korean immigrants construct meaning with a companion robot: A narrative analysis of user experiences. *International Journal of Human-Computer Interaction, 41*(5), 3259–3269. https://doi.org/10.1080/10447318.2024.2334124

Lee, O. E., Nah, K., Kim, E. M., Choi, N. G., & Park, D.-H. (2024). Exploring the use of socially assistive robot among socially isolated Korean American older adults. *Journal of Applied Gerontology, 43*(9), 1295–1304. https://doi.org/10.1177/07334648241236081

Lin, L., Liu, X., Cai, C., Zheng, Y., Li, D., & Hu, G. (2025). Urban–rural disparities in fall risk among older Chinese adults: Insights from machine learning-based predictive models. *Frontiers in Public Health, 13*, 1597853. https://doi.org/10.3389/fpubh.2025.1597853

MobilityWorks. (2025). *Assistive technology for people with limited mobility and dexterity*. MobilityWorks. https://www.mobilityworks.com

National Institutes of Health. (2026). Cognitive speed training over weeks may delay the diagnosis of dementia over decades. www.nih.gov/news-events/news-releases/cognitive-speed-training-over-weeks-may-delay-diagnosis-dementia-over-decades

National Science and Technology Council, Select Committee on Artificial Intelligence. (2023). *National artificial intelligence research and development strategic plan: 2023 update*. Office of Science and Technology Policy. www.nitrd.gov/pubs/National-Artificial-Intelligence-Research-and-Development-Strategic-Plan-2023-Update.pdf

OECD. (2024). *AI Principles*. OECD. www.oecd.org/en/topics/ai-principles.html

Olatunji, S. A., Shim, J. S., Syed, A., Tsai, Y.-L., Pereira, A. E., Mahajan, H. P., Mudar, R. A., & Rogers, W. A. (2025). Robotic support for older adults with cognitive and mobility impairments. *Frontiers in Robotics and AI, 12.* 1–15. https://doi.org/10.3389/frobt.2025.1545733

Perera, C. K., Gopalai, A. A., Gouwanda, D., & Nurzaman, S. G. (2024). A focused review on soft robotic exosuits for sitting to standing transfers. *Robotics Reports, 2*(1). 65–84. https://doi.org/10.1089/rorep.2023.0025

Riahi, T., Bappy, M. A. H., & Islam, M. M. (2025). ElderFallGuard: Real-time IoT and computer vision-based fall detection system for elderly safety. arXiv. https://arxiv.org/html/2505.11845v1

Satake, Y., Costello, H., Naran, N., Ishimaru, D., Ikeda, M., & Howard, R. (2025). Autonomous conversational agents for loneliness, social isolation, depression and anxiety in older people without cognitive impairment: Systematic review and meta-analysis. *medRxiv.* https://doi.org/10.1101/2025.10.15.25338078

Seaman, K., Ludlow, K., Wabe, N., Dodds, L., Siette, J., Nguyen, A., Jorgensen, M., Lord, S. R., Close, J. C. T., O'Toole, L., Lin, C., Eymael, A., & Westbrook, J. (2022). The use of predictive fall models for older adults receiving aged care, using routinely collected electronic health record data: A systematic review. *BMC Geriatrics, 22*, 210. https://doi.org/10.1186/s12877-022-02901-2

Serafimovska, A., Swavley, K., Zhang Qian Ao, A., Challinor, K. L., & Florio, T. (2025). Cognitive status assessment of older adults—test administration by conversational artificial intelligence (AI) chatbot: Proof-of-concept investigation. *Journal of Clinical and Experimental Neuropsychology, 47*(5), 472–484. https://doi.org/10.1080/13803395.2025.2542248

Shao, J., Pan, Y., Kou, W.-B., Feng, H., Zhao, Y., Zhou, K., & Zhong, S. (2024). Generalization of a deep learning model for continuous glucose monitoring–based hypoglycemia prediction: Algorithm development and validation study. *JMIR Medical Informatics, 12*. 1–10. https://medinform.jmir.org/2024/1/e56909

Sharkey, A. & Sharkey, N. (2012). Granny and the robots: Ethical issues in robot care for the elderly. *Ethics and Information Technology, 14*, 27–40. https://doi.org/10.1007/s10676-010-9234-6

Sørensen, L., Johannesen, D. T., Melkas, H., & Johnsen, H. M. (2024). Care-receivers with physical disabilities' perceptions on having humanoid assistive robots as assistants: A qualitative study. *BMC Health Services Research, 24*(523). 1–14 https://doi.org/10.1186/s12913-024-10857-9

Tan, M., Xiao, Y., Jing, F., Xie, Y., Lu, S., Xiang, M., & Ren, H. (2024). Evaluating machine learning-enabled and multimodal data-driven exercise prescriptions for mental health: A randomized controlled trial protocol. *Frontiers in Psychiatry, 15,* 1352420. https://doi.org/10.3389/fpsyt.2024.1352420

Tian, Y. J. (A.), Felber, N. A., Pageau, F., Roulet Schwab, D., & Wangmo, T. (2024). Benefits and barriers associated with the use of smart home health technologies in the care of older persons: A systematic review. *BMC Geriatrics, 24*, 152. https://doi.org/10.1186/s12877-024-04702-1

Umar, M. (2025). Digital trauma: Deepfake victimisation and AI-generated violence. *The Lancet. Psychiatry.* S2215-0366(25)00275-5. Advance online publication. https://doi.org/10.1016/S2215-0366(25)00275-5

Varidel, M., An, V., Hickie, I. B., Cripps, S., Marchant, R., Scott J., Crouse J. J., Poulsen A., O'Dea B., McKenna S., & Iorfino F. (2025). Causal AI recommendation system for digital mental health: Bayesian decision-theoretic analysis. *Journal of Medical Internet Research, 27*, e71305. https://doi.org/10.2196/71305

World Health Organization. (2023). *Global report on aging and health technology*. WHO.

Wright, J. (2023, January 9). *Inside Japan's long experiment in automating elder care.* MIT Technology Review. www.technologyreview.com/2023/01/09/1065135/japan-automating-eldercare-robots

Yang, Y., Wang, C., Xiang, X., & An, R. (2025). AI applications to reduce loneliness among older adults: A systematic review of effectiveness and technologies. *Healthcare, 13*(5), 446. https://doi.org/10.3390/healthcare13050446

Yen, H.-Y., Huang, C. W., Chiu, H.-L., & Jin, G. (2024). The effect of social robots on depression and loneliness for older residents in long-term care facilities: A meta-analysis of randomized controlled trials. *Journal of the American Medical Directors Association, 25*(6), 104979. https://doi.org/10.1016/j.jamda.2024.02.017

11.9 Support Materials

Lee, O. E. (2023, May 10). Would you talk to a robot when you feel lonely? |*TEDxUNCCharlotte* [Video]. YouTube. www.youtube.com/watch?v=k-SxUMNdlFA

You can watch how socially isolated older immigrants interacted with companion robots.

Part IV

Empowerment and Building Competencies

12 Human-Centered AI Design for the Common Good

Moon Sun Song and Othelia E. Lee

12.1 Introduction

We might ask: what happens when a novice competes with an expert? Popular culture often celebrates the underdog, like the biblical story of David and Goliath. But new artificial intelligence (AI) tools move us beyond speculation by making these comparisons dynamic and data-informed. To honor Serena Williams' retirement, Nike (2022) used AI to analyze years of her performance data and simulate a match between 17-year-old Serena in her early career and her present-day self.

Previously, we explored how deepfake technologies can pose serious risks to individuals and communities. Yet the same technologies that can be used to create harm can also be reimagined for protection and empowerment. One example is "Daisy," a 78-year-old "grandmother" persona developed as an AI voice agent to engage scam callers (O2, 2024). Daisy keeps scammers occupied in harmless conversation, reducing the likelihood that real, older adults become targets. Daisy illustrates how human-like, empathetic AI can be intentionally designed to safeguard vulnerable populations rather than exploit them.

Please access video 12.1 at www.routledge.com/9781041275459

Video 12.1 Human-Centered AI Created by a Social Worker

We would like to introduce Sensory Experience Integration, Immersion, and Representation (SEIIR www.routledge.com/9781041275459) as a prime example of human-centered AI (HCAI) created by a social worker (S.E.W. Gonzalez, personal communication, January 28, 2026). This research-driven methodology and software-supported workflow can embed authentic first-person sensory experience and accessibility directly into the creation of media, research artifacts, and digital narratives. Readers can watch how Dr. Gonzalez uses AI as supportive and amplifying tools. This SEIIR approach has excellent implications for disability justice, trauma-informed care, migration narratives, and community-based storytelling.

This kind of **Human-Centered AI (HCAI)** supports empowerment, self-reflection, and the enhancement of human potential, not by replacing people, but by helping them understand themselves. Let's consider how we can apply the

DOI: 10.4324/9781003755081-16

principles of HCAI to enhance client engagement, ethical decision-making, and service delivery in social work practice.

12.2 Principles of Human-Centered Design

AI integration in social work must advance the common good, guided by three principles: equitable access, relational integrity, and human autonomy (Reamer, 2025). **Equitable access** means building inclusive systems (such as those with multilingual tools and accessibility features) and auditing for bias to protect marginalized communities. **Relational integrity** ensures that AI enhances, rather than replaces, the human connection central to practice by offering contextualized, transparent support. **Human autonomy** requires safeguarding privacy and ensuring that major decisions remain with trained social workers. Together, these principles anchor a human-centered approach that promotes inclusiveness, transparency, and client agency in all AI-supported services.

12.2.1 Inclusiveness

Keeping with Universal Design principles, inclusiveness refers to a design philosophy that goes beyond making technology accessible to everyone, but also understanding and respecting the diverse cultural, linguistic, and digital literacy backgrounds and circumstances of people (Ahrweiler et al., 2025). Technological inclusiveness is about providing multiple interfaces (e.g., voice commands, large font, braille printout) to increase accessibility for people with limited digital literacy to use AI systems. Considering the user's cultural background and native language, it is important to design information delivery methods and interactions that do not cause prejudice or misunderstanding.

"Google's Flood Hub" is a public, AI-powered early warning system designed to provide real-time flood forecasts up to seven days before a flood occurs (Google Research, n.d.). It visualizes Google's flood forecasting models on an intuitive map and helps individuals, governments, disaster response agencies, and non-governmental organizations (NGOs) anticipate and respond to severe flood risks. Its design considers accessibility, inclusiveness, safety, and collaboration with impacted communities, hallmarks of responsible and people-first AI.

"ALERTCalifornia" is a public safety program designed to improve the state's ability to prepare for, respond to, and recover from wildfires (California Wildfire & Forest Resilience Task Force, n.d.). The platform deploys a 24/7 statewide network to provide real-time situational awareness. Developed by a multidisciplinary team, it incorporates feedback from firefighters, paramedics, foresters, pilots, researchers, and local communities, ensuring the system reflects real human needs. This program exemplifies how AI can serve society when built with human oversight and shared public benefit at its core.

Inclusiveness plays a more vital role in AI services for public purposes, such as child abuse-reporting systems. Since legal and social perceptions of neglect and emotional abuse vary depending on the culture, misunderstandings may arise if AI makes judgments by simply analyzing words.

To reduce these problems, AI systems must be capable of comprehensively judging the intensity, frequency, and context of "punishment" by referring to the family's cultural background data. There is a need for a structure that minimizes automatic judgment errors, provides interpretation that considers cultural and social contexts, and supports bilingual and culturally knowledgeable professionals to conduct final reviews (Keddell, 2022).

Let's explore a powerful example of equity-driven innovation: the multilingual AI chatbot now used by legal aid organizations in places like North Carolina and Nevada. This tool directly tackles the Access-to-Justice Gap, a systemic barrier for clients with limited English proficiency (LEP) and low incomes.

Using Generative AI, this chatbot translates complex legal jargons into simple, plain language, radically improving access and promoting client autonomy. By automating routine guidance, the AI frees up human staff to dedicate their time and expertise to the most complex, human-intensive cases, thus strengthening the capacity of the entire legal system (Legal Aid of North Carolina, 2024; Nevada Supreme Court, 2025).

12.2.2 Transparency

Transparency means AI must clearly show how and why it produces its output, especially in human services where decisions affect people's lives (OECD, 2019). When cultural or language differences influence whether behavior is labeled as child "abuse," transparency prevents misunderstandings. If an AI flags certain words or repeated actions, it should reveal the criteria behind that judgment so social workers and clients can evaluate or challenge it. This clarity allows people to correct cultural misinterpretations and builds trust in the system (UNESCO, 2021). Therefore, transparency ultimately supports meaningful collaboration between AI and humans.

Suppose that you are a social worker at the Child Protective Services (CPS) hotline. Every call is critical, but you have limited staff and time. Which reports are truly high-risk? Which families need immediate, in-person investigation? We can design an AI system (a machine learning model) that analyzes administrative data (e.g., family's prior history with social services, mental health records, substance abuse treatment records, or criminal justice system involvement) to calculate a risk score for reports of child neglect or abuse. The goal is to help screening staff prioritize their responses, ensuring that the highest-risk children get immediate attention, which is a clear argument for advancing the common good.

Let's dive into one of the most well-known, and most debated, applications of AI in human services: the use of predictive analytics in child welfare. The implementation of the Allegheny Family Screening Tool (AFST) is a masterclass in the delicate balance between innovation and ethics (Allegheny County Official Site, n.d.).

Box 12.1 The Allegheny Family Screening Tool (AFST)

The Ethical Safeguard: Transparency and Explainable AI

With AFST, the social worker receives a detailed explanation of *why* a particular risk score was generated. This concept, known as **Explainable AI (XAI),** is non-negotiable for human services.

Explainable Factors: The report explicitly lists the data points that contributed to the score, such as "repeated prior participation in social care," or "recent arrests of a household member." This report allows the social worker to understand the logic the model is using.

Social Work Takeaway: This level of transparency is vital. It allows the professional to check the AI's work and understand the differences between a "high-risk" flag based on a few minor infractions years ago, and one based on a recent pattern of severe issues.

The Core Principle: Human-in-the-Loop

The most important ethical design feature of AFST is that the AI does not make the final decision. The system serves only as a screening aid. The risk score and its explanation go to the human social worker, whose professional expertise and ethical judgment allow them to understand the context of the output in perspective.

Respect for Professional Judgment: A social worker is ethically empowered to override the score. If AFST determines a low-risk score, but a case worker's consultation with the client and professional intuition suggest a different course of action (perhaps based on non-quantifiable, nuanced contextual factors), the case worker has the full authority to conduct an in-depth investigation.

Relational Integrity: This is the practical application of our relational definition of AI. Technology *identifies* where help may be needed, but the *intervention* is part of the human, trusting, and empathetic social work process.

Equity and Algorithmic Bias

While AFST demonstrates innovative practice, it also highlights the most profound ethical challenge in AI: algorithmic bias and its impact on equity. Criticism leveled at AFST (and all predictive tools that rely on historical data) is that if its training data reflects a history of systemic bias, for example, if low-income families and families of color have been historically over-surveilled and disproportionately reported to CPS, then the algorithm will learn and reinforce that existing societal inequity.

> *Reflection Question*: If you were a social worker using AFST, how would you ensure that a high-risk score doesn't lead you to approach a family with a punitive bias, but rather with a focus on support and prevention?

The AI may unfairly classify certain families as "high-risk," not because they are inherently worse parents, but because they have had more negative interactions with biased systems like the police, emergency rooms, or public benefits programs. Predictive AI can be a powerful force for innovation by increasing efficiency, but it must be continuously audited for bias to prevent it from becoming a tool of oppression. Social workers are to ensure that the pursuit of the common good is not achieved at the expense of social justice and equity for marginalized populations.

12.2.3 Human Agency

Another important human-centered design principle that AI must follow to realize the common good is "human agency," or respecting the autonomy and choice of users. AI should not become an authority that decides a person's life for them, but an assistant that helps the person make their own choices and take responsibility for those choices (Reamer, 2025).

For example, if an AI tells a client, "You must get X service," the AI is impinging on the user's autonomy by not leaving the decision to the user. Instead, the AI says, "There are several options X.Y.Z., depending on your situation. The pros and cons of each are listed below." In this way, the client can choose according to their values, needs, and current situation. The user can take responsibility for their choices. AI only serves to organize information, help the user understand, and share viable options with the user.

Let's imagine a situation where a single-parent family receives social work counseling. If the AI analyzes the family's income, number of children, and area of residence and then categorically states, "Please apply for a childcare voucher," the parent may feel as if they have been "judged" by the system. However, if the AI instead says "In your current situation, several assistance options are available, including childcare vouchers, emergency livelihood assistance, and local community programs. The conditions and benefits of each are as follows," parents can make the choice that is best for them. In the process, they can feel a sense of autonomy as they are managing their own lives.

The principle of human agency is that AI should not "manage" people but should work in a way that "supports" people so that they may make informed decisions. This goes beyond simple functional differences and has deep ethical implications that AI should be designed in a way that respects human dignity and the right to self-determination. Let's consider Box 12.2 that shows how AI can be used in the healing process.

Box 12.2 AI for Healing: The Vivibot

Problems: Adolescents and young adults who have survived cancer often struggle with elevated levels of anxiety and depression post-treatment, yet face significant barriers (e.g., cost, location, and stigma to accessing consistent, long-term care). Hopelab's Vivibot provides a powerful model for using AI to bridge the equity gap in mental health support for vulnerable populations (Hopelab, 2019).

Interventions: The application of Vivibot demonstrates human-centered design focused on client agency and safety. Instead of trying to replace a human, the chatbot is designed as a "personal coach," utilizing techniques from positive psychology like gratitude and mindfulness. Available 24/7, its non-judgmental interface empowers users to assess their emotional state and actively build coping skills. Critically, the system maintains a strict ethical protocol by immediately flagging conversations that indicate a mental health crisis, ensuring a safe transition to a human expert when necessary.

Outcomes: After only four weeks of use, participants showed a significant reduction in anxiety levels. User feedback confirmed that the tool's non-judgmental nature was key to facilitating open emotional expression (Greer et al., 2019). This success demonstrates AI's immense potential to achieve measurable clinical outcomes and provide scalable solutions, thereby advancing social equity by making essential emotional support accessible to underserved communities.

Discussions: How does the "personal coach" role of Vivibot inform our discussion of AI's ethical boundaries, particularly regarding the need for crisis detection and the ultimate reliance on human expertise?

The potential of multimodal AI to address social isolation is striking. As Lee and colleagues (2025) demonstrated, robot-assisted life review psychoeducation can be highly effective for socially isolated, older immigrants. Participants interacted with a chatbot (a form of AI using natural language processing [NLP] and often integrated into a robot) to narrate their life stories. In the absence of close social ties, the chatbot provided a non-judgmental platform for the older adults to tell their stories. This not only supported the therapeutic work of the life review but also, by connecting participants with a shared intervention, fostered meaningful peer interactions within the group setting. This example highlights the critical role that HCAI plays in ensuring that technology is designed to prioritize human values and well-being, particularly when working with our most vulnerable populations.

12.3 Participatory Design and Community Co-Creation

Designing AI that truly supports human-centered practice requires approaches that honor the lived experiences, cultural contexts, and practical realities of the communities that social workers serve. To achieve this, participatory design and community co-creation are essential. These methods require the involvement of social workers, clients, and other stakeholders from the earliest stages of development, ensuring that the AI tools reflect real needs rather than assumptions made by developers (Ahrweiler et al., 2025).

12.3.1 Participatory Design in Social Work

Historically, social workers were treated mainly as end-users of technology, expected to adjust their practice to whatever system their agency adopted (Liu et al., 2025). Participatory design flips this dynamic. Instead of being passive consumers, social workers become active contributors, ethics experts, contextual advisors, and watchdogs who help shape how technology is built.

Their perspective matters because social workers understand far more than data points. They see the emotional realities of clients, the cultural nuances behind behavior, and the complex relationships that shape people's lives. These insights cannot be captured by AI through numbers alone. Their professional judgment helps ensure that sensitive situations are handled with care and that systems can respond to crises, emotional reactions, and unpredictable family dynamics.

Before AI systems are built, social workers can raise essential ethical questions such as, "Does this feature compromise privacy?" or "Could this criterion disadvantage certain groups?" They can also help test prototypes by grounding them in real-world scenarios. In child abuse-reporting tools, their expertise ensures that systems reflect cultural nuance, trauma-informed practice, and ethical decision-making rather than rigid checklists. Research shows that culturally competent, context-aware approaches reduce bias and improve accuracy, underscoring the importance of social work involvement (Mascari, 2022).

12.3.2 User (Client) as Co-Creator

The most transformative shift in participatory design is the intentional inclusion of the client (the very person the AI system is meant to serve) in the development process. Unlike traditional service systems which often position clients as passive recipients or reduce them to data points, co-creation approaches recognize them as experts in their own lived experiences, whose insights are essential for creating tools that understand real-world needs, cultural contexts, and everyday challenges (Agnello et al., 2025).

Consider a child welfare or social services intake system. A conventional AI model might analyze demographic data and automatically present output: "I recommend service X.Y.Z." However, algorithmic recommendations do not always capture clients' actual priorities, cultural expectations, family context, or emotional needs.

For instance, some individuals may prefer counseling over financial assistance, while others may struggle most with burdensome application processes. Participatory design directly addresses these limitations: when clients share feedback such as "the interface is too complicated," or "the wording feels culturally inappropriate," or "What I actually need is A.B.C.," the system evolves to become more humane, functional, and culturally responsive. Evidence shows that client input reduces miscommunication, increases cultural sensitivity, and makes systems more accurate and fairer toward marginalized populations (Gobat et al., 2025).

Client engagement also reinforces dignity, autonomy, and voice. When organizations actively involve clients in co-design, they strengthen trust and foster collaborative relationships. Co-creation therefore is not merely a design strategy: it is a rights-based approach that aligns technology development with the profession's commitment to dignity and social justice.

12.3.3 Community-Based Data Governance

Unlike traditional top-down models, where a finished product is handed to users after completion, participatory approaches center the design process around those most affected by the technology. By involving community members from the start, developers gain insights into cultural nuance, accessibility barriers, and ethical concerns that may otherwise have been overlooked. This collaborative, "bottom-up" model leads to AI systems that foster trust, empathy, and inclusion, rather than just delivering technical efficiency.

Data should no longer be recognized as a resource for engineers but as an asset of the community. Suppose that you want to develop a social work AI system for low-income families in your region. Traditionally, the agency would have collected residents' income, health, and family information and designed services based on this. However, in this process, residents did not know how their information was used or on what criteria they were judged, and they did not have the opportunity to express their opinions.

The community has the right to control their data and can clearly request that "income, health, and family information be used only for social work services." It goes beyond simply saying "I agree with the terms of service." Instead, it explains how the data is being used and continues the conversation with the community. Residents need to be able to say "service X is inconvenient" or "I want to know more about service Y and Z" at any time.

With this process, there is a committee with direct participation from community members to monitor and adjust how data is collected and used to ensure it is in line with local values and priorities. For example, the user could prompt: "Our region prioritizes child safety, so please handle relevant data more carefully." This structure is a key change that will ensure that technology works in a way that respects people's rights and voices.

12.3.4 Challenges and Opportunities of Community Partnership

Participatory design is a powerful approach but putting it into practice is challenging. When multiple stakeholders with competing interests come together, challenges inevitably arise. While these obstacles can create issues, they are not insurmountable: they can become opportunities to strengthen collaboration and create solutions that truly serve the common good.

One major challenge is power imbalance. Professional hierarchies often make it difficult to establish **equal partnerships** among developers, social workers, and clients. Each group brings unique expertise: developers understand technology, social workers know the field, and clients know their own lives best. Creating a structure where all voices carry equal weight requires intentional effort.

Time and funding pose additional barriers. Co-creation workshops and community consultations demand resources that public institutions and nonprofits often lack. Sustaining engagement over long development cycles can also be difficult; early participants may lose interest or face scheduling conflicts (Lipton et al., 2025).

Consider this example of homelessness prevention and affordable housing. Los Angeles County's Homelessness Prevention Unit (HPU) uses an AI-driven algorithm to analyze county data (such as physical and mental health, and benefits interactions) to flag individuals and families most at risk of losing housing within the next 12 months (PBS NewsHour, 2025). This proactive approach is ethically significant: it helps reach people who might otherwise remain invisible until a crisis occurs, ensuring a fairer distribution of preventive resources.

AI acts only as a finding mechanism, not a decision-maker. Once individuals are identified, human-centered case management, flexible financial assistance, and supportive services take over. This model illustrates how technology can enhance equity while preserving core social work values, shifting service delivery from reactive crisis response to proactive prevention.

Building preventive resources within communities is essential. Social workers play a critical role in educating stakeholders, especially developers, about ethical engagement and active listening. Starting small can help pilot a participatory design process on a manageable scale, such as testing one feature with a social worker and client in a specific region, then expanding based on results. Finally, acknowledging and rewarding participants for their time and contributions goes a long way toward sustaining motivation and trust.

12.4 Principles and Practices for Designing AI for the Common Good

The decisions made by AI in social work go beyond mere technical judgments and can be important choices that directly impact people's lives. Therefore, AI should not only present results but also provide stakeholders with a clear explanation of how the results were derived. This means revisiting the principles of transparency, explainability, and accountability.

12.4.1 Principles of Transparency, Explainability, and Accountability

12.4.1.1 Making the "Black Box" Transparent: A Practical Way to Explain

Many complex AI models, especially deep learning systems, are often referred to as "black boxes" because their inner workings are opaque. It's hard to understand why they make certain decisions. To solve this, we recommend several practical methods.

Whenever possible, use simpler and more interpretable models, such as decision trees or **rule-based systems** (Hsieh et al., 2024). AI determining housing subsidy eligibility may use a simple set of rules that are easy for both social workers and clients to understand (e.g., "If income is less than X and family size is Y, then eligible").

Even complex models can analyze which input factors had the greatest impact on the results. For example, the AI may recommend specific job training programs. The description might state that, "the following recommendation is primarily based on your past work experience and stated interests, with a low weight given to your age or location."

Providing explanations based on similar past examples, AI can explain its decisions by saying, "A recommendation for X mental health service was provided because the data shows that it has been highly effective with clients with similar stress levels and family situations" (Blessing et al., 2024).

12.4.1.2 Establish a Clear Chain of Accountability

If an AI system makes a mistake, who is responsible? In social work, this question is both technical and highly ethical. A clear chain of liability ensures that errors can be corrected and damage mitigated. AI should serve as a **decision support tool** rather than a decision-maker. Human social workers should be ultimately responsible for all decisions, especially those that affect the well-being of their clients, having the final say to ignore or change the AI's recommendations (Cheung, 2024).

All decisions made by the AI should be meticulously recorded. This **audit trail** should include the data used, the output of the model, and the final work of the human. This allows for a clear review of past decisions and helps identify any systemic biases or errors.

Agencies should develop clear policies that outline who is responsible for the outcomes when using AI. This includes specifying who manages appeals, who investigates errors, and what actions are taken to remedy the harm caused by flawed algorithms (Perron et al., 2025). COMPAS in Box 12.3, an AI tool for crime prediction, provides profound ethical insights and lessons regarding accountability.

Box 12.3 AI Crime Prediction Tools and Legal Accountability

In some U.S. courts and correctional facilities, the Correctional Offender Management Profiling for Alternative Sanctions (COMPAS) system has been used to predict the likelihood of recidivism. This AI tool generates a "risk score" that is determined by the person's legal history and personal data. This score influences decisions about bail, sentencing, and parole (Larson et al., 2023).

***Problems**:* ProPublica's 2016 investigation revealed troubling racial bias in COMPAS. Black defendants were disproportionately labeled as "high-risk," even when they did not reoffend, while white defendants who did reoffend were often classified as low-risk. These errors raised serious concerns about fairness and equity in the justice system.

Accountability: The controversy sparked critical questions about who is accountable when AI influences legal decisions.

System Developer (Northpointe): The company refused to disclose its algorithm, citing trade secrets. This "black box" approach made it nearly impossible to find the source of the bias or hold the developer accountable.

System User (Judge): Judges claimed that the AI score was only a reference and that final decisions were theirs. However, the predictive score is likely shaped by judicial reasoning in significant ways.

Legal Liability: When defendants challenged sentences or bail decisions influenced by COMPAS, courts ruled that the AI was merely a "tool" and that ultimate responsibility rested with the human decision-maker.

This COMPAS case clearly illustrates the complexity of AI accountability. While technology itself was flawed, the legal system was unable to hold the AI or its developer accountable, reaching the vague conclusion that the responsibility lies with the final judgment of human users.

This incident offers important lessons for social workers when adopting AI. It should be made clear that AI is just a tool, and that human users are ultimately responsible for decisions made and actions taken based on recommendations (separation of responsibilities), and that AI system developers have an ethical obligation to be transparent about how their AI works and potential biases (duty of transparency). Therefore, AI systems must be regularly audited to ensure that decisions are fair. Any biases found that lead to unfair outcomes must be corrected immediately.

12.4.2 Designing Accessible Interfaces for All Users

AI systems in human services should be accessible to everyone, regardless of background, ability, or digital literacy. AI which is technologically advanced but not available to the target audience is a failure. Designing for inclusivity and accessibility is a key principle, not an afterthought.

Considering both health literacy and digital literacy of clientele, social workers need to use jargon-free language. Interfaces and descriptions should use simple and clear phrasing that can be easily understood by clients possessing varying levels of literacy. For example, instead of "model-driven predictive analytics," simply state "a tool that helps predict which services might be most helpful."

Not everyone has a smartphone or high-speed internet. AI services should be accessible through various channels, such as basic text messaging services, voice-activated phone lines, and in-person kiosks. AI and its interface must be culturally sensitive and available in multiple languages. It is important to understand that concepts and requirements can vary greatly depending on the cultural group. Finding resources for immigrant communities should include services that specifically meet their unique needs, such as legal aid or language-specific support groups for asylum seekers.

12.4.3 Putting Ethical Guidelines and Assessment Tools into Practice

To ensure that AI is designed and implemented ethically, social work organizations must adopt formal guidelines and evaluation tools. This is essential for maintaining professional standards and public trust.

Like the Institutional Review Board (IRB), which oversees research on human topics, social service agencies are required to establish an AI Ethics Review Board. This committee consists of social workers, community members, ethicists, and technicians. Their role is to review and approve the design and deployment of new AI systems, ensuring they align with ethical principles (Gobat et al., 2025).

Before an AI system is deployed, it must be rigorously evaluated for fairness and bias. This requires testing model performance across demographic subgroups (e.g., race, gender, and income) to ensure that predictions do not systematically disadvantage any population. Researchers emphasize that fairness evaluations must examine disparities in model outcomes and identify potential harms before real-world implementation (Barocas et al., 2023).

Evaluation must also include a **social impact assessment**, which expands the focus beyond technical accuracy to consider broader community effects. This involves asking questions like: does this AI empower or disempower clients? and what unintended social consequences might arise? Scholars argue that fairness is a sociotechnical issue, meaning that responsible evaluation must account for societal context, community well-being, and downstream impacts, not just model metrics (UNESCO, 2021).

12.5 The Future of Social Work Integrating HCAI

The integration of HCAI expands beyond technological innovation. It means fundamental change that redefines the essence of human services. Instead of fearing that technology will replace human intuition and empathy, we are moving toward a future where AI and social workers work together.

12.5.1 Harmonizing Humans and Technology: Redefining the Role of Social Workers

AI transforms the role of social workers by taking over routine administrative tasks, allowing social workers to focus on what matters most, that is, supporting people. While AI handles data entry, eligibility checks, and resource-matching, social workers can devote more time to building relationships, conducting deeper assessments, and offering emotional support.

Their role also expands from case management to strategic leadership. With AI identifying trends (e. g., rising homelessness or increased opioid use), social workers can respond quickly, direct resources effectively, and even inform policy decisions. Rather than acting as the sole authority, social workers can collaborate with AI. When AI presents service options, practitioners can guide clients through them, strengthening informed choice and enhancing client autonomy.

To illustrate, using an AI image generator, play therapy offers an innovative way to help neurodivergent children express feelings that are difficult to verbalize. When a child feels overwhelmed, the therapist can invite them to imagine a place where they feel completely safe and describe it in detail, perhaps a forest of soft pillows or a sky made of glitter. The therapist then uses AI tools to create this sensory-friendly environment, saving the image as a calming visual tool for future moments of stress.

Similarly, for children who struggle with social cues or transitions, the therapist can co-create "Social Stories" by generating images where the child or a favorite animal is the hero navigating a challenging situation, such as entering a noisy classroom. These images allow the therapist to guide the child through "what happens next," building predictive thinking and reducing anxiety, especially with neurodivergent children.

Older adults often struggle to maintain regular exercise routines, especially when muscle strength declines and physical activity become more challenging. HCAI can help transform these experiences. Imagine an indoor cycling machine equipped with an AI-powered screen that adapts to each user's preferences. Instead of staring at a blank wall, users could ride through breathtaking landscapes, rolling hills, forest paths, and oceanside views. Even more powerful, the system could personalize the scenery to reflect a user's hometown or meaningful places from their past. These familiar images evoke nostalgia, joy, and connection, motivating older adults to stay active and promoting both physical and emotional well-being.

HCAI can also support people during some of life's most painful moments. Emerging technologies using text, images, and voice can create comforting messages for individuals experiencing profound grief. While not a substitute for human connection or professional support, tools like **personalized text-to-speech** can help bereaved individuals feel less alone, especially those grieving the sudden loss of a spouse, child, or close friend. Even though users understand that the message is not "real," many people still find solace in hearing a familiar voice or receiving a gentle reminder of love, encouragement, or shared memories.

These examples highlight a core principle of HCAI: technology designed with compassion can strengthen motivation, emotional resilience, and connection. When guided by ethical practice, AI can become a partner, not a replacement, in promoting human dignity and well-being.

12.5.2 Continuous Learning and Innovation: Adapting to the Evolving Technological Landscape

The rapid pace of technological change means that social workers cannot rely on one-time training sessions. The future of social work demands a commitment to continuous learning and a culture of ethical innovation. This goes beyond mere skill acquisition to encompass critical thinking, collaboration, and a spirit of experimentation. We will further discuss AI literacy for social workers in Chapter 14.

Social workers are no longer isolated professionals. They should actively collaborate with data scientists, engineers, and designers. Social workers' experience in the field provides practical insights into technology developers, and this collaboration creates a feedback loop, helping guide the development of technology with realistic and innovative solutions to real-world problems. Technology evolves into a field-oriented tool through the experience of social workers.

The future of social work does not end with the embrace of technology. Through continuous learning and ethical innovation, social workers must become change agents of reconstructing technology to be human-centered. This change is not just an adaptation but an evolution that simultaneously strengthens professionalism for the common good.

12.6 Critical Thinking Questions

1 How does human-centered AI design and development differ from traditional technology-driven approaches?
2 What criteria must AI meet to be considered supporting the "common good" and "human-centered?"
3 How can conflicts be resolved when different parties engage in AI design?
4 What policies or regulations are needed to support ethical AI development?

12.7 Summary

The adoption of AI technology in social work is more than enhancing efficiency: it raises important questions about how we embed ethical values into technology. Human-centered design is the overarching answer to this question, offering a path for AI to truly realize the common good. We explored how human-centered design that promotes inclusiveness, transparency, and client agency in all AI-supported services can be applied to AI development. Ethical considerations and social responsibility are presented as key elements of AI design. Finally, we suggested that capacity-building and education can help scale human-centered AI practices. Next, let's examine development and implementation of AI from a global perspective.

12.8 Empowerment-Focused Activities

12.8.1 Developing AI Ethics and Human-Centered Design Assessment Scale

Based on what you have learned in this chapter, rate how well your organization's current AI systems or operational policies align with each item on a scale of 1 (Strongly Disagree) to 5 (Strongly Agree).

Table 12.1 Human-Centered Design Assessment Scale

Category	*Criteria*	*1*	*2*	*3*	*4*	*5*
Participation and Agency	*Participatory Design*: Are there formal procedures in place to gather and incorporate feedback from clients and community members in the early stages of AI development?					
	Human Agency: Does AI support clients in making their own decisions rather than making choices for them?					
	Data Governance: Do clients and the community understand how their data is used, and do they have the right to opt out or exercise control over it?					
Trust and Explainability	*Transparency:* Is the AI's decision-making process disclosed so that users do not perceive the system as a "black box?"					
	Explainability: Does the AI provide the reasoning behind its outcomes in "Plain Language" that is easily understood by clients?					
	Inclusivity: Is accessibility (e.g., multilingual support, visual aids) sufficiently ensured for digitally marginalized groups?					
Professional Responsibility	*Accountability*: Is there a clear line of responsibility for AI errors, and are all final decisions reviewed and approved by a human social worker?					
	Role Optimization: Does the AI effectively reduce repetitive administrative tasks, allowing social workers to focus more on building relationships with clients?					
	Ethical Training: Do practitioners receive regular continuing education on AI ethics and data security?					

12.8.2 Audit of Local AI Services for "Human-Centeredness"

Overview: Select one public AI service currently in use and conduct an Ethical Impact Assessment.

Objective: Critically analyze whether the selected service respects the dignity of its users or if it marginalizes human context in favor of technical efficiency.

Deliverables: Human-Centeredness Score: Visualized via a "Radar Chart" and Improvement Proposal

References

Agnello, D. M., Anand-Kumar, V., An, Q., de Boer, J., Delfmann, L. R., Longworth, G. R., Loisel, Q., McCaffrey, L., Steiner, A., & Chastin, S. (2025). Co-creation methods for public health research—Characteristics, benefits, and challenges: A Health CASCADE scoping review. *BMC Medical Research Methodology, 25*, 60. https://doi.org/10.1186/s12874-025-02514-4

Ahrweiler, P., Späth, E., Siqueiros-García, J. M., Capellas, B. L., & Wurster, D. (2025). Inclusive technology co-design for participatory AI. In P. Ahrweiler (Eds.), *Participatory artificial intelligence in public social services. Artificial intelligence, simulation and society.* Springer. https://doi.org/10.1007/978-3-031-71678-2_2

Allegheny Family Screening Tool. (n.d.). Allegheny County, PA. www.alleghenycounty.us/Services/Human-Services-DHS/DHS-News-and-Events/Accomplishments-and-Innovations/Allegheny-Family-Screening-Tool

Barocas, S., Hardt, M., & Narayanan, A. (2023). *Fairness and machine learning*. https://fairmlbook.org/?utm_source=copilot.com

Blessing, E., Abil, R., Porter, K., & Lewis, F. (2024). Explainable AI: Interpreting and understanding machine learning models. HAL Id: hal-04972111. https://hal.science/hal-04972111v1

California Wildfire & Forest Resilience Task Force. (n.d.). ALERTCalifornia: Using AI to stay ahead of wildfires and other disasters. https://wildfiretaskforce.org/alertcalifornia-launches-to-provide-essential-tools-to-understand-and-adapt-to-wildfires-and-natural-disasters

Cheung, B. C. (2024). Transparency and accountability in AI systems: Safeguarding well-being in the age of algorithmic decision-making. *Frontiers in Human Dynamics, 6*. 1–11. https://doi.org/10.3389/fhumd.2024.1421273

Gobat, N., Slack, C., Hannah, S., Salzwedel, J., Bladon, G., Burgos, J. G., Purvis, B., Molony-Oates, B., Siegfried, N., Cheah, P. Y., Conway, M., Kamuya, D., Davies, A., Johnson, T., Tholanah, M., Mugamba, S., Mutengu, N. L., Machingaidze, S., Schwartz, L., Rägo, L., … von Harbou, K. (2025). Better engagement, better evidence: Working in partnership with patients, the public, and communities in clinical trials with involvement and good participatory practice. *The Lancet. Global Health, 13*(4), e716–e731. https://doi.org/10.1016/S2214-109X(24)00521-7

Google Research. (n.d.). *Flood forecasting: AI for information & alerts*. https://sites.research.google/floodforecasting/

Greer, S., Ramo, D., Chang, Y. J., Fu, M., Moskowitz, J., & Haritatos, J. (2019). Use of the chatbot "Vivibot" to deliver positive psychology skills and promote well-being in young people after cancer treatment: Randomized controlled feasibility trial. *JMIR Mhealth and Uhealth, 7*(10). 1–13. https://doi.org/10.2196/15018

Hopelab. (2019, November 6). Hopelab's Vivibot, the first chatbot designed for young adult cancer survivors, can improve mental well-being of users. *Cision PR Newswire*. www.prnewswire.com/news-releases/hopelabs-vivibot-the-first-chatbot-designed-for-young-adult-cancer-survivors-can-improve-mental-well-being-of-users-300951573.html

Hsieh, W., Bi, Z., Jiang, C., Liu, J., Peng, B., Zhang, S., Pan, X., Xu, J., Wang, J., Chen, K., Feng, P., Wen, Y., Song, X., Wang, T., Liu, M., Yang, J., Li, M., Jing, B., Ren, J., … Liang, C. X. (2024). A comprehensive guide to explainable AI: From classical models to LLMs. arXiv. https://arxiv.org/html/2412.00800v2

Keddell, E. (2022) On decision variability in child protection: Respect, interactive universalism and ethics of care. *Ethics and Social Work, 17*(1), 4–19. https://doi.org/10.1080/17496535.2022.2073381

Larson, J., Mattu, S., Kirchner, L., & Angwin J. (2023). *How we analyzed the COMPAS recidivism algorithm, ProPublica*. www.propublica.org/article/how-we-analyzed-the-compas-recidivism-algorithm

Lee, O. E., Nah, K., Kim, K., & Ahn, H. (2025). From hardship to harmony: Life reviews of Korean American immigrants facilitated by companion robots. *Research on Aging.*

48(5-6), 286–298. 1640275251379367. Advance online publication. https://doi.org/10.1177/01640275251379367
Legal Aid of North Carolina. (2024). *LANC-LIA*. https://legalaidnc.org/lia/
Lipton, B., Dickinson, H., Bailie, J., Hewitt, B., Kavanagh, A., Aitken, Z., & Shields, M. (2025). Collaborating with young people: Identifying the barriers and facilitators in co-designed research. *Health Expectations, 28*(3), e70308. https://doi.org/10.1111/hex.70308
Liu, C., Zhong, M., He, M., Wang, X., Gan, H., Cao, P., Wang, C., & Lou, Y. (2025). Research on co-creation of community public cultural spaces through generative dynamic workflows. *Systems, 13*(5), 316. https://doi.org/10.3390/systems13050316
Mascari, L.H. (2022). Navigating cultural considerations and disclosure of child maltreatment. *Journal of Health Service Psychology, 48*, 185–194. https://link.springer.com/article/10.1007/s42843-022-00074-5
Nevada Supreme Court (2025). *Nevada judiciary expands free legal resources with self-help website*. Administrative Office of the Courts. https://nvcourts.gov/aoc/aoc_news/nevada_judiciary_expands_free_legal_resources_with_self-help_website
Nike. (2022). *Never done evolving, ft. Serena [Case study]*. YouTube. www.youtube.com/watch?v=2ehJczf2FEk
O2. (2024, November 14). *AI Scambaiters: O2 creates AI granny to waste scammers' time*. YouTube. www.youtube.com/watch?v=RV_SdCfZ-0s
OECD. (2019). *Transparency and explainability (Principle 1.3)*. OECD.AI. Retrieved from https://oecd.ai/en/dashboards/ai-principles/P7
PBS NewsHour. (2025, October 28). *Dana Vanderford and Fred Theus, homelessness prevention unit*. [Video]. www.pbs.org/newshour/brief/536751/dana-vanderford-and-fred-theus
Perron, B. E., Goldkind, L., Qi, Z., & Victor, B. G. (2025). Human services organizations and the responsible integration of AI: Considering ethics and contextualizing risk(s). *Journal of Technology in Human Services, 43*(1), 20–33. https://doi.org/10.1080/15228835.2025.2457045
Reamer, F. G. (2025). *Artificial intelligence in the behavioral health professions ethical and risk management issues*. NASW Press.
UNESCO. (2021). *Recommendation on the ethics of artificial intelligence*. United Nations Educational, Scientific, and Cultural Organization. www.unesco.org/en/articles/recommendation-ethics-artificial-intelligence

12.9 Support Materials

12.9.1 The AI Social Worker

www.theaisocialworker.com/about

The AI Social Worker was created to help social workers navigate advances in practice—without sacrificing care. With a foundation in ethical standards for human services professionals, they provide tools and training to support those doing the real, hard, transformative work every day.

12.9.2 Mindgard—"The Shadow of AI in Identifying Welfare Blind Spots"

https://mindgard.ai/resources/shadow-ai-is-a-blind-spot

This resource explores the concept of Shadow AI—AI tools used in organizations without proper oversight or governance. It explains why unmonitored AI can create ethical, privacy, and security risks, and offers practical insights on how professionals can identify and manage these blind spots. For social workers, this article highlights the importance of transparency and accountability when integrating AI into practice, ensuring client data and rights remain protected.

Please access video 12.2 at www.routledge.com/9781041275459

Video 12.2 How to Build Human-Centered AI?

Please access video 12.3 at www.routledge.com/9781041275459

Video 12.3 Human-Centered AI of the Social Workers, for the Social Workers, and by the Social Workers

13 Global Perspectives on AI and Social Work

Othelia Lee

Box 13.1 AI for Environmental Protection of the Amazon

In Brazil and Peru, Indigenous organizations have partnered with technology groups to use AI and satellite imagery to track deforestation and illegal mining in the Amazon rainforest. The systems employ machine learning to detect land-use changes in near real time, generating alerts that Indigenous communities can use in legal advocacy and territorial defense. Unlike conventional "top-down" conservation models, these AI tools are deployed under Indigenous leadership, ensuring that data serves community-defined goals of land stewardship and cultural survival.

Box 13.1 shows how Indigenous and other minority communities are actively shaping AI for environmental justice, while resisting extractive uses of their data. It also highlights how AI can reinforce traditional ecological knowledge when guided by **data sovereignty**. This chapter examines why a global perspective is essential, highlights regional and national approaches to AI, explores ethical and human rights considerations, reviews illustrative case studies, and outlines strategies for education and capacity building.

AI is a global phenomenon that is rapidly reshaping multiple dimensions of society, including the ways in which social workers engage with individuals, families, and communities. While much of the early scholarship on AI has been concentrated in technology hubs in North America and Europe, the implications of these innovations extend far beyond national borders. Social work, as an internationally grounded profession rooted in the values of social justice, human rights, and dignity, must engage with AI through a global lens.

13.1 Why Global Perspectives?

AI technologies do not exist in isolation. As a matter of fact, they are products of global supply chains, transnational corporations, and shared infrastructures such as cloud computing. An app developed in Silicon Valley may be downloaded in

DOI: 10.4324/9781003755081-17

New Delhi, Rio de Janeiro, or Nairobi within seconds, shaping local human service practices. For social workers, this interconnectedness means that adopting a purely national or regional view risks overlooking both opportunities and challenges that transcend borders.

The primary reason a global perspective is necessary is the uneven distribution of technological resources. Bentley and colleagues (2024) argue that **structural barriers** (e.g., income, age, geographic location, and digital access) significantly influence individuals' digital confidence and their engagement with AI technologies. Without addressing these disparities, the benefits of AI will remain unevenly distributed, particularly disadvantaging populations in low- and middle-income countries.

High-income countries often lead in developing and regulating AI tools, while low- and middle-income countries may lack infrastructure such as stable internet, data storage, or regulatory frameworks (Shams et al., 2025). Yet these same contexts may benefit most from **leapfrogging technologies** that bypass traditional barriers. Instead of building expensive telephone infrastructure, they went straight to mobile networks, gaining communication access much more quickly and at lower cost.

For example, mobile-based AI tools are enabling mental health screening in rural Kenya, where access to mental health professionals is extremely limited (Hoque et al., 2020). Mobile-based tools are increasingly used to deliver mental health services to low-resource communities, highlighting the potential of mobile AI technologies to support screening, diagnosis, and follow-up care in rural and underserved regions.

Let's consider some examples of how AI technology is implemented to innovate social work practice in other countries. A study integrating multisource geospatial data and deep learning techniques evaluated China's poverty reduction efficiency from 2016 to 2019. Yao and colleagues (2024) report significant progress in targeting aid effectively, with regional disparities highlighted for future policy focus. This contrasts with the U.S., where AI-based social service targeting is fragmented across states and agencies, and with Europe, where strong social protection systems reduce reliance on predictive analytics.

A pilot qualitative study explored the feasibility and cultural acceptability of SMS-based mental health promotion among young women in urban slums in India (Chandra et al., 2014). The findings support the use of mobile text messages in local languages to address mental health needs in underserved populations.

New Zealand piloted a predictive risk model known as the Vulnerable Children PRM, which aimed to identify children at high risk of maltreatment using administrative data (Dare, 2013). While the model showed potential for targeted resource allocation, ethical evaluations raised concerns about stigmatization, privacy, and the risk of misclassification. Recommendations emphasized voluntary engagement, minimal intervention, and careful dissemination of risk scores to avoid harm.

Globalization brings ethical concerns. Technologies developed in one cultural context may be exported to another without considering local needs or values, potentially reinforcing structural inequalities. Therefore, a **global perspective** allows social workers to critically evaluate whose voices are shaping AI development and who is being left behind.

Table 13.1 AI Front-Runners and Disparities

Dimension	*Leading Countries*	*Disparities and Challenges*
Total Investment	U.S., China	Europe invests less; Asia emerging (South Korea, UAE)
Research and Innovation	UK, France, Germany, South Korea, Japan, Singapore	Regulatory burden may slow adoption (EU); talent gaps in some EU countries
Enterprise Adoption	Denmark, Sweden (25%+); Belgium regions (30%+)	Turkey, Hungary, SMEs lag significantly
Governance Focus	EU: AI Act, ethics frameworks	U.S. and China prioritize speed and innovation over regulation
Urban–Rural Divide	High in capital regions (e.g., London vs Guerrero in Mexico)	Regional rural lag within countries impacting equitable access

13.2 AI Adoption Landscape: Tales of Two Countries

United States and China remain the dominant forces in global AI development. The U.S. leads with vast private-sector investment (nearly $471 billion from 2013 to 2024) and substantial public funding (Voronoi, 2025), while China is rapidly closing gaps through aggressive state support. China's total AI investment in 2025 was ¥890 billion (≈$125 billion; Second Talent, 2025). China also leads global AI patenting (roughly 60% of the world's AI patents; *Global Times*, 2025).

Beyond these two giants, other Organisation for Economic Co-operation and Development (OECD) countries also stand out. According to a recent global AI vibrancy ranking, countries like the U.K., India, U.A.E., France, Germany, South Korea, Japan, and Singapore are notable for their AI maturity in areas such as research, infrastructure, governance, and innovation (Fattorini et al., 2024). Table 13.1 presents a portrait of AI adoption across OECD countries, with both front-runners and disparities highlighted.

Over the past two decades, China has rapidly positioned itself as a global leader in AI, investing heavily in research, infrastructure, and applications across industries. The turning point came with the 2017 "New Generation Artificial Intelligence Development Plan" issued by the State Council, which set ambitious goals for China to become the world's primary AI innovation hub by 2030 (Webster et al., 2017). This plan mobilized massive state funding, private sector investment, and academic–industry collaboration. China's approach has emphasized scale, speed, and integration, leveraging vast datasets collected through state and corporate platforms.

In contrast, the U.S. has pursued a more market-driven model, where private companies such as Google, Microsoft, and OpenAI spearhead innovation with comparatively less centralized government oversight (Federal Trade Commission, 2025). Europe, by contrast, has taken a regulatory-first approach, prioritizing human-centered design and ethical safeguards, as reflected in the European Union's AI Act (2024).

Disparities in AI Adoption are apparent across countries in terms of scale of investment, governance, and innovation. OECD-wide, AI adoption reflects a dynamic interplay of investment, strategy, ethics, and institutional capacity. Countries like the U.S., China, the UK, and South Korea are technological trailblazers, while Germany and France emphasize responsible leadership (Gooding et al., 2024). Yet, regional and enterprise-level disparities risk leaving vulnerable populations, and human services agencies, without access to AI's potential. This creates a "two-speed" system where innovation hubs surge ahead while others risk dependency on imported AI technologies.

This triangulation—China's scale and state support, the U.S.'s private-sector dominance, and Europe's regulatory caution—creates distinct pathways for AI's integration into human services. For social work professionals, understanding this uneven global landscape is essential: it frames where AI can most effectively bolster human services, where ethical vigilance is needed, and where capacity building is most urgent to avoid deepening inequalities.

The OECD reports significant internal disparities within countries and regions. Eastern Europe and Southern Europe lag adoption leaders. Capital regions like London, Seoul, and Brussels dominate innovation hubs, while rural and disadvantaged areas (e.g., Guerrero in Mexico) lag in adoption capacity (OECD, 2023). AI expertise is concentrated in a few hubs, leaving workforce gaps in countries like Greece, Portugal, and parts of Eastern Europe.

For social work, these internal disparities in AI adoption and landscapes have profound implications. AI adoption remains concentrated among larger, ICT-intensive firms. Smaller agencies and nonprofits may struggle to adopt AI, emphasizing the need for capacity-building, equitable infrastructure, and collaborative technology platforms (OECD, 2023). This disparity threatens to widen productivity gaps across economies unless infrastructure and skills training are expanded. The OECD report warns that without targeted infrastructure investment and workforce training, these gaps could exacerbate productivity inequalities across regions and sectors.

13.3 Regional and National Approaches

As shown in these examples, different regions have developed distinct approaches to their adoption of AI, shaped by cultural, political, and economic contexts. Now, let's further examine regional and national approaches to adopt and adapt AI.

13.3.1 Europe: Human-Centered Regulation and Social Policy Integration

Europe has taken a more regulatory approach, emphasizing human-centered AI and **General Data Protection Regulation** (GDPR). The European Parliament's Artificial Intelligence Act establishes harmonized rules for the development, deployment, and use of AI systems across the EU. It emphasizes transparency, accountability, and the protection of fundamental rights, including privacy and nondiscrimination (Vardas et al., 2025). As we discussed in Chapter 7, the Act categorizes AI systems by risk level and imposes stricter obligations on high-risk applications, including requirements for human oversight, data governance, and clear documentation of system functionality (Busch et al., 2024).

Social workers in Europe often encounter AI tools framed as public services rather than private ventures, which may better align with social work's values of equity and access. Yet, there is investment gaps. Nordic countries (Denmark, Sweden) and Belgium show exceptionally high enterprise adoption rates—with over 25%–30% of firms integrating AI into operations, while middle-income OECD members (e.g., Turkey, Hungary) struggle with scaling. Moreover, regulatory pressure: EU's strict governance may slow commercialization compared to the U.S. and Asia.

13.3.2 Asia-Pacific: Rapid Adoption, Cultural Contexts, and Local Innovation

Asia is characterized by rapid tech adoption in countries like China, South Korea, Japan, and India and government-led AI initiatives in social services. Healthcare applications in China include AI diagnostic imaging, hospital triage, and predictive analytics. These resemble U.S. hospital systems, but China's scale allows faster deployment in rural and urban clinics.

China has invested heavily in AI for health and education, though its integration into social policy raises questions about surveillance and individual rights (Woods, 2025). Education employs AI-powered adaptive learning systems, with a strong uptake in after-school tutoring and university monitoring (Cui et al., 2018). Facial recognition and surveillance are deeply integrated into urban infrastructure, used for law enforcement, access to services, and financial transactions (Wang, 2021).

China, Japan, and South Korea have pioneered the use of socially assistive robots (SARs) in elder care, reflecting cultural norms around aging and filial piety. Elder care makes use of AI-enabled robots and monitoring systems, an area in which they share leading roles, given their rapidly aging populations. SARs such as Xiao You or Hyodol engage older adults through companionship, cognitive games, and medication reminders (Lee et al., 2023). Western contexts are experimenting with SARs more cautiously, often framed by ethical debates on dignity and autonomy.

A systematic review of 163 empirical studies found that smart home health technologies (SHHTs)—including sensors, wearable devices, and AI-enabled systems—can support aging-in-place by enabling continuous remote monitoring. These technologies help reduce caregiver burden and improve older adults' independence, though barriers such as usability and cost remain (Tian et al., 2024). These innovations are increasingly being tested in Europe and North America, raising questions about cultural adaptation and transferability.

Now, let's turn our attention to the global regions where AI is less developed because of limited resources. Yet, some of these regions pioneered to demonstrate community-based innovation and there are many lessons to be learned.

13.3.3 Africa: Opportunities for Leapfrogging and Challenges of Infrastructure

Africa faces infrastructure challenges but also represents a site of innovation. Despite persistent infrastructural challenges, African nations have emerged as dynamic sites of technological innovation, particularly in the deployment of AI to address pressing social and economic issues. This dual reality, marked by resource limitations and creative adaptation, has catalyzed the development of AI-enabled mobile platforms that support poverty alleviation, agricultural productivity, public health, and psychosocial interventions.

AI technologies integrated into mobile platforms have demonstrated significant potential in advancing development goals across multiple sectors. Mobile-based AI systems are increasingly utilized to identify economically vulnerable populations, facilitate the distribution of financial aid, and support microfinance initiatives. Notably, platforms such as "M-Pesa" have transformed financial inclusion by enabling secure mobile banking services for underserved communities (Ndung'u, 2021).

AI applications in agriculture assist smallholder farmers by optimizing planting schedules, monitoring soil conditions, and accessing shared machinery. "Zenvus," an agritech startup in Nigeria, uses AI-powered sensors to monitor soil moisture, temperature, and nutrient levels. These insights help smallholder farmers optimize planting schedules and reduce input waste, leading to yield improvements of over 20% in pilot regions (Muhammed, 2025). Similarly, "Hello Tractor" connects farmers to shared machinery via a digital platform, improving access to mechanization and boosting productivity across over 4.5 million acres in 20 African countries (Hello Tractor, 2023). These innovations contribute to increased crop yields and improved livelihoods.

Community-driven initiatives are also emerging. An AI tool developed by researchers from the University of California, supported by Microsoft and AMREF, uses satellite imagery, weather data, and health records to predict food insecurity in Kenya. The tool has been trialed since 2023 and helps identify households most in need, enabling a more equitable distribution of aid (Adedunmola, 2025).

"Babyl" Rwanda, a subsidiary of Babylon Health, launched an AI-powered triage tool that significantly enhanced healthcare delivery in Rwanda. The tool supports nurses in collecting patient symptoms, guiding triage decisions, and streamlining referrals. It has been fully localized to Rwanda's language, epidemiology, and healthcare pathways, and is used in both call centers and public health facilities. By 2023, Babyl was providing over 3,000 virtual consultations daily to more than 2.5 million registered users, demonstrating its scalability and impact on healthcare access in remote and underserved areas (Byamukama et al., 2024).

In contexts where professional social workers are scarce, AI-driven text-messaging programs offer scalable solutions for psychosocial support. These systems leverage **natural language processing** (NLP) to deliver empathetic responses, facilitate crisis intervention, and provide referrals to appropriate services. For instance, UNICEF's "U-Report" platform has been deployed across Africa to provide scalable psychosocial support through AI-powered chatbots and SMS-based systems.

In Zambia, the U-Report Mental Health Chatbot was launched to address rising adolescent depression (Mwela, 2025). It offers free, confidential support via SMS and WhatsApp, using NLP to guide users through modules on emotional regulation, stress management, and stigma reduction. The chatbot is designed to be empathetic and accessible even on basic mobile phones, making it effective in remote and underserved areas.

The integration of AI into mobile platforms across Africa illustrates a pragmatic and innovative response to systemic challenges. In social work, these technologies present new opportunities to extend the reach of psychosocial services, particularly in resource-constrained environments. Future research should examine the ethical, cultural, and contextual dimensions of AI deployment to ensure equitable and culturally responsive practice.

13.3.4 Latin America: Community-Based Approaches and Inequality Concerns

Latin America is emerging as a dynamic arena for AI innovation. A notable regional initiative, Latam-GPT, spearheaded by Chile's National Center for Artificial Intelligence (CENIA) together with over 30 institutions, aims to create a large-language model trained on culturally and linguistically diverse datasets, with a special focus on Indigenous languages like Rapa Nui (Dhankhar, 2025). This open-source effort is intended to power region-specific applications in education and healthcare, challenging the dominance of English-centric AI systems.

A 2025 survey by Read AI found that 84% of Brazilian professionals are excited about the future of work with AI, indicating strong public trust and enthusiasm for AI adoption, significantly above the global average. The "LAURA" platform, developed in Brazil, uses AI to monitor ICU patients and detect early signs of sepsis. It analyzes over 2.5 million patient records and serves more than 200,000 patients monthly, reducing mortality by approximately 25% through real-time alerts and collaborative care strategies (fAIrLAC, n.d.).

Clínica Alemana in Chile has integrated AI into its pathology and imaging departments. AI tools are used to detect lesions related to fractures and strokes, enhancing diagnostic accuracy and enabling earlier interventions (Arce, 2024).

In Mexico, the social development agency SEDESOL joined with machine learning experts to refine the delivery of social services by detecting underreporting in household surveys and generating multidimensional poverty profiles (Sankaran et al., 2017). The system helped improve the targeting of social programs for over 7.4 million individuals, demonstrating the potential of AI to refine service delivery and support vulnerable populations.

AI is being used as a tool for urban planning and climate justice. In Honduras, researchers have used machine learning with satellite imagery to map informal settlements in Tegucigalpa, aiding more inclusive resource planning (Bayle & Silvani, 2020). The project aims to support more inclusive urban planning by creating the first informal settlements census in the city, addressing gaps in traditional data collection methods. In Mexico and Colombia, participatory AI models are informing climate resilience strategies, such as assessing vulnerability in informal urban settlements, while emphasizing ethical governance and community involvement (Ramirez Garcia, 2025).

A national-level analysis of Brazil's Zero Hunger program used quasi-experimental methods to assess the impact of social protection investments. Dyngeland and colleagues (2020) reported that collaboration between social workers and data scientists helped improve food production and educational outcomes, though effects on child malnutrition and infant mortality were mixed.

Argentina's AI solution PROMETEA, developed by the Public Prosecutor's Office in Buenos Aires, automates legal document analysis and precedent identification. It has significantly reduced Argentina's bureaucratic backlog, with examples including the automation of 1,000 rulings in just 26 days—tasks that would otherwise take over 100 days to process manually (Cerda, 2025). PROMETEA exemplifies scalable, high-impact AI use in legal systems, improving access to justice while maintaining human oversight.

Several AI applications streamline public-facing services. Brazil's federal government has implemented AI-powered chatbots on its Gov.br portal, which spans nearly 5,000 public services. These chatbots use Large Language Models (LLMs) to interact with citizens, clarify doubts, and direct them to appropriate services, significantly improving accessibility and reducing wait times (de Melo et al., 2024).

Hemominas, Brazil's largest blood bank, launched an AI-powered virtual assistant to actively engage blood donors via WhatsApp, email, and its website. The chatbot monitors blood stock levels and contacts registered donors to schedule appointments, increasing donation rates and streamlining logistics (Fundação Hemominas, 2025). These examples reflect how conversational AI tools are being adapted to diverse communities and institutional settings.

Camanchaca, a Chilean seafood company, developed "Elon," a generative AI assistant using Google Cloud's PaLM 2 model. Elon enables employees to access enterprise data through natural language queries, improving internal decision-making and customer service responsiveness (Hanley & Giang, 2023).

Latin America is charting its own path in AI, oriented toward inclusive, justice-driven deployment in human services. From healthcare diagnostics (LAURA), social welfare targeting (Mexico's SEDESOL) to urban resilience mapping and civic engagement tools, the region's AI efforts are defined by contextual responsiveness and ethical intention. At the same time, they remain less cohesive compared to the U.S. model, which is shaped more by private enterprise and established regulations. For global social work, these Latin American innovations offer instructive contrasts: they highlight the potential for AI to serve underserved populations through culturally grounded design and underscore the importance of regulation, ethics, and inclusivity.

13.3.5 Indigenous and Minority Communities: The Question of Data Sovereignty

The rapid expansion of AI carries both promise and risk for Indigenous and minority communities worldwide. While AI can support improved access to health, education, and social services, it also raises critical concerns about cultural autonomy, systemic bias, and control over community data. These issues are especially pressing because the effectiveness and fairness of AI systems depend directly on the data used to train them.

AI models are usually trained on large-scale datasets dominated by voices, languages, and experiences from majority populations. This structural imbalance risks rendering Indigenous and minority communities "invisible" in AI systems. For instance, NLP models often exclude Indigenous languages, limiting their ability to serve speakers of Māori, Quechua, or First Nations languages (Jones et al., 2023). As we have learned, predictive analytics in welfare or child protection may misclassify or over-surveil minority families, reproducing historic patterns of inequity in public systems. Another challenge is **algorithmic bias**: when AI is trained on skewed or incomplete datasets, it produces outputs that reinforce stereotypes and systemic discrimination. For example, automated decision-making tools in housing allocation, credit scoring, or social service eligibility may unfairly disadvantage minority groups if cultural and socioeconomic contexts are not accounted for (Zou & Khern-am-nuai, 2023).

In response, Indigenous scholars and activists have emphasized the principle of **data sovereignty**, the right of a people to govern the collection, ownership, and use of their own data (Redden & Kwan-Lafond, 2023). This concept is rooted in international frameworks such as the United Nations Declaration on the Rights of Indigenous Peoples (UNDRIP), which affirms Indigenous peoples' rights to self-determination and cultural preservation. Data sovereignty ensures that information about Indigenous communities is not simply extracted for commercial or governmental use but remains under local control to serve community priorities (Walter & Suina, 2019).

The CARE Principles of Indigenous Data Governance (**Collective benefit, Authority to control, Responsibility, Ethics**) provide a widely recognized framework for advancing this vision (Hudson et al., 2023). These principles move beyond the conventional FAIR guidelines (Findable, Accessible, Interoperable, Reusable) to emphasize justice, equity, and collective wellbeing.

When guided by principles of sovereignty and inclusion, AI can empower Indigenous and minority communities rather than harm them. AI-driven translation and speech recognition tools are being adapted to preserve endangered languages, such as efforts to build Māori language chatbots in New Zealand (Taiuru, 2023) and Cree language digital tools in Canada (Gupta & Boulianne, 2020).

Project Guacamaya is a collaborative initiative involving Indigenous communities, research institutions, and technology partners. This project uses machine learning and satellite imagery to monitor deforestation in the Amazon rainforest, particularly in Colombia, where Indigenous lands are under threat (Smith, 2024). The initiative combines daily satellite images, bioacoustics, and Amazon-specific AI models to detect ecological changes and support conservation efforts.

Khan and colleagues (2025) explored how AI models trained on culturally specific health data, when governed by Indigenous communities, can enhance diagnosis and treatment outcomes. The authors advocate for the Two-Eyed Seeing approach, integrating Indigenous knowledge systems with AI to ensure culturally safe, ethical, and effective healthcare delivery. They emphasize that community-controlled data governance is essential to avoid replicating colonial harm and to build trust in AI systems.

Social work's ethical commitment to cultural competence, anti-oppressive practice, and social justice aligns with the push for data sovereignty. Advocating for community consent in data collection, supporting culturally grounded AI tools, and critiquing exclusionary or biased systems are all professional responsibilities.

The development of AI must not replicate colonial dynamics of resource extraction in the form of data. Instead, centering data sovereignty ensures that Indigenous and minority communities shape how AI technologies are designed, deployed, and governed.

13.4 Implications for Global Social Work

China's experience illustrates the potential of AI to transform human services at scale, but it also highlights the risks of surveillance, inequity, and weakened privacy protections. In contrast, European practices stress human rights and ethical safeguards, while the U.S. approach balances innovation with ongoing debates about algorithmic bias. A global perspective is thus essential for social workers to understand both the possibilities and the limitations of AI integration into child welfare, mental health, gerontology, and poverty alleviation.

When we apply global perspective, data privacy and algorithmic bias become intensified. In Europe, the GDPR provides robust safeguards, while many low-income countries lack equivalent protection. This disparity can result in vulnerable populations being subject to data extraction without informed consent. Predictive analytics used in U.S. child welfare systems have been shown to disproportionately label Indigenous families as "high risk," reflecting entrenched systemic inequities. When exported globally, such systems may replicate or intensify discrimination.

From a human rights perspective, AI can both advance and threaten access to services. Tools that provide mental health counseling through chatbots can dramatically expand care in underserved regions, but if designed without cultural sensitivity, they may reinforce stigma or alienation. Global case studies presented here underscore that while AI holds promise for improving efficiency and expanding access, its application must always be critically evaluated for cultural fitness, ethical integrity, and its impact on human dignity.

For social workers to engage with AI, education and capacity building are essential. Many practicing social workers currently lack even basic digital literacy, let alone familiarity with AI systems. Without this foundation, social work professionals are at risk being sidelined in discussions that will profoundly shape their practice areas. Building AI literacy requires understanding the social implications of algorithms, the cultural context of data, and the ways technology intersects with systemic inequality. Specific training programs must therefore be multilingual, culturally relevant, and adaptable to different regional contexts.

Professional associations such as International Federation of Social Workers (IFSW), the International Association of Schools of Social Work (IASSW), and regional networks can provide platforms for knowledge sharing. Cross-national partnerships between universities, NGOs, and governments can foster the development of curricula that prepare the next generation of social workers to critically evaluate and shape AI tools.

Capacity building also includes policy advocacy. Social workers must play a role in influencing how governments regulate AI, ensuring that policies prioritize social justice and human dignity. In low-resource contexts, this may mean advocating for investment in digital infrastructure so that vulnerable populations are not further marginalized.

13.5 Critical Thinking Questions

1 Why do global disparities in AI development matter for social work and human services?
2 How do the U.S., European, and Chinese approaches to AI development differ in their underlying values and priorities? What implications might these differences have for social work practice and policy?
3 Why is cultural context important when applying AI to human services? Can you think of examples where AI solutions designed in one region might not work effectively, or ethically, in another?
4 How might ethical principles conflict with state or corporate interests in different regions?
5 What lessons can social workers in your own country draw from China's state-driven AI model, the U.S.'s private-sector dominance, and Europe's regulatory focus? How can these lessons be applied to strengthen social services locally?
6 What types of education, training, or cross-disciplinary collaboration in your country would help social workers develop the knowledge and skills to engage with AI responsibly and effectively?

13.6 Summary

AI presents both opportunities and challenges for social work, and its influence is undeniably global. By adopting a global perspective, social workers can learn from diverse regional approaches, identify ethical pitfalls, and leverage innovations that align with human rights. Whether in child protection, mental health, or elder care, AI must be applied with cultural sensitivity and ethical vigilance. Education and capacity building are crucial to ensuring that the profession is prepared not just to respond to AI, but to shape its development in service of the common good.

13.7 Empowerment-Focused Activities

13.7.1 Simulation: Writing a UN AI Governance Recommendation

Objective: Integrate advocacy and global social work perspective.
Activity: Students form country delegations to a mock "UN Social Work and AI Ethics Council."
Each delegation proposes a brief policy statement

- Protect human rights in AI use.
- Support equitable access and participation.
- Regulate data justice and transparency.

Class votes on shared recommendations to submit to a "UN declaration."

Learning outcome: Link macro-level advocacy with practice-level values.

13.7.2 Case Analysis: Global AI Governance Models

Objective: Compare how countries handle AI governance and its human rights impact.

Activity: Assign small groups a different region: EU, U.S., China, Global South (e.g., Kenya, Brazil, India). Each group researches:

- How AI is regulated or guided.
- Human rights challenges (privacy, bias, surveillance).
- Social work implications.

Groups present short posters or infographics in class.

Use a "World Café" setup where students rotate tables to discuss each region's approach.

Learning outcome: Recognize global diversity and ethical tensions in AI governance.

References

Adedunmola, A. (2025, February 10). *AI tool developed to predict, prevent food insecurity in Kenya.* Jarida Africa. https://kigalijournal.com/ai-tool-developed-to-predict-prevent-food-insecurity-in-kenya/

Arce, D. (2024, November 22). *How AI is integrating and transforming health and education in Latin America.* AméricaEconomía. www.americaeconomia.com/en/node/289559

Bayle, F., & Silvani, D. E. (2020). Case study: Mapping potential informal settlements areas in Tegucigalpa with machine learning to plan ground survey. arXiv. https://doi.org/10.48550/arXiv.2006.14490

Bentley, S. V., Naughtin, C. K., McGrath, M. J., Irons, J. L., & Cooper, P. S. (2024). The digital divide in action: How experiences of digital technology shape future relationships with artificial intelligence. *AI and Ethics, 4*, 901–915. https://doi.org/10.1007/s43681-024-00452-3

Busch, F., Kather, J. N., Johner, C., Moser, M., Truhn, D., Adams, L. C., & Bressem, K. K. (2024). Navigating the European Union Artificial Intelligence Act for healthcare. *NPJ Digital Medicine, 7*, Article 1213. https://doi.org/10.1038/s41746-024-01213-6

Byamukama, S., Maas, J., & Pfisterer, S. (2024, May 20). *Lessons learned from Babyl: Scaling digital healthcare solutions in Rwanda (DCCC learning paper).* Digital Connected Care Coalition. www.digitalconnectedcarecoalition.org/wp-content/uploads/2024/05/DCCC-learning-paper-Lessons-learned-from-Babyl.pdf

Cerda, L. (2025). *Prometea: Revolutionizing judicial efficiency in Argentina through artificial intelligence powered legal solutions.* Inter-American Law Review. https://inter-american-law-review.law.miami.edu/prometea-revolutionizing-judicial-efficiency-in-argentina-through-artificial-intelligence-powered-legal-solutions/

Chandra, P. S., Sawmya, H. R., Mehrotra, S., & Duggal, M. (2014). 'SMS' for mental health—Feasibility and acceptability of using text messages for mental health promotion among young women in urban slums in India. *Asian Journal of Psychiatry, 11*, 59–65. https://doi.org/10.1016/j.ajp.2014.06.008

Cui, W., Xue, Z., & Thai, K.-P. (2018). Performance comparison of an AI-based adaptive learning system in China. *2018 Chinese Automation Congress (*CAC*), 3170–3175*. https://doi.org/10.1109/CAC.2018.8623327

Dare, T. (2013, September 23). *Predictive risk modelling and child maltreatment: An ethical review*. Ministry of Social Development of New Zealand. www.msd.govt.nz/documents/about-msd-and-our-work/publications-resources/research/predictive-modelling/00-predicitve-risk-modelling-and-child-maltreatment-an-ethical-review.pdf

de Melo, M. K., dos Reis, S. A., Di Oliveira, V., Faria, A. V. A., de Lima, R., Weigang, L., Salm Junior, J. F., Souza, J. G. M., Freitas, V., Brom, P. C., Kimura, H., Cajueiro, D. O., da Silva, G. L., & Celestino, V. R. R. (2024). *Implementing AI for enhanced public services Gov.br: A methodology for the Brazilian federal government*. ScitePress. www.scitepress.org/Papers/2024/129970/129970.pdf

Dhankhar, S. (2025, June 18). *Latam-GPT aims to preserve Indigenous languages with AI*. yPredict. https://ypredict.ai/news/latam-gpt-aims-to-preserve-indigenous-languages-with-ai/

Dyngeland, C., Oldekop, J. A., & Evans, K. L. (2020). Assessing multidimensional sustainability: Lessons from Brazil's social protection programs. *Proceedings of the National Academy of Sciences, 117*(34), 20511–20519. https://doi.org/10.1073/pnas.1920998117

fAIrLAC. (n.d.). *LAURA: Plataforma de inteligencia artificial para salvar vidas*. Inter-American Development Bank. https://fairlac.iadb.org/laura-br

Fattorini, L., Maslej, N., Perrault, R., Parli, V., Etchemendy, J., Shoham, Y., & Ligett, K. (2024). The global AI vibrancy tool. https://doi.org/10.48550/arxiv.2412.04486

Federal Trade Commission. (2025, January 17). *FTC issues staff report on AI partnerships & investments study*. Federal Trade Commission. www.ftc.gov/news-events/news/press-releases/2025/01/ftc-issues-staff-report-ai-partnerships-investments-study

Agência Minas Gerais. (2025, January 28). *Hemominas inicia testes com assistente virtual para captar doadores de sangue.*. www.agenciaminas.mg.gov.br/noticia/hemominas-inicia-testes-com-assistente-virtual-para-captar-doadores-de-sangue

Global Times. (2025, April 24). China becomes world's top holder of AI patents: WIPO. Retrieved from www.globaltimes.cn/page/202504/1332783.shtml

Gooding, P., van Kolfschooten, H., & Centola, F. (2024). *Artificial intelligence in mental healthcare*. Mental Health Europe. www.mentalhealtheurope.org/wp-content/uploads/2025/02/Study-on-AI-in-mental-health-care-final-for-publication.pdf

Gupta, V., & Boulianne, G. (2020). Speech transcription challenges for resource constrained indigenous language Cree. In *Proceedings of the 1st Joint SLTU and CCURL Workshop (SLTU-CCURL 2020)* (pp. 362–367). European Language Resources Association (ELRA). https://aclanthology.org/2020.sltu-1.51.pdf

Hanley, M., & Giang, M. (2023, December 4). Camanchaca innovates its employee experience with real-time generative agents. *Google Cloud Blog*. https://cloud.google.com/blog/products/ai-machine-learning/camanchaca-innovates-its-employee-experience-with-real-time-generative-agents

Hello Tractor. (2023). *Growing together*. https://hellotractor.com/

Hoque, M. R., Rahman, M. S., Nipa, N. J., & Hasan, M. R. (2020). Mobile health interventions in developing countries: A systematic review. *Health Informatics Journal, 26*(4), 2792–2810. https://doi.org/10.1177/1460458220937102

Hudson, M., Carroll, S. R., Anderson, J., Blackwater, D., Cordova-Marks, F. M., Cummins, J., David-Chavez, D., Fernandez, A., Garba, I., Hiraldo, D., Jäger, M. B., Jennings, L. L., Martinez, A., Sterling, R., Walker, J. D., & Rowe, R. K. (2023). Indigenous Peoples' rights in data: A contribution toward Indigenous research sovereignty. *Frontiers in Research Metrics and Analytics, 8*. 1–8. https://doi.org/10.3389/frma.2023.1173805

Jones, P.-L., Mahelona, K., Duncan, S., & Leoni, G. (2023, August 23). Kia tangata whenua: Artificial intelligence that grows from the land and people. *Ethical Space: International Journal of Communication Ethics, 2023*(2/3). 1–19. https://doi.org/10.21428/0af3f4c0.9092b177.

Khan, A., McKinney, V., & Mendez, I. (2025). Two-Eyed seeing and artificial intelligence: Enhancing healthcare delivery in Indigenous communities requires an ethical and culturally relevant public health framework. *Canadian Journal of Public Health. 116*, 883–886. https://doi.org/10.17269/s41997-025-01037-1

Lee, O. E. K., Nam, I, Chon, Y., Park, A., & Choi, N. (2023). Socially assistive humanoid robots: Effects on depression and health-related quality of life among low-income, socially isolated older adults in South Korea. *Journal of Applied Gerontology, 42*(3), 367–375. https://doi.org/10.1177/07334648221138283

Muhammed, J. (2025, March 1). AI for agriculture: The African perspectives. *African Leadership Magazine.* www.africanleadershipmagazine.co.uk/ai-for-agriculture-the-african-perspectives/

Mwela, N. N. (2025, May 15). *Opening up: U-Report Zambia activates mental health chatbot for World Mental Health Action Day.* UNICEF Zambia. www.unicef.org/zambia/stories/opening-u-report-zambia-activates-mental-health-chatbot-world-mental-health-action-day

Ndung'u, N. S. (2021). *A digital financial services revolution in Kenya: The M-Pesa case study.* African Economic Research Consortium. https://aercafrica.org/old-website/wp-content/uploads/2021/03/AERC-MPesa-Case-Study.pdf

Organisation for Economic Co-operation and Development (OECD). (2023). *OECD employment outlook 2023: Artificial intelligence and the labour market.* OECD Publishing. https://doi.org/10.1787/08785bba-en

Ramirez Garcia, L. A. (2025, July). *See how AI can transform informal settlements in Latin America.* Weforum. www.weforum.org/stories/2025/07/how-ai-is-transforming-informal-settlements-in-latin-america/

Read AI. (2025, May 15). *Brazil survey: 68% of Brazilians use AI everyday but only 31% have formal access and training at work—and they want more.* Read AI. www.read.ai/post/brazil-survey-68-of-brazilians-use-ai-everyday-but-only-31-have-formal-access-and-training-at-work--and-they-want-more

Redden, M., & Kwan-Lafond, D. (2023). *Indigenous data sovereignty: Moving toward self-determination and a future of good data.* Ecampusontario.pressbooks.pub. https://doi.org/10.5206/OMRK6926

Sankaran, K., Garcia-Olano, D., Javed, M., Alcala-Durand, M. F., De Unánue, A., van der Boor, P., Potash, E., Sánchez Avalos, R., Alberro Encinas, L. I., & Ghani, R. (2017). Applying machine learning methods to enhance the distribution of social services in Mexico. arXiv. https://doi.org/10.48550/arXiv.1709.05551

Second Talent. (2025, September 16). Top 50+ Chinese AI investment statistics [2025]. Retrieved from www.secondtalent.com/resources/chinese-ai-investment-statistics/

Shams, R. A., Zowghi, D., & Bano, M. (2025). AI and the quest for diversity and inclusion: A systematic literature review. *AI and Ethics, 5*, 411–438. https://doi.org/10.1007/s43681-023-00362-w

Smith, E. (2024, September 25). *Project Guacamaya uses daily satellite images, Amazon-specific AI models in battle against deforestation.* Source LATAM. https://news.microsoft.com/source/latam/features/ai/project-guacamaya-rainforest-deforestation/?lang=en

Taiuru, K. (2023). *Te Reo Māori: The Māori language revitalisation and adaption with AI.* Taiuru & Associates Ltd. www.taiuru.co.nz/maori-language-revitalisation-with-ai/

Tian, Y. J. (Angelina), Felber, N. A., Pageau, F., Roulet Schwab, D., & Wangmo, T. (2024). Benefits and barriers associated with the use of smart home health technologies in the care of older persons: A systematic review. *BMC Geriatrics, 24*, 152. https://doi.org/10.1186/s12877-024-04702-1

Vardas, E. P., Marketou, M., & Vardas, P. E. (2025). Medicine, healthcare and the AI Act: Gaps, challenges and future implications. *European Heart Journal – Digital Health, 6*(4), 833–839. https://doi.org/10.1093/ehjdh/ztaf041

Voronoi. (2025, April 21). The United States is the AI capital of the world. Retrieved from www.voronoiapp.com/technology/The-United-States-is-the-AI-Capital-of-the-World-4744

Walter, M., & Suina, M. (2019). Indigenous data, Indigenous methodologies, and Indigenous data sovereignty. *International Journal of Social Research Methodology, 22*(3), 233–243. https://doi.org/10.1080/13645579.2018.1531228

Wang, L. L. (2021). Face recognition in law enforcement: A comparative analysis of China and the United States. *Open Journal of Social Sciences, 9*(10), 498–506. https://doi.org/10.4236/jss.2021.910036

Webster, G., Creemers, R., Kania, E., & Triolo, P. (2017). *Full translation: China's "new generation artificial intelligence development plan" (2017).* DigiChina; Stanford University. https://digichina.stanford.edu/work/full-translation-chinas-new-generation-artificial-intelligence-development-plan-2017/

Woods, D. (2025). AI as a tool for surveillance: China's concave trilemma. *Journal of Chinese Political Science. 30*, 1–35. https://doi.org/10.1007/s11366-025-09907-8

Yao, Y., Zhou, J., Sun, Z., Guan, Q., Guo, Z., Xu, Y., Zhang, J., Hong, Y., Cai, Y., & Wang, R. (2024). Estimating China's poverty reduction efficiency by integrating multi-source geospatial data and deep learning techniques. *Geo-Spatial Information Science*, *27*(4), 1000–1016. https://doi.org/10.1080/10095020.2023.2165975

Zou, L., & Khern-am-nuai, W. (2023). AI and housing discrimination: The case of mortgage applications. *AI and Ethics, 3*, 1271–1281. https://doi.org/10.1007/s43681-022-00234-9

14 AI Literacy for Social Workers in the Future

Othelia E. Lee

14.1 AI Literacy and Digital Literacy for Social Workers

When used with intention and care, AI can serve as a supportive partner in a profession long marked by high workloads and burnout. By automating routine tasks and easing documentation burdens, AI has the potential to give social workers what they repeatedly say they need most: more time for meaningful human connection. Early evidence suggests that AI-supported documentation tools can reduce after-hours work and lighten administrative load (Albrecht et al., 2025). For these reasons, AI is increasingly being adopted across healthcare and human services to provide clinicians with timely resources, assist with recommendations, and even help predict health-related risks and outcomes (Vasey et al., 2021).

At the same time, AI systems generate responses based on the data and design choices that shape them, meaning that polished, confident, and eloquent outputs may still contain inaccuracies, distortions, or biased assumptions (Ratwani et al., 2024). Because clients and communities can be directly affected by these errors, social workers must approach AI tools with a critical lens. Responsible integration requires ongoing evaluation, transparency, and ethical vigilance, especially as these tools are still emerging.

While AI is rapidly finding its way into practice settings, social work education has not kept pace. Very few social work programs currently offer structured opportunities for students to meaningfully engage with AI tools, often due to concerns about ethics, equity, or preparedness. As a result, many new practitioners enter the profession without the AI literacy needed to navigate technologies that are already reshaping service delivery (Ahn et al., 2025). This chapter takes up that charge by outlining how we can build the capacities future social workers need to use AI responsibly in service of human rights and the common good.

Digital literacy refers to the capacity to access, understand, and critically use digital tools and information. For social workers, this includes everything from managing electronic case files to engaging with clients through telehealth platforms and understanding the implications of AI in service delivery (Adelore & Ojedeji, 2021).

What defines the **AI literacy** necessary for social workers? AI literacy involves understanding how intelligent systems work, recognizing their limitations, and evaluating their impact on individuals and communities (Taylor-Beswick, 2023).

DOI: 10.4324/9781003755081-18

The rationale for including AI in social work education stems from the growing presence of digital systems in assessment, case management, mental health support, and policy analysis. AI is already being used to identify patterns in service delivery, predict client needs, and support decision-making in complex cases (Ahn et al., 2025). As these technologies become embedded in practice, social workers must be prepared to critically engage with them, not just as users, but as advocates for ethical, equitable, and human-centered design.

14.1.1 Digital Tools and Competencies Across Practice Levels

The urgency of digital/AI literacy in social work stems from the rapid integration of technology into nearly every aspect of practice. From virtual counseling sessions to algorithmic decision-making, digital tools are reshaping how services are delivered. Without adequate digital/AI literacy, social workers risk falling behind in their ability to advocate effectively, protect client confidentiality, and ensure equitable access to services (Adelore & Ojedeji, 2021).

Social work profession is at a pivotal moment where technological competence must be paired with ethical awareness to prepare learners for the realities of contemporary practice. It is essential for practitioners to understand how these tools apply across the micro, mezzo, and macro levels of practice. Each level presents unique opportunities and challenges, requiring tailored competencies to ensure ethical, effective, and equitable service delivery (Table 14.1).

Micro-Level Practice: Supporting Individuals Through Technology. At the micro level, digital tools such as teletherapy platforms, client-facing mobile apps, and AI-powered chatbots have become increasingly common in clinical and case management settings. These technologies can enhance accessibility, reduce barriers to care, and offer flexible support options for clients who may face geographic, financial, or mobility constraints. Moreover, digital literacy is essential, not only for social workers but also for clients, to ensure that technology enhances therapeutic relationships (Zgoda & Shane, 2018).

Mezzo-Level Practice: Engaging Communities and Organizations. At the mezzo level, digital tools such as social media platforms, nonprofit data analytics, and online support groups enable practitioners to expand outreach, foster community engagement, and evaluate program effectiveness. Social media can be used to raise awareness about mental health resources or mobilize support for local initiatives. Social workers must be equipped to critically assess digital content, manage organizational data responsibly, and facilitate inclusive online spaces that reflect the values of equity and empowerment.

Macro-Level Practice: Driving Systemic Change Through Technology. At the macro level, digital tools such as online advocacy campaigns, predictive analytics, and interactive policy platforms empower practitioners to amplify marginalized voices and influence decision-making processes. For instance, predictive analytics can help identify areas of need in a community, guiding resource allocation and policy development (Minoi et al., 2025).

Table 14.1 Digital/AI Tools and Competencies across Practice Levels

Practice Level	*Digital Tools*	*Benefits*	*Risks*	*Ethical Considerations*
Micro	Teletherapy, client apps, chatbots	Increased accessibility, flexible support, personalized care	Privacy concerns, digital divide, reduced interpersonal connection	Confidentiality, informed consent, cultural responsiveness
Mezzo	Social media outreach, nonprofit analytics, online groups	Enhanced outreach, data-driven program evaluation, community engagement	Misinformation, data mismanagement, exclusion of digitally underserved groups	Responsible data use, inclusive communication, equity in access
Macro	Digital campaigns, predictive analytics for community planning	Amplified advocacy, informed policy decisions, strategic resource allocation	Algorithmic bias, lack of transparency, ethical misuse of data	Transparency, community involvement, justice-oriented data practices

14.1.2 Core Dimensions of Digital and AI Literacy

To guide the development of these literacy, educators and practitioners can draw on established frameworks such as the UNESCO Digital Literacy Global Framework. This model outlines key competencies across areas like information and data literacy, communication and collaboration, digital content creation, safety, and problem-solving (UNESCO, 2018). Integrating such frameworks into social work education ensures that students are not only digitally capable but also critically aware and ethically grounded.

Therefore, digital and AI literacy for social workers encompasses four core dimensions:

1 *Technical Literacy*: Understanding how to use digital tools, platforms, and systems effectively, including case management software, telehealth platforms, and data analytics tools.
2 *Critical Literacy*: The ability to question and evaluate digital content, including recognizing misinformation, assessing algorithmic bias, and understanding the limitations of AI systems.
3 *Ethical Literacy*: Applying social work values to digital contexts, including safeguarding client privacy, ensuring informed consent, and advocating for transparency in AI systems.
4 *Cultural Literacy*: Recognizing how digital tools interact with cultural identities and social structures and ensuring that technology use is inclusive and respectful of diverse populations.

14.2 Reframing Digital and AI Literacy as a Core Competency

The Council on Social Work Education (CSWE, 2022) has emphasized the importance of technology in its Educational Policy and Accreditation Standards (EPAS), calling for competency-based education that includes the ethical use of digital tools. Digital and AI literacy aligns directly with these standards, supporting the development of critical thinking, ethical practice, and culturally responsive service delivery in the AI era. As technology evolves, so must the competencies of social workers, ensuring they are prepared to meet the needs of clients in digital environments.

14.2.1 AI Literacy Goals for Social Workers

AI literacy is a foundational competency for social workers in the digital age. It begins with the ability to understand core AI concepts in plain language and extends to recognizing how these technologies shape decision-making in human services (Taylor-Beswick, 2023). Social workers must be able to define AI and distinguish its subareas, including:

- *Machine learning*: systems that learn from data to make predictions or decisions.
- *Natural language processing (NLP):* tools that understand and generate human language.
- *Robotics*: machines that perform tasks autonomously or semi-autonomously.

Beyond technical understanding, AI literacy involves the ability to recognize bias, fairness, and accountability issues in AI systems. Social workers should be able to read and interpret AI systems are not neutral. They reflect the values, assumptions, and biases of their creators and the data they are trained on. Algorithmic bias, for example, can reinforce systemic inequities if not carefully addressed.

AI literacy includes identifying ethical risks such as surveillance, privacy violations, and algorithmic inequities, especially when these tools are used in sensitive areas like child welfare, mental health, or public welfare benefits (Ahn et al., 2025). It also involves advocacy for ethical standards that protect client autonomy, promote transparency, and address the digital divide (Gooding et al., 2024). AI literacy is not about becoming a technologist—it's about becoming a thoughtful, informed advocate who can interpret AI-generated data responsibly and ensure that technology serves the common good.

14.2.2 Competencies for Ethical AI Practice

The NASW Standards for Technology in Social Work Practice emphasize that ethical and effective use of technology is integral to competent practice (NASW, 2017). Ethical engagement with AI requires a set of interrelated competencies that reflect the values and standards of the social work profession.

Collaborative Skills. Social workers must be prepared to collaborate with technologists, policymakers, data scientists, engineers, and communities. These partnerships are essential for designing and implementing AI tools that meet real-world needs.

Critical Thinking. Practitioners must be able to evaluate the benefits and harms of AI tools, assessing claims about their effectiveness, fairness, and impact. This includes questioning assumptions, analyzing evidence, and considering unintended consequences.

Equity and Justice Orientation. AI systems can reinforce existing inequalities if not carefully designed and monitored. Social workers must be able to identify digital divides, recognize algorithmic discrimination, and advocate for marginalized groups in digital contexts (Gooding et al., 2024).

Ethical Reasoning. Social workers should be able to apply ethical principles to AI-related dilemmas, such as whether to use predictive analytics in child protection or how to respond to biased algorithmic assessments.

Practice Integration. Finally, social workers must learn to use AI responsibly in assessment, intervention, and evaluation. This means understanding when and how AI tools can support human judgment and ensuring that technology enhances client-centered care. Central to this integration is the principle of "Human-in-the-loop" decision-making: social workers must remember that AI analysis should never be accepted as the final judgment. Instead, practitioners must exercise their final decision-making authority by critically synthesizing AI insights with the core values of the social work profession and the unique, lived context of each client.

AI competency framework provides a roadmap for preparing social workers to navigate the ethical, technical, and relational dimensions of AI in practice. By fostering AI literacy and ethical reasoning, educators can empower students to become compassionate, critically engaged professionals who advocate for justice in the digital world.

14.2.3 Barriers and Equity Challenges in Social Work Practice

Because these literacies are not isolated skills but interconnected competencies that support holistic, ethical, and effective practice in a digital world, there are many challenges and barriers to overcome. One of the most pressing challenges is the **digital divide**, which refers to unequal access to digital tools and internet connectivity. The digital divide disproportionately affects marginalized communities, limiting access to education, healthcare, and employment opportunities. Bridging this divide means advocating for access to technology, supporting digital skill development, and ensuring that digital tools do not reinforce systemic inequalities (Ahn et al., 2025).

Another significant barrier is **algorithmic bias**. AI tools used in social services (e. g., predictive risk models or automated eligibility systems) can unintentionally replicate and reinforce existing social inequalities (Ratwani et al., 2024). Without careful oversight, AI systems may produce outcomes that disadvantage clients based on race, gender, disability, or socioeconomic status. Box 14.1 offers a check list for social workers can use.

Box 14.1 Algorithmic Bias Recognition Checklist for Social Workers

Purpose and Power: Why Is This AI Being Used?

- What decision or recommendation does the tool make (risk score, eligibility, prioritization, prediction)?
- Does the AI support human judgment—or does it effectively replace it?
- Who benefits most from this tool: clients, agency efficiency, funders, or policymakers?
- Are high-stakes outcomes involved (child removal, benefits denial, incarceration, housing access)?

Data Origins: Who Is (and Isn't) Represented?

- Do we know where the data came from (public records, case files, healthcare, policing, education)?
- Were certain groups over-surveilled in the data (e.g., low-income families, racial minorities)?
- Are marginalized populations missing or underrepresented?
- Is the data historical, reflecting past discrimination?

Equity Impact: Who Is Harmed If It's Wrong?

- What happens if the AI makes a false positive (labels someone high-risk incorrectly)?
- What happens if it makes a false negative (misses someone who needs help)?
- Are harms unevenly distributed across race, gender, disability, age, or immigration status?
- Are vulnerable clients punished more severely for errors?

Transparency and Explainability: Can It Be Understood?

- Can staff explain in simple language how the AI reaches conclusions?
- Can clients receive a meaningful explanation for decisions affecting them?
- Is the system described as a "black box"?
- Are explanations limited to technical jargon?

Human Oversight: Can Social Workers Override It?

- Are social workers allowed and encouraged to override AI recommendations?
- Is there a formal process to challenge or correct AI outputs?
- Are workers pressured to follow AI results to avoid liability?
- Does disagreement with the AI require extra justification?

Accountability: Who Is Responsible for Harm?

- Who is accountable if the AI causes harm—the vendor, agency, or worker?
- Are there clear appeal mechanisms for clients?
- Has the system been independently audited for bias?
- Is there ongoing monitoring, not just one-time evaluation?

Language and Framing: How Are Clients Described?

- Does the AI use deficit-based language (risk, threat, burden)?
- Are clients framed as problems to be managed rather than people to be supported?
- Does the system ignore structural factors (poverty, racism, housing shortages)?
- Are behaviors interpreted without social context?

Cultural Humility and Disability Sensitivity

- Does the system account for cultural differences in communication or family structure?

- Are disabilities incorrectly treated as risk indicators?
- Are neurodivergent behaviors misinterpreted as noncompliance?
- Is language access considered?

Consent and Client Awareness

- Do clients know AI is being used in decisions about them?
- Is consent informed, not buried in fine print?
- Can clients opt out or request human review?
- Are privacy protections clearly explained?

Ethical Alignment with Social Work Values

- Does the AI promote dignity and worth of the person?
- Does it advance social justice rather than efficiency alone?
- Does it respect self-determination?
- Would you feel comfortable explaining its use to a client, supervisor, or ethics board?

One-Minute Bias Test for Practice
Ask yourself: "If this tool were used primarily on wealthy, white, able-bodied clients—would it still be acceptable?"

If the answer is no, bias is likely present.

These structural challenges are not merely technical: they are deeply rooted in social, economic, and cultural inequalities. Understanding these barriers is critical for social workers committed to justice, inclusion, and ethical practice. Now let's consider strategies to cope with these challenges.

14.3 Curriculum Integration Strategies

Boetto (2025) proposes the EPIC (Ethics, Policy, Intersectoral collaboration, and Community engagement) model, as a framework for integrating AI into social work education and practice. This EPIC model emphasizes the importance of preparing students to navigate the opportunities and risks posed by AI while upholding the core values of the profession. Social work educators face a critical opportunity, and responsibility, to prepare learners for a future shaped by digital transformation. Integrating AI into social work education is not merely about teaching technical skills: it is about fostering ethical awareness, critical thinking, and a commitment to equity in a rapidly evolving landscape (Taylor-Beswick, 2023). Let us introduce three approaches for curriculum innovation: infusion into existing courses, stand-alone courses, and practicum experiences.

14.3.1 Infusion into Existing Courses

One accessible and flexible strategy is to embed AI-related content into the core social work curriculum. This approach allows learners to explore the implications of AI within familiar disciplinary contexts such as ethics, policy, research, and direct practice.

In policy courses, learners might examine algorithmic decision-making in child welfare or predictive policing, critically evaluating how these systems impact marginalized communities. In practice courses, students can explore chatbot-assisted counseling scenarios, considering both the potential for increased access and the limitations of machine-mediated empathy. In research courses, students can learn how AI tools analyze large social datasets, while grappling with questions of bias, representation, and data justice (Barsky, 2017).

A sample assignment might include a Policy Brief on AI in Social Services, where students write a 3–4-page memo evaluating the risks and benefits of predictive analytics in public benefits programs. This encourages learners to apply policy analysis skills while engaging with real-world technological developments.

14.3.2 Stand-Alone Courses or Modules

Another strategy is to develop dedicated courses or modules focused on AI and its intersection with social work. These elective offerings can provide deeper engagement with the technical, ethical, and advocacy-related dimensions of AI.

A sample course titled "AI and Social Work Practice for the Common Good" could be designed with the following learning objectives. At the completion of the course, students will:

- Demonstrate AI literacy by explaining core concepts such as algorithms, machine learning, and NLP.
- Critically evaluate AI tools used in social services for their ethical implications.
- Propose strategies to advocate for equitable and transparent AI use in practice settings.

Assignments might include an Ethical Dilemma Analysis, where learners analyze a case in which predictive AI flagged families for child protection risk. Using the NASW Code of Ethics, students would recommend an action plan that balances technological efficiency with human rights.

Another assignment could be a Team Project, where students design a prototype (e.g., chatbot script or data visualization) to address a community need, fostering creativity and interdisciplinary collaboration (Gooding et al., 2024). These courses can be enriched through partnerships with departments such as computer science, information studies, and public health, promoting interdisciplinary learning and innovation. We present a sample syllabus in support materials (Box 14.2).

14.3.3 Practicum and Experiential Learning

Practicum offers a powerful avenue for students to engage directly with AI systems in practice settings. Agencies using predictive analytics, chatbot counseling, or assistive robotics can provide rich learning environments for students to observe, reflect, and contribute.

Learners might participate in technology impact audits, interviewing practitioners, clients, and administrators about how an AI tool shapes service delivery. They could also conduct student-led ethics reviews of agency technologies, applying ethical frameworks to assess risks and benefits (Rodríguez Martínez et al., 2024). Reflective supervision is essential in these placements, helping students process ethical dilemmas and align their experiences with social work values.

Integrating AI into social work education is a dynamic and necessary step toward preparing compassionate, critically engaged practitioners. Whether through infusion into existing courses, stand-alone offerings, or practicum-based learning, these curriculum strategies support the development of AI literacy aligned with the CSWE EPAS, including competency-based education, ethical practice, and technological proficiency (CSWE, 2022).

14.4 Teaching Approaches and Examples

Preparing social work students for a future shaped by AI requires thoughtful, inclusive, and experiential teaching strategies. AI literacy is not just about understanding algorithms: it's about cultivating ethical awareness, critical thinking, and commitment to social justice in digital contexts. We introduce several teaching approaches.

14.4.1 Icebreaker: "AI in Everyday Life" Mapping Exercise

To begin building AI awareness, educators can invite students to reflect on how AI already appears in their daily lives, through recommendation systems, chatbots, health apps, and smart devices. In this mapping exercise, learners identify these technologies and then draw parallels to their potential applications in human services. This activity fosters curiosity and helps demystify AI by connecting it to familiar experiences, laying the groundwork for deeper exploration.

14.4.2 Case-Based Learning: Ethical Dilemmas in Predictive Analytics

Case-based learning allows learners to grapple with real-world ethical challenges. For example, a case study on predictive analytics in juvenile justice can prompt students to debate whether AI improves fairness or amplifies racial disparities. Through structured discussion, learners examine algorithmic bias, data ethics, and the implications of automated decision-making. This approach encourages critical engagement and ethical reasoning, core competencies in social work practice (Barsky, 2017).

14.4.3 Critical Media Analysis: Deconstructing AI Narratives

Students can also engage in critical media analysis, examining how AI is portrayed in news media and popular culture. By analyzing the coverage of AI in social care, students learn to identify biases, sensationalism, and gaps in reporting. This activity promotes media literacy and helps students develop a nuanced understanding of the public discourse around technology and human services.

14.4.4 Cross-Disciplinary Collaboration: Designing AI with Social Values

Collaboration across disciplines enriches learning and fosters innovation. Social work students can partner with peers in computer science or public health to co-develop AI prototypes grounded in social values. These projects could include designing ethical chatbot scripts, developing inclusive data dashboards, or proposing community-based AI interventions. Such partnerships model the interdisciplinary nature of modern social work and promote mutual learning (Taylor-Beswick, 2023).

14.4.5 Project-Based Learning: AI-Informed Interventions

In project-based learning, learners design small-scale interventions using AI tools. Examples include creating chatbots to connect clients with resources or building data visualizations for nonprofit organizations. These hands-on projects allow students to apply theoretical knowledge in practical ways, fostering creativity, problem-solving, and community engagement.

14.4.6 Simulation and Role-Play: Practicing with AI Tools

Simulations and role-play offer immersive experiences that build empathy and confidence. Students can practice client engagement using socially assistive robots or AI chatbot systems, rotating roles as a client, a social worker, and AI chatbot. This activity helps students explore communication dynamics, identify strengths and limitations of AI tools, and reflect on ethical considerations in digital interactions.

14.4.7 Classroom Activities for Experiential Learning

Furthermore, social work educators can implement a variety of classroom activities to deepen learning by incorporating experiential learning. Here we provide some ideas.

Class Debate: “Can AI reduce social work caseloads without compromising ethics?” Divide the class into two groups to make an argument from each side. This encourages learners to articulate and defend diverse perspectives.

AI Tool Evaluation Worksheet: Students assess a real-world AI system for transparency, bias, equity impact, and client experience.

Community Engagement Simulation: Students role-play presenting AI-driven tools to a client advisory board, practicing advocacy and communication.

Competency Portfolio: Students compile reflection essays, project reports, and peer feedback to demonstrate growth in AI literacy and ethical practice.

Innovative teaching methods are already transforming social work education as demonstrated in scholarship in teaching. Simulations and **Virtual Reality** (VR) have emerged as powerful training tools that foster empathy, decision-making, and confidence in practice. Virtual simulations allow students to engage with realistic scenarios (e.g., home visits or crisis interventions) within a safe, controlled environment. These tools bridge the gap between theoretical knowledge and practical application, helping students develop role expectancy and professional identity (Lanzieri et al., 2021).

Digital storytelling is also gaining attraction as a pedagogical method that enhances critical thinking and engagement. Learners create personal narratives using multimedia tools, reflecting on their placement experiences and evolving professional identities. Davey and Benjaminsen (2021) found that digital storytelling promotes deep reflection, collaboration, and identity formation, even in large, online learning environments.

Podcasting has been used to make abstract or intimidating topics, such as social policy, more accessible and emotionally resonant, encouraging students to engage critically with complex content. Besser and colleagues (2022) present case studies showing how podcasting enhances student engagement, critical thinking, and content retention.

14.5 Assessment and Evaluation of AI Competency in Social Work

It is essential to develop meaningful and inclusive assessment strategies that reflect both technical understanding and ethical engagement. Assessments should not only measure knowledge but also foster reflection, critical thinking, and commitment to equity. Grounded in the CSWE EPAS, competency-based assessments offer a framework for evaluating student growth across AI literacy, ethical reasoning, and practice integration (CSWE, 2022).

14.5.1 Competency-Based Assessments Aligned with CSWE Standards

Competency-based education emphasizes the demonstration of skills and values in real-world contexts. In the realm of AI, this means assessing students' ability to:

- Understand and explain key AI concepts.
- Apply ethical reasoning to technology-related dilemmas.
- Advocate for equitable and transparent use of AI in social services.
- Collaborate across disciplines and engage with communities affected by digital systems.

Box 14.2 AI Competency Checklist

Readers should be able to demonstrate the following after completing their assignment

AI Literacy (Knowledge)

Explain key AI applications (chatbots, predictive analytics, teletherapy tools).
Differentiate benefits and limitations of AI in direct and community practice.

Ethical Reasoning (Values)

Identify confidentiality, consent, and data equity concerns in AI use.
Apply the NASW Code of Ethics to AI-related dilemmas.

Equity and Justice Orientation (Values/Skills)

Recognize the risks of algorithmic bias, surveillance, and the digital divide.
Propose strategies to mitigate inequities in AI deployment.

Critical Thinking (Skills)

Evaluate AI tools critically rather than accepting them at face value.
Integrate professional judgment with AI-informed recommendations.

Practice Integration (Skills)

Suggest appropriate ways to use AI to enhance, not replace, therapeutic relationships.
Identify how AI can strengthen mezzo-level service delivery and macro-level advocacy.

A variety of assessment formats can be used to support diverse learning styles and promote deep engagement. We provide some examples here:

Short Quiz: A brief assessment covering foundational AI literacy concepts such as algorithms, machine learning, and automation. This helps ensure baseline understanding and vocabulary.
Reflection Journal: Students reflect on ethical risks and equity implications presented in a vignette. Ongoing entries encourage students to explore how AI intersects with their evolving professional identity and values.
Case Analysis: Students select a vignette involving AI in social services (e.g., predictive analytics in child welfare) and outline how they would intervene, applying ethical reasoning and client-centered approaches.

Policy Brief (1–2 pages): Students recommend safeguards for a mental health AI system at the macro level, considering transparency, accountability, and human rights.
Capstone Project: Students design a policy advocacy brief or practice innovation that incorporates AI to promote equity. This project allows for creativity, interdisciplinary thinking, and real-world relevance.
Team Projects: Students work collaboratively to evaluate real-world AI tools used in social services. They assess transparency, bias, and client experience, and present findings to peers or community stakeholders.

14.5.2 Rubrics for Student Learning Outcomes

Rubrics provide clarity and consistency in evaluating student work. Suggested criteria include:

- *AI Literacy*: Accuracy in explaining AI concepts and terminology.
- *Ethical Reasoning*: Application of the NASW Code of Ethics to AI-related dilemmas, including considerations of privacy, bias, and equity.
- *Practice Application*: Realistic, client-centered proposals that demonstrate thoughtful integration of AI into assessment, intervention, or evaluation.

Rubrics should also include space for peer feedback, self-assessment, and reflective commentary, reinforcing the importance of continuous learning and ethical growth (Table 14.2).

Assessment in AI-integrated social work education must go beyond technical proficiency. It should cultivate ethical awareness, critical thinking, and a deep commitment to justice. By using diverse, competency-based strategies, educators can support students in becoming thoughtful, compassionate professionals who are prepared to navigate the complexities of AI in human services.

14.6 Challenges and Considerations

Despite growing interest in AI, many social work programs face significant barriers to implementation. One of the most pressing challenges is faculty readiness. Many educators report feeling underprepared to teach AI-related content, citing a lack of training, resources, and confidence in navigating technical subjects (Taylor-Beswick, 2023). Faculty development is essential to ensure that instructors can guide students through both the technical and ethical dimensions of AI.

Access disparities also pose a serious concern. Smaller or underfunded programs may lack the infrastructure to support AI education, including access to digital tools, interdisciplinary partnerships, and professional development opportunities. These disparities risk widening the gap between institutions and limiting students' exposure to emerging technologies (CSWE, 2022).

Another challenge is the risk of "techno-optimism," a trusting embrace of AI as a solution to complex social problems. While innovation is important, it must be balanced with ethical scrutiny. Social work educators must help students

Table 14.2 Rubric for Evaluation

Criteria	*Exceeds Expectations (A)*	*Meets Expectations (B–C)*	*Needs Improvement (D–F)*
AI Literacy	Accurately explains AI tools with clear, applied examples in mental health/substance use.	Explains most AI tools but with limited detail or unclear applications.	Demonstrates minimal understanding; confuses terms or misses key tools.
Ethical Reasoning	Consistently applies NASW Code to AI dilemmas; articulates nuanced ethical trade-offs.	Identifies ethical issues but analysis is surface-level or lacks depth.	Fails to identify or misinterprets ethical issues.
Equity and Justice Orientation	Clearly identifies risks of bias, digital divide, and surveillance; proposes thoughtful mitigation strategies.	Recognizes risks but offers few or generic strategies for addressing them.	Ignores or overlooks equity concerns.
Critical Thinking	Critically evaluates AI applications with balanced pros/cons and professional judgment.	Provides some critical analysis but leans toward uncritical optimism or skepticism.	Accepts or rejects AI tools without analysis.
Practice Integration	Demonstrates strong ability to integrate AI into micro, mezzo, and macro practice appropriately.	Applies AI in one practice level but inconsistently across others.	Shows limited ability to connect AI with practice levels.

critically evaluate AI tools, recognizing both their potential and their limitations. This includes addressing student anxieties about technology, particularly fears of being replaced by machines or losing the human-centered nature of their profession. Creating space for dialogue and reflection can help students integrate AI into their professional identity with confidence and clarity.

To move forward, social work education must adopt a proactive and inclusive approach to AI literacy. One promising direction is the development of continuing education modules for practicing social workers. These offerings can help bridge the gap between academic learning and real-world application, ensuring that professionals remain informed and empowered as technologies evolve.

There is also a growing need for accreditation guidelines that define AI competencies within social work education. Establishing clear standards can support curriculum development, promote consistency across programs, and ensure alignment with ethical and professional values (Gooding et al., 2024).

Partnerships between schools of social work and the tech industry offer another avenue for innovation. Collaborative projects can foster mutual learning, support the development of socially responsible AI tools, and provide students with hands-on experience in interdisciplinary settings.

On a global scale, educators are beginning to explore international competencies for AI in social work, including partnerships with institutions focused on AI and social justice at global levels. These efforts can promote cross-cultural dialogue, share best practices, and ensure that AI literacy reflects diverse perspectives and global realities.

Finally, a robust research agenda is needed to evaluate the outcomes of AI education in social work. Empirical studies should examine how AI literacy impacts learning, ethical reasoning, and practice readiness, providing evidence to guide future curriculum design and policy development.

14.7 Critical Thinking Discussion Questions

1. Are you ready to meet the needs of clients in digital environments? How can you prepare for working in human services in the future?
2. What does AI literacy and competence mean to you?
3. Can you identify knowledge, skills, and values that make you successful in your future social work practice?
4. What are curriculum innovation strategies that you can work on?
5. What is project-based learning to build AI literacy and competency for social work students, and why is it important in today's social work education?

14.8 Summary

From immersive simulations to AI literacy, technologies are reshaping how future social workers learn, reflect, and engage with complex social issues. These educational innovations reflect a broader commitment to preparing social workers for a digital future, one that is grounded in empathy, ethics, and equity. By integrating technology thoughtfully into the curriculum, educators can ensure that students are not only competent in digital tools but also critically engaged with their social and ethical dimensions. Teaching AI in social work isn't just about tools: it's about values, advocacy, and preparing social workers to lead in shaping AI for the common good. By addressing challenges with compassion and foresight, and by embracing future directions with integrity and collaboration, social work education can empower students to become ethical, informed, and justice-oriented professionals in a digital age.

References

Adelore, O. O., & Ojedeji, S. O. (2021). Digital literacy: Key to equity and social justice in a tech-dependent world. In P. A. Robinson, K. V. Williams, & M. Stojanović (Eds.). *Global citizenship for adult education* (1st ed.). Routledge. https://doi.org/10.4324/9781003050421-40

Ahn, E., Choi, M., Fowler, P., & Song, I. H. (2025). Artificial intelligence (AI) literacy for social work: Implications for core competencies. *Journal of the Society for Social Work and Research, 16*(1). 9–26. https://doi.org/10.1086/735187

Albrecht, M., Shanks, D., Shah, T., Hudson, T., Thompson, J., Filardi, T., … Smith, T. R. (2025). Enhancing clinical documentation with ambient artificial intelligence: A quality improvement survey assessing clinician perspectives on work burden, burnout, and job satisfaction. *JAMIA Open, 8*(1), ooaf013. https://doi.org/10.1093/jamiaopen/ooaf013

Barsky, A. E. (2017). Social work practice and technology: Ethical issues and policy responses. *Journal of Technology in Human Services, 35*(1), 8–19. https://doi.org/10.1080/15228835.2017.1277906

Besser, E. D., Blackwell, L. E., & Saenz, M. (2022). Engaging students through educational podcasting: Three stories of implementation. *Technology, Knowledge and Learning, 27*, 749–764. https://doi.org/10.1007/s10758-021-09503-8

Boetto, H. (2025). Artificial intelligence in social work: An EPIC model for practice. *Australian Social Work*, 1–14. https://doi.org/10.1080/0312407X.2025.2488345

Council on Social Work Education (CSWE). (2022). 2022 educational policy and accreditation standards for baccalaureate and master's social work programs. www.cswe.org/getmedia/bb5d8afe-7680-42dc-a332-a6e6103f4998/2022-Educational-Policy-and-Accreditation-Standards-(EPAS).pdf

Davey, N. G., & Benjaminsen, G. (2021). Telling tales: Digital storytelling as a tool for qualitative data interpretation and communication. *International Journal of Qualitative Methods, 20*. 1–10. https://doi.org/10.1177/16094069211022529

Gooding, P., van Kolfschooten, H., & Centola, F. (2024). *Artificial intelligence in mental healthcare*. Mental Health Europe. www.mentalhealtheurope.org/wp-content/uploads/2025/02/Study-on-AI-in-mental-health-care-final-for-publication.pdf

Lanzieri, N., McAlpin, E., Shilane, D., & Samelson, H. (2021). Virtual reality: An immersive tool for social work students to interact with community environments. *Clinical Social Work Journal, 49*(2), 207–219. https://doi.org/10.1007/s10615-021-00803-1

Minoi, J.-L., Suleiman, N., & Purnomo, R. A. (2025). Digital advocacy strategies with data analytics framework: A case study for effective campaigns. *Journal of Advanced Research in Applied Sciences and Engineering Technology, 54*(2), 157–171. https://doi.org/10.37934/araset.54.2.157171

National Association of Social Workers, Association of Social Work Boards, Council on Social Work Education, & Clinical Social Work Association. (2017). *NASW, ASWB, CSWE, & CSWA standards for technology in social work practice*. www.socialworkers.org/Practice/NASW-Practice-Standards-Guidelines/Standards-for-Technology-in-Social-Work-Practice

Ratwani, R. M., Sutton, K., & Galarraga, J. E. (2024). Addressing AI algorithmic bias in health care. *JAMA, 332*(13), 1051–1052. https://doi.org/10.1001/jama.2024.13486

Rodríguez Martínez, A., Amezcua Aguilar, M. T., Cortés Moreno, J., & Jiménez Delgado, J. J. (2024). Ethical issues related to the use of technology in social work practice: A systematic review. *SAGE Open, 14*(3), 1–14. https://doi.org/10.1177/21582440241274842

Taylor-Beswick, A. M. L. (2023). Digitalizing social work education: Preparing students to engage with twenty-first century practice need. *Social Work Education, 42*(1), 44–64. https://doi.org/10.1080/02615479.2022.2049225

UNESCO Institute for Statistics. (2018). *A global framework of reference on digital literacy skills for indicator 4.4.2* (UIS Information Paper No. 51). UNESCO Institute for Statistics. https://unesdoc.unesco.org/ark:/48223/pf0000265403

Vasey, B., Ursprung, S., Beddoe, B., et al. (2021). Association of clinician diagnostic performance with machine learning–based decision support systems: A systematic review. *JAMA Network Open, 4*(3), e211276. https://doi.org/10.1001/jamanetworkopen.2021.1276

Zgoda, K., & Shane, K. (2018). Digital literacy in social work education: A case study incorporating technology and social media within the social work curriculum. *Journal of Nonprofit Education and Leadership, 8*(1), 32–40. https://doi.org/10.18666/JNEL-2018-V8-I1-8350

14.9 Support Materials

Remember, Andrew we met in Chapter 1? He is back to offer tips and ideas for social workers in various roles.

Please access this video at www.routledge.com/9781041275459

Video 14.1 A Social Worker Who Wears Many Hats

Box 14.3 Sample Syllabus

Course Title: AI and Social Work Practice for the Common Good: Ethics, Equity, and Innovation
Level: MSW/Graduate
Credits: 3
Instructor: [Name]
Prerequisites: Intro to Social Work Research Methods or equivalent
Course Format: Lecture, seminar discussion, experiential activities, and project-based learning

Course DescriptionThis course introduces social work students to AI as it relates to social work values, ethics, and practice. Students will gain AI literacy, critically analyze applications in human services, and develop competencies to ethically and equitably integrate AI into social work practice. Emphasis will be placed on promoting social justice, protecting vulnerable populations, and shaping AI for the common good.
Learning ObjectivesBy the end of the course, students will be able to:

1 Demonstrate AI literacy by explaining key concepts (algorithms, machine learning, predictive analytics, NLP, robotics).
2 Critically analyze ethical, cultural, and equity issues raised by AI in human services.
3 Apply the NASW Code of Ethics and social justice frameworks to real-world AI dilemmas.
4 Evaluate and assess AI tools for transparency, bias, accountability, and client-centeredness.
5 Collaborate across disciplines to propose socially responsible AI applications.
6 Advocate for policies that promote fairness, equity, and inclusion in AI adoption in social work.

Required Texts/Readings

- Selected scholarly articles and reports (provided via Learning management system (LMS)).
- Case studies of AI in social services (child welfare, mental health, aging, disability services).
- Supplemental readings from computer science, ethics, and policy studies.

Course Assignments and Evaluation

- Reflective Journals: Weekly 1–2 page reflections on readings/discussions.
- AI Ethical Dilemma Paper: Short paper analyzing an ethical scenario using NASW Code of Ethics.
- AI Tool Evaluation Report: Group project evaluating a real-world AI system (bias, equity, client impact).
- Policy Brief: Individual paper recommending guidelines for ethical AI use in a social service domain.
- Capstone Project: Design a practice, policy, or advocacy initiative that integrates AI for social good.

Weekly OutlineWeek 1—Introduction to AI and Social Work

- Topics: What is AI? Why does it matter for social work? Myths vs realities.
- Activity: *AI in My Life* mapping exercise.
- Reading: Introductory AI literacy articles.

Week 2—Foundations of AI Literacy

- Topics: Algorithms, machine learning, data, and automation .
- Activity: AI "explain it to a client" exercise.
- Reading: AI basics for human services professionals.

Week 3—Ethics and the NASW Code

- Topics: Ethical implications of AI: privacy, consent, transparency.
- Activity: Case discussion—predictive analytics in child welfare.

Week 4—Equity, Bias, and Algorithmic Discrimination

- Topics: How AI can reinforce or challenge inequities.
- Activity: Analyze case of racial bias in predictive risk models.
- Reading: Articles on algorithmic bias and fairness.

Week 5—AI in Social Work Practice (Micro Level)

- Topics: Chatbots, therapeutic AI, socially assistive robots, virtual agents.
- Activity: Role-play session with chatbot simulation.

Week 6—AI in Social Work Practice (Mezzo Level)

- Topics: AI in community services, nonprofits, schools, and healthcare.
- Activity: Small group analysis of AI pilot programs in nonprofits.

Week 7—AI in Policy and Macro Practice

- Topics: Predictive analytics in policing, benefits systems, housing allocation.
- Activity: Debate: *Can AI reduce inequities in public benefits administration?*
- Reading: Reports on AI in government.

Week 8—Global Perspectives

- Topics: U.S. (private-sector led), EU (regulation-focused), China (state-led).
- Activity: Comparative analysis of global AI strategies and their implications for social services.

Week 9—Client Perspectives and the Digital Divide

- Topics: Digital inclusion, older adults, disability access, language equity.
- Activity: Student-led interviews (or case vignettes) on client experiences

Week 10—Interdisciplinary Collaboration

- Topics: Working with technologists, policymakers, and communities.
- Activity: Joint project brainstorming (social work + computer science teams, if feasible).
- Reading: Human-centered AI design articles.

Week 11—Regulation, Policy, and Advocacy

- Topics: AI governance frameworks, data privacy laws, and advocacy strategies.
- Activity: Draft policy position statement in small groups.

Week 12—Designing AI for the Common Good

- Topics: Principles of ethical design, participatory approaches, community co-design.
- Activity: Workshop: Designing AI prototypes guided by social work values.

Week 13—Student Capstone Project Development

- Topics: Project work time and consultations with instructor.
- Activity: Peer review of project drafts.

Week 14—Capstone Presentations and Future Directions

- Topics: Students present final projects.
- Discussion: Future of AI in social work practice, education, and research.

Index

Note: Tables are indicated by **bold**.

For Product Safety Concerns and Information please contact our EU representative GPSR@taylorandfrancis.com
Taylor & Francis Verlag GmbH, Kaufingerstraße 24, 80331 München, Germany

www.ingramcontent.com/pod-product-compliance
Ingram Content Group UK Ltd.
Pitfield, Milton Keynes, MK11 3LW, UK
UKHW022022180926
475701UK00005B/979
9781041275459